About This Book

Imagine yourself waking up one morning to the arrival of a fascinating people unlike any you had ever seen, who could do things you never thought possible and had riches beyond your imagining. These were a friendly people, and although you didn't understand what they said, they led you to believe that they wanted to live with you in peace. Then picture how you would feel when you realized that the strangers had weapons that could kill from afar, that through lies and trickery they were stealing your land and all you owned and that they squandered the wealth of the nature you revered while poisoning you with rum and disease.

Imagine all that and you begin to feel what the Indians must have felt in 1609 when Henry Hudson first sailed into New York harbor ... wonder, awe and horror ... as the end of their way of life arrived on the incoming tide.

The History of **THE INDIAN TRIBES OF HUDSON'S RIVER**, written in 1872 by E.M.Ruttenber, begins with Hudson's arrival, as the author carefully reconstructs the history of the dozens of tribes along the Hudson River included in the great nations of the Lenni Lenap Mahicans and the Iroquois. Every sachem (or ki identified, and the location, origins, customs traditions of each tribe are documented. Prior to thi only had the history of the Indian tribes which occi the Hudson Valley never been written, but any incid references treated them as fragmentary bands wit any organization. Now we can see that nothing c

have been farther from the truth.

Starting with the migration of the Lenni Lenape and the Iroquois from the West across the Mississippi, their displacement of the Algonquins and subsequent settlement in the East is recounted. Also, all their battles, treaties, and alliances are documented up to and through the establishment of the Iroquois Confederacy. (That pinnacle of Indian Law was "borrowed from" heavily by our founding fathers when they wrote our constitution. So much for the theory that the Indians were unorganized savages!)

Significant attention is paid to the various tribal interactions with the colonists and how these affected each nationality's struggle for controlling interest in the New World. While the Dutch controlled the Hudson Valley they maintained a neutrality with the Indian tribes. When the English gained control of the lower reaches of the Hudson, they allied with the Iroquois, while, to the North, the French created formidable opposition to them when they allied with the Hurons. As other tribes alligned themselves on either side, the Indians became little more than pawns in the white man's struggle, and the stage was set for years of bloody battles for control of the wealth of the new world.

Then, in the year 1700, a short-lived and short-tempered peace prevailed. That ends the first half of E.M.Ruttenber's monumental work, The History of the **INDIAN TRIBES OF HUDSON'S RIVER to 1700**. A second volume, dated 1700 - 1850, will be published by HOPE FARM PRESS in the fall of 1992. That begins with the tenuous peace of 1700 and then quickly continues with the Indian's destructive alliance with the Europeans during the French and Indian Wars and the Revolutionary War. The sad truth is that, no matter which side won, the Indians were destined to lose. In the end, a loving, trusting, ancient people were subjugated, corrupted and driven from the land they loved by ever-strengthening waves of European settlers.

HISTORY

of

INDIAN TRIBES
of
HUDSON'S RIVER

THEIR

ORIGIN, MANNERS AND CUSTOMS; TRIBAL,
AND SUB-TRIBAL ORGANIZATIONS; WARS,
TREATIES, ETC., ETC.,

to 1700

BY

E. M. RUTTENBER

1872

HOPE FARM PRESS

1992

THIS PUBLICATION IS A
FACSIMILE REPRINT
OF THE ORIGINAL BOOK

HOPE FARM PRESS
& BOOKSHOP
7321 RT 212
SAUGERTIES NY 12477

ISBN 0-910746-98-2

MADE IN U.S.A.

PREFACE.

———•———

HE pioneer in new fields of historic inquiry
encounters many obstacles from which those
who follow the more beaten paths of investigation are exempt, and especially so if the inquiry
involves conclusions differing materially from those
which have been generally accepted. The experience
of the author in prosecuting the investigations, the
results of which have been embodied in the work which
is now submitted to the public, have been no exception
to this rule. Not only had the history of the Indians
who occupied the valley of Hudson's river never been
written, but the incidental references to them, in the
histories of nations more prominent at a later period —
treating them as mere fragmentary bands without
organization or political position among the aboriginal
nations — being regarded as erroneous, the inquiry
involved the rejection, to a very great extent, of the
conclusions of others, and the investigation and ana-
lyzation of original sources of information. To
extract the truth and embody it in consistent narrative,
has involved no little labor and research, and the
careful weighing of words; and, although the results

1

may not be stated in the clearest terms or the most
flowing rhetoric, nor entirely without error, they are
nevertheless believed to fully sustain the conclusion
that the tribes in question have a history which enti-
tles them to a high rank in the annals of aboriginal
nations, and which assigns to them native abilities as
distinguished, eloquence as pure, bravery and prowess
as unquestionable, as was possessed by those who, preserved for a greater time in their national integrity by
their remoteness from civilization, became of more
esteem in their relations to the government but less
noble in their purposes.

It has been the object of the author to trace the history of the Indians from the earliest period; to show
their original position in the family of nations, and that
which they subsequently maintained; the wrongs which
they suffered, and the triumphs which they won; their
greatness and their decay. In the narrative, liberal use
has been made of current histories, so far as their statements were found to be in accordance with the facts.
Acknowledgment, it is believed, has been fully made,
and even to an extent which is not customary. Very
full notes have been introduced for the purpose of
explaining the text and enabling the reader to judge
of the correctness of the conclusions drawn therefrom.
As far as possible the narrative has been divested of
the recitation of events which do not pertain to it,
and though necessarily running beyond the limits of
the territory regarded as the valley of the Hudson,
has been as closely confined to it as possible, too
closely perhaps, as it is believed that the eastern

Indians have the same claim to consideration as a confederacy as the western.

The work is submitted to the judgment of the public, with a desire that the author may be lost in the theme which he has presented, and the truth of history vindicated in behalf of a people that have left behind no monuments to their memory save those erected by their destroyers.

NEWBURGH, N. Y.

The Half Moon off Yonkers.

Indian Tribes of Hudson's River.

CHAPTER I.

HUDSON IN THE MAHICANITUK — HIS INTERCOURSE WITH THE INDIANS — THEIR TRADITIONS CONCERNING HIS VISIT.

SAILING under the auspices of the Dutch West India Company, HENRY HUDSON, an intrepid English navigator, moored his vessel, the Half Moon, on the morning of September 3d, 1609, in the waters of the river which now bears his name. Lingering off Sandy Hook a week, he passed through the Narrows, and anchored in what is now Newark bay. On the 12th, he resumed his voyage, and slowly drifting with the tide, anchored over night, on the 13th, just above Yonkers, the great river stretching on before him to the north and giving to his ardent mind the hope that he had at last discovered the gateway to the Eastern seas. On the 14th, he passed Tappan and Haverstraw bays, and sailed through the majestic pass guarded by the frowning Donderberg, and anchored at night near West Point, in the midst of the sublimest scenery of the mountains. On the morning of the 15th, he entered Newburgh bay, and reached Katskill; on the 16th, Athens; on the 17th, Castleton; on the 18th, Albany. Here he remained several days, sending an exploring boat as far as Waterford, and sadly learning that he had reached the head of navigation, and that the Eastern passage was yet an unsolved problem. His return voyage began on the 23d; on the 25th,

he anchored in Newburgh bay; reached Stony point on the
1st of October; on the 4th, Sandy Hook, and sailed from thence

Newburgh Bay.

to Europe, bearing with him the information which he had collected, not the least of which in importance was that in relation
to the native lords whom he had met on the banks of the river
he had discovered, and who then broke the silvery surface of
its waters with their light canoes and awoke the echoes of its
mountain sides with their wild choruses, of whose power it was
an emblem, on the waters of which, as they faded away in the
north, was wafted their war shallops into tributaries that
stretched on to the lakes and the great river of Canada, bearing
with them the prestige of savage supremacy.

Hudson first met the Indians near the Narrows, where they
came on board his vessel " clothed in mantles of feathers and
robes of fur, the women, clothed in hemp, red copper tobacco
pipes, and other things of copper they did wear about their
necks;" of arms they brought none, their mission was peace;
but he "durst not trust them." Suspicion breeds suspicion,
and suspicion leads to violence. Sending an exploring boat up
the river the next day, it was attacked, on its return to the ship,

and one of the English sailors, John Coleman, was killed by an arrow shot in the throat.[1] He was buried upon the adjacent beach, the first European victim of an Indian weapon on the Mahicanituk. The offense which had been committed by himself and his companions is not stated, but may be inferred. They were far from the ship, the night came on and a thick cloud of rain and fog settled over them ; seeing their condition, the Indians sprang to their boats to rescue them, fear seized them, the savage was more dreaded then the tempest, a falcon shot was hurled at the approaching canoes, the swift arrow replied, and "in the fight one man was slain and two more hurt." Day after day the Indians came on board, brought tobacco and Indian wheat, and oysters and beans, "making show of love," but he "durst not trust them." They brought their women and children with them, but he "durst not trust them." At Yonkers they came on board in large numbers ; here he detained two of them, and dressed them in red coats, and though they jumped from the ports and swam away, their detention was not the less a violation of the laws of hospitality, so they regarded it, for when they had reached the shore they called to him "in scorn."

At Katskill he found a "very loving people and very old men." They brought on board "Indian corn, pumpkins, and tobacco," and used him well. At Castleton they were very sociable, and the "master's mate went on land[2] with an old savage, a governor of the country, who carried him to his house and made him good cheere." "I sailed to the shore," he says, "in one of their canoes, with an old man who was chief of a tribe consisting of forty men and seventeen women. These I saw there in a house well constructed of oak bark, and circular in shape, so that it had the appearance of being built with an

---

[1] Coleman's point is the monument to this occurrence.

[2] It has been assumed on the authority of a quotation alleged by De Laet to have been made from a journal kept by Hudson, that the place of this visit was in latitude 42° 18', or in the vicinity of the present city of Hudson. (*N. Y. Hist. Soc. Coll.*, 1, 300). The journal kept by Juet was not only the official record of the voyage, but is very precise in its statements as to who visited the shore in this, and in other instances. He does not give the latitude, but from the ship's log it would seem that the place was "six leagues higher," up the river than that fixed by De Laet, and that it was at Schodac or Castleton.— *O'Callaghan*, 1, 37 ; *Brodhead*, 1, 31 ; *Collections of the New York Historical Society*, 2d Ser. 1, 326.

arched roof. It contained a large quantity of corn and beans of last year's growth, and there lay near the house, for the purpose of drying, enough to load three ships, besides what was growing in the fields. On our coming to the house two mats were spread out to sit upon, and some food was immediately served in well-made wooden bowls. Two men were also dispatched at once, with bows and arrows, in quest of game, who soon brought in a pair of pigeons which they had shot. They likewise killed a fat dog,¹ and skinned it in great haste, with shells which they had got out of the water. They supposed that I would remain with them for the night; " but when they saw that he desired to return to the ship and that he would not remain, they supposed he "was afraid of their bows and arrows, and taking their arms they broke them in pieces and threw them in the fire."

At Albany, Hudson repaid the old governor for his entertainment. The Indians flocked to visit his vessel, and he determined to try some of their chief men to see " whether they had any treachery in them." " So they took them down into the cabin, and gave them so much wine and *aqua vitæ* that they were all merry. In the end one of them was drunk, and they could not tell how to take it." At night they all departed, except the old man who had taken the *aqua vitæ*; " he slept all night quietly." On the following day they came again, and when they saw that their chief had recovered from his debauch they were glad. They returned to their castle and " brought tobacco and beads " and gave them to Hudson, " and made an oration, and showed him all the country round about." " Then they sent one of their company on land again, who presently returned and brought a great platter full of venison, dressed by themselves," and caused Hudson " to eat with them ; then they made him reverence, and departed, all save the old man " who had found the Indian's paradise with the white man's rum. But he took his departure the next day, and two days after returned, bringing " another old man with him " from the place where " the loving people " had first been met. He too brought belts of wampum beads and gave them to Hudson, " and shewed

¹ Probably a black bear.

him all the country thereabout, as though it were at his command. So he made the two old men dine with him, and the old man's wife; for they brought two old women, and two young maidens of the age of sixteen or seventeen years with them, who behaved themselves very modestly." No doubt more wine was served at this dinner, but the *aqua vitæ* was evidently omitted, for the party took their departure at one o'clock.

On his return voyage "the loving people" met Hudson again, and "would have him go on land and eat with them;" but the wind was fair, and he would not yield to their request. Very sorrowfully the old man, who had made the request in behalf of himself and his people, left the ship, although comforted with presents and with the assurance that his new friends would come again. Passing down through the Highlands, the Half Moon was becalmed off Stony point, and "the people of the mountains" came on board and wondered at the "ship and weapons." One canoe kept "hanging under the stern," and its occupant was soon detected in pilfering from the cabin windows. When detected, he had secured a "pillow and two shirts, and two bandeliers;" but the "mate shot at him, and struck him on the breast, and killed him." The Indians were frightened and fled away, some in their canoes, others jumping into the water. A boat was lowered to recover the articles which they had taken, when one of them who was in the water seized hold of it "thinking to overthrow it," but "the cook seized a sword and cut off one of his hands and he was drowned." At the head of Manhattan island the vessel was again attacked. It was here that Hudson had attempted to kidnap two young men, who, on their escape, had called to him "in scorn" at their betrayal. One of these men, accompanied by his friends, now came out to the ship in their canoes. They were not suffered to enter the vessel, and falling behind it, discharged their arrows at it; "in recompense whereof" six muskets replied "and killed two or three of them." The Indians retreated, and from a point of land renewed the attack; but "a falcon shot" killed two of them, and "the rest fled into the woods;" "yet they manned off another canoe, with nine or ten men," through which a falcon shot was sent, killing one of its occupants. Then the sailors discharged their muskets, and "killed three or four more of them." " So they went their way," and the Half Moon was hurried down into the bay, "clear from all danger," carrying thence to Holland, in Hudson's simple narrative, an epitome of the subsequent history of the intercourse of the Indians with the Europeans ; the clash of customs, the violence, the intoxicating cup.

To most of the Indians the advent of Hudson's ship was a strange spectacle. For over an hundred years the white-winged messengers of the old world had been wafted by them; in the further south, the white man was not a stranger, but not before had his sails been folded on the breast of their waters, nor the voice of trumpet and cannon reverberated through their solitudes. All this was new and strange; the Great Spirit had come to them ; the signals of a mighty change passed before their vision. Their traditions repeat that almost with the appearance of Hudson in the lower bay, they began to collect on the shores and headlands, gazing in astonishment on the strange sight ; that when they first saw the Half Moon they " did not know what to make of it, and could not comprehend whether it came down from heaven or from the devil." Some of them " even imagined it to be a fish, or some monster of the sea, and accordingly a strange report of it soon spread over the land." It was at length agreed among them " that, as this phenomenon moved towards the land, whether it was an animal or not, or any thing that had life in it," would soon be apparent. Runners from the shore went back and forth, and messengers were sent to the chiefs of the country to send in their warriors. As the ship approached they concluded it was " a large canoe or house, in which the great Manitto himself was, and that he was probably coming to visit them." Every thing was put in order to entertain him ; " the best of victuals was prepared, and plenty of meat for sacrifice procured, and idols or images examined and put in order, to appease him in case he was angry." Other runners soon arriving, declared it to be a " large house of various colors, full of people, yet of quite a different color from themselves, that they dressed in a different manner, and that one, in particular, appeared altogether red, which must be the Manitto himself." The crew of the Half Moon soon hailed them with a loud shout, which so frightened them that some were for running away, yet they feared to give offense and remained.

Meanwhile Hudson kept on his course, and the Indians continued to collect on the banks of the river, expressing their curiosity in the strongest manner. Establishing intercourse at last, they ventured on board the ship, where they were saluted " in a friendly manner, and they returned the salute after their manner." " They are lost in admiration both as to the color of the skin of these whites, as also of their manner of dress ; yet most as to the habit of him who wore the red clothes, which shone with something they could not account for. He must be the Great Manitto, but why should he have a white skin?" Then they sat down to eat with their strange visitant, " a large and elegant *hockback* was brought forward by one of the Manitto's servants, and something poured from it into a small cup or glass, and handed to the Manitto. He drank it, had the cup refilled, and had it handed to the chief next to him to drink. The chief receives the glass, but only smells at it, and passes it on to the next chief, who does the same. The glass thus passes through the circle without the contents being tasted by any one, and is on the point of being returned again to the red-clothed man, when one of their number, a spirited man and great warrior, jumps up, harangues the assembly on the impropriety of returning the glass with the contents in it ; that the same was handed them by the Manitto in order that they should drink it, as he himself had done before them ; that this would please him ; but to return what he had given to them might provoke him, and be the cause of their being destroyed by him. And that since he believed it for the good of the nation that the contents offered them should be drank, and as no one else was willing to drink it, he would, let the consequence be what it might ; that it was better for one man to die than for a whole nation to be destroyed. He then took the glass, and, bidding the assembly a farewell, drank it off. Every eye was fixed on their resolute companion, to see what an effect this would have upon him ; and he soon beginning to stagger about, and at last dropping to the ground, they bemoan him. He falls into a sleep, and they view him as expiring. He awakes again, jumps up, and declares that he never before felt so happy as after he had drank of the cup. He wishes for more. His wish is granted ; and the whole assembly soon join him, and become intoxicated. Then the man with the red clothes distributed presents to them of beads, axes, hoes, stockings, and other articles, and made them understand that he would return home and come again to see them, bring them more presents and stay with them awhile, but should want a little land to sow some seeds, in order to raise herbs to put in their broth."

But from their dream of trusting love they had a speedy awakening. Their traditions state that the promise made by Hudson to return again was fulfilled the following season, and that they " rejoiced much at seeing each other again ; but the whites laughed at them, seeing that they knew not the use of the axes, hoes, etc., they had given them, they having had those hanging to their breasts as ornaments, and the stockings they had made use of as tobacco pouches. The whites now put handles or helves in the former, and cut trees down before their eyes, and dug the ground, and showed them the use of the stockings. Here a general laughter ensued among the Indians, that they had remained for so long a time ignorant of the use of so valuable implements, and had borne with the weight of such heavy metal hanging to their necks for such a length of time. They took every white man they saw for a Manitto, yet inferior and attendant to the supreme Manitto, to wit : to the one which wore the red and laced clothes.

" Familiarity daily increasing between them and the whites, the latter now proposed to stay with them, asking them only for so much land as the hide of a bullock would cover or encompass, which hide was brought forward and spread on the ground before them. That they readily granted this request ; whereupon the whites took a knife, and beginning at one place on this hide, cut it up into a rope not thicker than the finger of a little child, so that by the time this hide was cut up, there was a great heap ; that this rope was drawn out to a great distance, and then brought round again, so that the ends might meet; that they carefully avoided its breaking, and that upon the whole it encompassed a large piece of land; that they were surprised at the superior wit of the whites, but did not wish to contend with them about a little land, as they had enough; that they and the whites lived for a long time contentedly together, although the whites asked from time to time, more land of them and proceeding higher up the Mahicanituk,[1] they believed they would soon want all the country."

[1] The Iroquois, it is said, called the river the Cohatatea, while the Mahicans and the Lenapes called it the Mahicanituk or " the continually flowing waters." The Dutch gave it the name of Mauritius river, as early as 1611, in honor of their stadt-holder, Prince Maurice, of Nassau. Hudson called it the River of the mountains, a name which the French adopted in Rio de Montagne. The English first gave it the name of Hudson's river by which, it from the Connecticut or East river, and from the Delaware or South river, it has since been known.

Henry Hudson.

CHAPTER II.

Origin, Manners and Customs, etc.

THE origin of the North American Indians, is a subject which has engrossed the attention of learned
men for over two hundred years, and yet the
question, " By whom was America peopled ? "
remains without satisfactory answer.   In 1637, Thomas
Morton wrote a book to prove that the Indians were of Latin
origin.   John Joselyn held, in 1638, that they were of Tartar
descent.   Cotton Mather inclined to the opinion that they
were Scythians.   James Adair seems to have been fully convinced that they were descendants of the Israelites, the lost
tribes ; and, after thirty years residence among them, published
in 1775, an account of their manners and customs, from which
he deduced his conclusions.[1]   Dr. Mitchill, after considerable
investigation, concluded " that the three races, Malays, Tartars
and Scandinavians, contributed to made up the great American
population, who were the authors of the various works and antiquities found on the continent."   DeWitt Clinton held, that
" the probability is, that America was peopled from various
quarters of the old world, and that its predominant race is the
Scythian or Tartarian."   Calmet, a distinguished author, brings

[1] " Observations and arguments in proof
of the American Indians being descended
from the Jews : 1. Their division into
tribes. 2. Their worship of Jehovah. 3.
Their notion of a theocracy. 4. Their
belief in the ministration of angels. 5.
Their language and dialects. 6. Their
manner of counting time. 7. Their pro-
phets and high priests. 8. Their festivals, fasts and religious rites. 9. Their
daily sacrifice. 10. Their ablutions and
anointings. 11. Their laws of unclean-
ness. 12. Their abstinence from unclean
things. 13. Their marriages, divorces,
and punishments of adultery. 14. Their
several punishments   15. Their cities of
refuge.   16. Their purifications and ceremonies preparatory to war   17. Their
ornaments.   18. Their manner of curing
the sick.   19. Their burial of the dead.
20. Their mourning for the dead.   21.
Their raising seed to a departed brother.
22. Their choice of names adapted to
their circumstances and the times.   23.
Their own traditions, the accounts of our
English writers, and the testimony which
the Spanish and other authors have given
concerning the primitive inhabitants of
Peru and Mexico."— *Adair.*

forward the writings of Hornius, son of Theodosius the Great, who affirms that " at or about the time of the commencement of the Christian era, voyages from Africa and Spain into the Atlantic ocean were both frequent and celebrated ; " and holds that " there is strong probability that the Romans and Carthagenians, even 300 B. C., were well acquainted with the existence of this country," adding that there are " tokens of the presence of the Greeks, Romans, Persians, and Carthagenians, in many parts of the continent." The story of Madoc's voyage to America, in 1170, has been repeated by every writer upon the subject, and actual traces of Welsh colonization are affirmed to have been discovered in the language and customs of a tribe of Indians living on the Missouri. Then the fact is stated that " America was visited by some Norwegians," who made a settlement in Greenland, in the tenth century. Priest, in his *American Antiquities*, states that his observations had led him " to the conclusion that the two great continents, Asia and America, were peopled by similar races of men."

It is not necessary to add to this catalogue. Men equally learned with those whose opinions have been quoted, see no obstacle in the way of an opinion that America received her population as she did her peculiar trees, and plants, and animals, and birds. The geologist examines the relics of the west, and where imagination fashions artificial walls, he sees but crumbs of decaying sandstone, clinging like the remains of mortar to blocks of greenstone that rested on it; discovers in parallel intrenchments a trough that subsiding waters have ploughed through the centre of a ridge, and explains the tessellated pavement to be but a layer of pebbles aptly joined by water; and, examining the mounds, finds them composed of different strata of earth, arranged horizontally to the very edge, and ascribes their creation to the power that shaped the globe into vales and hillocks.[1] The mounds, it is true, may have been selected by the aborigines as the site of their dwellings, fortifications, or burial places; but the mouldering bones, from hillocks which are crowned by trees that have defied the storms of many centuries, the graves of earth from which they are dug, and the

[1] *Hitchcock.*

feeble fortifications that are sometimes found in their vicinity, afford no special evidence of connection with other continents.[1] "Among the more ancient works" of the west, says another writer,[2] "there is not a single edifice, nor any ruins which prove the existence, in former ages, of a building composed of imperishable materials. No fragment of a column, nor a brick, nor a single hewn stone large enough to have been incorporated into a wall, has been discovered. The only relics which remain to inflame the curiosity, are composed of earth."

To add force to this sweeping blow at the beautiful theories that have been woven, the learned Agassis disputes the idea of the unity of the races through Adam; while other writers pretty clearly demonstrate that the theory of the lost tribes of Israel has no foundation in fact. Dr. Lawrence, in his *Lectures on Physiology, Zoology, and the Natural History of Man,* sums up the whole argument by saying that, "in comparing the barbarian nations of America with those of the eastern continent, we perceive no points of resemblance between them, in their moral institutions or in their habits, that are not apparently founded in the necessities of human life."

This is apparently the reasonable conclusion of the whole matter, for to pass intelligent judgment, the aborigines of America must be taken as they were found, and not as they may have appeared after years of association with Europeans, an association necessarily producing a mingling of ancient customs with those learned from missionaries, or copied under the impulse of imitation. These early lessons were taught by men of all nations, the Dutch, the French, the Spanish, and the English, and, before their advent, by the Norwegians. It would be strange indeed, under all the circumstances, if the aborigines did not have grafted upon them some resembling features of all nations. Sir William Johnson, than whom no man had better opportunity to form a correct judgment, after considering the whole matter, concluded that all theories were defective for this reason; saying, that the Indians residing next to the English settlements had lost a great part of their traditions, and had so

[1] Warren in *Delafield's Antiquities.*   [2] *Drake's Picture of Cincinnati.*

blended their customs with those of the Europeans as to render it " difficult if not impossible to trace their origin or discover their explication," while those further removed had nevertheless been visited by traders, and especially by French Jesuits, who had " introduced some of their own inventions which the present generation confound with their ancient customs."[1] Until many of the nations of the old world can satisfactorily explain the origin of their own race, it is hardly worth while to endeavor to make our aborigines any further kindred with them than that the same Almighty Power called them into being and endowed them with common instincts.

Verazzano,[2] who sailed along the coast of North America in 1524, speaks of the natives whom he met in the harbor of New York, as " not differing much," from those with whom he had intercourse at other points, " being dressed out with the feathers of birds of various colors." His description being the earliest is of the most merit, for at that time they were untainted by association with Europeans. In person, he says, they were of good proportions, of middle stature, broad across the breast, strong in the arms, and well-formed. Among those who came on board his vessel were " two kings more beautiful in form and stature than can possibly be described ; one was about forty years old, the other about twenty-four." " They were dressed," he continues, " in the following manner: The oldest had a deer's skin around his body, artificially wrought in damask figures, his head was without covering, his hair was tied back in various knots ; around his neck he wore a large chain ornamented with many stones of different colors. The young man was similar in his general appearance." In size, he says: " they exceed us," their complexion tawny, inclining to white, their faces sharp, their hair long and black, their eyes black and sharp, their expression mild and pleasant," " greatly resembling the antique." The women, he says, were " of the same form and beauty, very graceful, of fine countenances and pleasing appearance in manners and modesty." They wore no clothing " except a deer skin ornamented like those of the men." Some

[1] *Documentary History of New York*, iv, 431. [2] *Collections of the New York Historical Society*, 2d Series, i, 45.

3

had "very rich lynx skins upon their arms, and various ornaments upon their heads, composed of braids of hair," which hung down upon their breasts on each side. The older and the married people, both men and women, "wore many ornaments in their ears, hanging down in the oriental manner." In disposition they were generous, "giving away" whatever they had; of their wives they were careful, always leaving them in their boats when they came on ship-board, and their general deportment was such that with them, he says, "we formed a great friendship." [1]

Hudson's experience with them, in 1609, was somewhat different, but his references to their personal appearance are similar. "This day," he says, "many of the people came aboard, some in mantles of feathers, and some in skins of divers sorts of good furs. Some women also came to us with hemp. They had red copper tobacco pipes, and other things of copper they did wear about their necks."

The Dutch historians, Wassenaar, Van der Donck, and others, agree that the natives were generally well-limbed, slender around the waist, and broad-shouldered ; that they had black hair and eyes, and snow white teeth, resembling the Brazilians in color, or more especially "those people who sometimes ramble through Netherland and are called Gipsies ; " were very nimble and swift of pace, and well adapted to travel on foot and to carry heavy burthens. " Generally," says one writer, "the men have no beards, some even pluck it out. They use very few words, which they previously well consider. Naturally they are quite modest and without guile, but in their way haughty enough, ready and quick witted to comprehend or learn, be it good or bad. As soldiers, they are far from being honorable, but perfidious and accomplish all their designs by treachery ; they also use many stratagems to deceive their enemies, and execute by night almost all their plans that are in any way hazardous. The thirst for revenge seems innate in them; they are very pertinacious in self-defense, when they cannot escape ; which, under other circumstances, they like to do ; and they make little of death, when it is inevitable, and despise

[1] *Collections of the New York Historical Society*, 2d Series, I, 46.

all tortures that can be inflicted on them at the stake, exhibiting no faint-heartedness, but generally singing until they are dead. Their clothing is described as having been most sumptuous. The women ornamented themselves more than the men. " All wear around the waist a girdle made of the fin of the whale or of sewant." The men originally wore a breech-cloth, made of skins, but after the Dutch came those who could obtain it wore " between their legs a lap of duffels cloth half an ell broad and nine quarters long," which they girded around their waists, and drew up in a fold "with a flap of each end hanging down in front and rear." In addition to this they had mantles of feathers, and at a later period decked themselves with "plaid duffels cloth " in the form of a sash, which was worn over the right shoulder, drawn in a knot around the body, with the ends extending down below the knees. When the young men wished to look especially attractive, they wore "a band about their heads, manufactured and braided, of scarlet deer hair, interwoven with soft shining red hair." " With this head-dress," says Van der Donck, " they appear like the delineations and paintings of the Catholic saints," and, he adds, " when a young Indian is dressed in this manner he would not say *plum* for a bushel of plums. But this decoration is seldom worn unless they have a young woman in view."

The dress of an Indian belle was more attractive than any which civilized life has produced. Says the writer last quoted, " The women wear a cloth around their bodies, fastened by a girdle which extends below their knees, and is as much as an under coat ; but next to the body, under this coat, they wear a dressed deer skin coat, girt around the waist. The lower body of this skirt they ornament with great art, and nestle the same with strips which are tastefully decorated with wampum. The wampum with which one of these skirts is ornamented is frequently worth from one to three hundred guilders. They bind their hair behind in a club of about a hand long, in the form of a beaver's tail, over which they draw a square cap, which is frequently ornamented with wampum. When they desire to be fine they draw a headband around the forehead, which is also ornamented with wampum, etc. This band confines the hair smooth, and is fastened behind, over the club, in a beau's knot. Their head dress forms a handsome and lively appearance. Around their necks they wear various ornaments, which are also decorated with wampum. Those they esteem as highly as our ladies do their pearl necklaces. They also wear hand bands or bracelets, curiously wrought, and inter-woven with wampum. Their breasts appear about half covered with an elegantly wrought dress. They wear beautiful girdles, ornamented with their favorite wampum, and costly ornaments in their ears. Here and there they lay upon their faces black spots of paint. Elk hide moccasins they wore before the Dutch came, and they too were most richly ornamented." Shoes and stockings they obtained from the Dutch, and also bonnets.

Plurality of wives was, to some extent, in vogue among them. " The natives," says Van der Donck, " generally marry but one wife and no more, unless it be a chief who is great and powerful ; such frequently have two, three or four wives, of the neatest and handsomest of women, and who live together without variance." Minors did not marry except with the advice of their parents or friends. Widowers and widows followed their own inclinations. Their marriage ceremonies were very simple. Young women were not debarred signify-ing their desire to enter matrimonial life. When one of them wished to be married she covered her face with a veil and sat covered as an indication of her desire. If she attracted a suitor, negotiations were opened with parents or friends, pre-sents given and the bride taken.

Chastity was an established principle with married females. To be unchaste during wedlock was held to be very disgraceful. " Many of the women would prefer death, rather than submit to be dishonored." No Indian would keep his wife, however much he loved her, when he knew she was unchaste. Divorce frequently came from disagreements, and was a simple form. The wife was handed her share of the goods and put out of doors by the husband, and was then free to marry another. In cases of separation the children followed the mother, and were frequently the cause of the parents coming together again. The man who abandoned his wife without cause left her all her property, and in like manner the wife the husband's. Foul and impertinent language was despised by them. All romping, caressing and wanton behavior they spoke of with contempt, as indirect alurements to unchastity, and reproved such conduct in the Netherlanders. The Dutch made wives of many of them and retained them, refusing to leave them for females of their own country.

Most of the diseases incident to females of the present day were unknown to them. Before confinement it was their custom to retire to a secluded place near a brook, or stream of water, and prepare a shelter for themselves with mats and covering and food, and await delivery "without the company or aid of any person." After their children were born, and especially if they were males, they immersed them some time in the water, no matter what the temperature, and then swathed them in warm clothing and gave them great attention. Several days after delivery they returned to their homes, but until the child was weaned, had no commerce with their husbands, holding it to be disgraceful and injurious to their offspring.

In sickness they were very faithful to each other, and when death occurred the next of kin closed the eyes of the deceased. The men made no noise over the dead, but the women made frantic demonstrations of grief, striking their breasts, tearing their faces, and calling the name of the deceased day and night. Their loudest lamentations were on the death of their sons and husbands. On such occasions they cut off their hair and burned it on the grave in the presence of all their relatives, painted their faces pitch black, and in a deer's skin jerkin mourned the dead a full year. In burying their dead the body was placed in a sitting posture, and beside it were placed a pot, kettle, platter, spoon, money and provisions for use in the other world. Wood was then placed around the body, and the whole covered with earth and stones, outside of which palisades were erected, fastened in such a manner that the tomb resembled a little house.[1] To these tombs great respect was paid, and to violate them was deemed an unpardonable provocation.

---

[1] *Documentary History of New York*, iv, 127.

Their fare or food was poor and gross, "for," says one Dutch writer, "they drink water, having no other beverage." They eat the flesh of all sorts of game, "even badgers, dogs, eagles, and similar trash which Christians in no way regard." All sorts of fish were eaten, as well as "snakes, frogs and such like." Their mode of cooking without removing the entrails was not palatable to the Dutch. In addition to their meats they made bread of Indian meal and baked it in hot ashes, and make a "pap or porridge, called by some sapsis, by others dundare (literally boiled bread), in which they mixed beans of different color which they raised." The maize from which their bread and sapsis were made was raised by themselves, and was broken up or ground in rude mortars. They observed no set time for meals. Whenever hunger demanded, the repast was prepared. Beavers' tails, the brains of fish, and their sapsis,[1] ornamented with beans, were their state dishes and highest luxuries. They knew how to preserve meat and fish by smoking, and when on a journey or while hunting, carried with them corn roasted whole. At their meals they sat on the ground.

Their occupations were hunting, fishing and war. When not on the war path they repaired to the rivers and caught fish or to the forests and hunted deer, fawns, hares and foxes, "and all such," says the narrator who adds, "the country is full of game ; hogs, bears, leopards, yea, lions, as appears by the skins which were brought on board." The beaver was most highly prized by them, not only for its food and fur, but for the medicinal uses of the oil obtained. The women made clothing of skins, prepared food, cultivated the fields of corn, beans and squashes, made mats, etc., but the men never labored until they became too old for the field, when they remained with the women and made mats, wooden bowls and spoons, traps, nets, arrows, canoes, etc.

Their houses were for the most part built after one plan, differing only in lengths. They were formed by long, slender hickory saplings set in the ground, in a straight line of two rows, as far asunder as they intended the width to be and con-

---

[1] "The crushed corn is daily boiled to a pap which is called *suppaen*."

tinued the rows as far as they intended the length to be. The poles were then bent towards each other in the form of an arch and secured together, giving the appearance of a garden arbor. Split poles were then lathed up the sides and roof, and over this was bark, lapped on the ends and edges, which was kept in its place by withes to the lathings. A hole was left in the roof for smoke to escape, and a single door of entrance was provided. Rarely exceeding twenty feet in width, these houses were sometimes a hundred and eighty yards long. " In those places," says Van der Donck, "they crowd a surprising number of persons, and it is surprising to see them out in open day." From sixteen to eighteen families occupied one house, according to its size. A single fire in the centre served them all, although each family occupied at night its particular division and mats.

Their castles were strong, firm works, and were usually situated on the side of a steep, high hill, near a stream of water with a level plain on the crown of the hill. This plain was enclosed with a strong stockade, which was constructed by laying on the ground large logs of wood for a foundation, on both sides of which oak palisades were set in the ground, the upper ends of which crossed each other and were joined together: against the rude assaults of rude enemies , these castles were a safe retreat. Inside of their walls they not unfrequently had twenty or thirty houses, so that a clan or tribe could be provided for in winter. Besides their strongholds, they had villages and towns which were enclosed or stockaded. The latter usually had woodland on one side and corn land on the other. Near the water sides and at fishing places they not unfrequently had huts for temporary occupancy; but in the winter they were found in their castles which were rarely, if ever, left altogether.

Their weapons of war were the spear, the bow and arrows, the war club and the stone hatchet, and in combat they protected themselves with a square shield made of tough leather. A snake's skin tied around the head, from the centre of which projected the tail of a bear or a wolf, and a face not recognizable from the variety of colors in which it was painted, was their uniform. Their domestic implements were of very rude construction. Fire answered them many purposes and gained for them the name of Fireworkers. By it they not only cleared lands, but shaped their log canoes and made their wooden bowls. Some of their arrows were of elegant construction and tipped with copper, and when shot with power would pass through the body of a deer as certainly as the bullet from the rifle. The more common arrows were tipped with flint, as well as their spears, and required no little patience and skill in their construction. When they came to obtain guns from the Dutch they were remarkably expert with them.

Their money consisted of white and black zewant (wampum),[1] which was " nothing more nor less than the inside little pillars of the conch shells " which the sea cast up twice a year. These pillars they polished smooth, drilled a hole through the centre, reduced them to a certain size, and strung them on threads. Gold, silver or copper coins they had none. Their standards of value were the hand or fathom of wampum, and the *denotas* or bags which they made themselves for measuring and preserving corn. Such was their currency and such their only commercial transactions. To obtain wampum they made war and took captives for whom they demanded ransom, or made the weaker tribes tributaries to the stronger.

[1] There were two kinds of wampum in early use by the Indians, as a standard of value, the *purple* or black and the *white*. The purple was made from the interior portions of the *venus mercenaria*, or common conch. The white was wrought out of the pillar of the periwinkle. Each kind was converted into a kind of bead, by being rounded and perforated, so as to admit of being strung on a fibre of deer's sinew. This was replaced after the discovery, by linen thread. The article was highly prized as an ornament, and as such constituted an object of traffic between the sea coast and the interior tribes. It was worn around the neck ; also as an edging for certain pieces of their garments ; and when these strings were united, they formed the broad wampum belts by which solemn public transactions were commemorated. As a substitute for gold and silver coin, its price was fixed by law. Three *purple* beads of wampum, or six of *white*, were equal to a stuyver among the Dutch, or a penny among the English. Some variations, however, existed in its value, according to time and place. A single string of wampum of one fathom, ruled at five shillings in New England, and is known in New Netherland to have reached as high as four guilders, or one dollar and sixty-six cents. The old wampum was made by hand and was an exceedingly rude article. After the discovery, the Dutch introduced the lathe in its manufacture, polished and perforated it with exactness, and soon had the monopoly of the trade. The principal place of its manufacture was at Hackensak, in New Jersey. The principal deposit of sea-shells was Long Island, where the extensive shell banks left by the Indians, in which it is difficult to find a whole shell, show the immense quantities that were manufactured.

They were not skilled in the practice of medicines, notwithstanding the general belief on that subject. They knew how
to cure wounds and hurts, and treated simple diseases successfully. Their general health was due more to their habits than
to a knowledge of remedies. Their principal medical treatment was the sweating bath. These were literally earthen
ovens, into which the patient crept, and around which heated
stones were placed to raise the temperature. When the patient
had remained under perspiration for a certain time he was taken
out and immersed suddenly in cold water, a process which
served to cure or certainly cause death. The oil which they
obtained from beavers was used in many forms and for many
purposes ; among others for dizziness, for trembling, for the
rheumatism, for lameness, for apoplexy, for toothache, for
earache, for weak eyes, for gout, and for almost all ills. The
Dutch took to this remedy and attached to it great value.

As the term is generally understood, they had no religion,
but in its place a rude system in which they looked

" Through nature up to nature's God."

Good and evil spirits they recognized, and to them appealed in
sacrifice and fires. Their minister or priest was called *kitzi-
naeka*. It was his duty to visit the sick and exorcise the evil
spirits ; or, failing, to see the usual rites for the dead performed.
He had no home of his own, but lodged were it pleased him,
or where he last officiated ; was not permitted to eat any food
prepared by a married woman, but that only which was cooked
by a maiden or an old woman, and altogether lived " like a
Capuchin." [1] To the sun, moon and stars they paid particular
attention. The first moon following that at the end of February they greatly honored. They watched its coming and
greeted its advent with a festival, at which they collected from
all quarters and reveled " in their way with wild game or fish,"
and drank clear river water to their fill. This was their new
year ; this moon the harbinger of spring. The harvest moon,
or the new moon in August, they also honored with a feast, in

---

[1] Wassenaar, *Documentary History of New York*, III, 28.

acknowledgment of the product of their fields and their success in the chase.

They fully recognized the existence of God, who dwelt beyond the stars, and in a life immortal expected to renew the associations of this life.[1]   But to them God had less to do with the world than did the devil, who was the principal subject of their fears, and the source of their earthly hopes.   No expeditions of hunting, fishing or war were undertaken unless the devil was first consulted, and to him they offered the first fruits of the chase, or of victory.   "On such occasions," says one of the early writers, "conjurors act a wonderful part.   These

Devil Worship.

tumble, with strange contortions, head over heels, beat themselves, leap, with a hideous noise, through and around a large fire.[2]   Finally they set up a tremendous caterwauling, when the devil, as they say, appears in the shape of a ravenous or harmless animal; the first betokens something bad, the other good; both give information respecting coming events, but obscurely, which they attribute to their own ignorance, not understanding the devil's right meaning when matters turn out differently."   For the spiritual they cared nothing; but directed

[1] The belief of *Maikans* regarding the separation of the soul, is, that it goes up westward on leaving the body.   There it is met with great rejoicing by the others who died previously; there they wear black otter or bear skins, which among them are signs of gladness.   They have no desire to be with them.—*Wassenaar.*

[2] This dance of the Indians was called *kinte-kaying.*   It was observed on the

their study principally to the physical, "closely observing the seasons." Their women were the most experienced star-gazers, scarce one of whom could not name them all, give the time of their rising and setting, their position, etc., in language of their own. *Taurus* they described as the horned head of a big wild animal inhabiting the distant country, but not theirs; that when it rose in a certain part of the heavens, then it was the season for planting. The firmament was to them an open book wherein they read the laws for their physical well-being, the dial plate by which they marked their years.

They were not without government and laws, although both partook of the nomadic state. They had chief and subordinate rulers, and general as well as local councils. Their sachem was their local ruler and representative. Their general councils were composed of the sachems of different families or clans. But these councils assembled only in case of war, or other matters requiring concerted action. In all other respects the tribes or clans acted independently, and declared war and made peace without reference to their neighbors, unless the contest was such that assistance was desirable, in which case invitations to alliance were sent out by messengers. All obligations acquired their force from the acceptance of presents. In making agreements or sending messages they took as many little sticks as there were conditions or parties in their proposals.[1] If the contracting parties agreed on all, each party, at the conclusion, laid his presents at the feet of the other. If the presents be mutually accepted, the negotiation is firmly concluded, but if not, no further proceedings were had unless the applicant changed the conditions and the presents. On occasions of importance, a general assembly was held at the house of the chief

eve of engaging in expeditions of war or hunting. When taken prisoners and about to suffer torture, they asked permission to dance the *kinte-kaye*. The first dance witnessed by the Europeans was by the savages assembled on the point of land just above Newburgh, which still bears the name of *Dans kammer*, or dance chamber.

[1] "As to the information which you observe I formerly transmitted to the governor of New York, concerning the belt and fifteen bloody sticks sent by the Missiosagaes, the like is very common, and the Indians use sticks as well to express the alliance of castles as the number of individuals in a party. These sticks are generally about six inches in length and very slender, and painted red if the subject is war, but without any peculiarity as to shape.—*Documentary History of New York*, IV, 437.

sachem in order that a full explanation might be made. At these assemblies the will of the sachem was supreme, for although permitting full debate, mutiny was punished by death.

Lands held by them were obtained by conceded original occupation or by conquest. If conquered, original right ceased and vested in the conquerors; if reconquered, the title returned to its original owners. This rule they applied also to the sale of lands to the Dutch. As often as they sold to the latter and subsequently drove off the settlers, so often was repurchase necessary, and, if it was not made, cause of grievance and future war remained. Some respect was paid to the rights of property, and whenever it was stolen, it was ordered returned.[1] Although the reputation attaches that they were a "thieving set," yet the fact is that in almost every stated case the Dutch were the aggressors, the Indians only making reprisals for that of which they had been despoiled.

Rank was known among them; nobles, who seldom married below their rank, as well as a commonalty.[2] These conditions were hereditary, for although one of the commonalty might rise to prominence, the sachemship descended as long as any one was found fit to rule, and regents frequently governed in the name of a minor. The oldest or first of a household or family represented it "with or unto the chief of the nation." Military distinction was conferred by merit without regard to families or birth. The lowest might become a chief, but the rank died with its possessor, unless his posterity followed in his footsteps, in which case his titles were transmitted. Those of hereditary rank, however, were not esteemed, unless they were distinguished for activity, bravery and understanding, and such they honored greatly.

Their armies, or warriors, were composed of all their young men, among whom were even boys of fifteen, and were not without some of the forms of organization and discipline known to civilized nations. Each clan or canton had its war chiefs,

[1] "Notwithstanding misdemeanors are not punished, wicked acts are of rare occurrence. Stolen property, whenever discovered, is ordered by the chief to be restored. If any one commit that offense (stealing) too often, he is stripped bare of his goods." — *Documentary History,* IV, 129; *Wassenaar, Ib.,* III, 44.

[2] "Though this people do not make such a distinction between man and man as

or captains, as the Europeans called them,[1] who stood in rank according to the services by which they had distinguished themselves, the one highest in the qualifications of prudence, cunning, resolution, bravery, and good fortune, had powers equivalent to a commanding general. In times of war, the tribes were under rigid martial law; nothing was done without the consent of the war captains; no warrior could leave the troop without forfeiting his honor and the highly esteemed advantages of promotion.

To begin a war was called "taking up the hatchet," and could not be done without what were regarded as the most just and important reasons. The death of a warrior at the hands of a neighboring tribe, was not always a cause for war. The murderer could be surrendered or the offense atoned by presents; but when a warrior was killed and scalped, or when, as with the *Mohawks*, the hatchet was left sticking in the head of the victim, it was regarded as a declaration of war. In such cases the war captains summoned their followers and addressed them: " The bones of your murdered countrymen lie uncovered; they demand revenge at our hands, and it is our duty to obey them; their spirits loudly call upon us, and we must satisfy them; still greater spirits watching over our honor, inspire us with a resolution to go in pursuit of the murderers of our brethren. Let us go and devour them! Do not sit inactive! Follow the impulse of your hereditary valor! Anoint your hair! Paint your faces! Fill your quivers! Make the woods echo with your voices! Comfort the spirits of the deceased, and revenge their blood!" The work of preparation for the field was speedily performed; the weapons of war were collected, a pouch of parched corn and maple sugar prepared, and the body painted black. Then came the war·dance and

other nations, yet they have high and low families; inferior and superior chiefs, whose authority remains hereditary in the houses. The military officers are disposed of only according to the valorous prowess of each person."— *Documentary History of New York*, IV, 128.

[1] A captain among the Indians, is what we should call a commander or general. He has several subordinate officers, in proportion to the number of troops under his command. The rank of captain is neither elective nor hereditary. The first occasion to this appointment is generally a dream, early in life, which a young man or his friends interpret as a destiny for the office of captain. He therefore endeavors to attain the necessary qualifications for this dignity, and to prove his prowess by feats of valor.— *Loskiel.*

war song;[1] and the paths of the forest received the avenging horde, to return to peace only when compelled by necessity or the intervention of mediators.

The ceremonies of war and peace were somewhat different when the alliance of one tribe with another was called. In such cases an embassy was dispatched bearing a piece of tobacco, a belt of wampum, and a hatchet with a red handle. The tobacco invited a friendly smoke and consideration, the belt described by certain figures the tribe against whom alliance was desired, and the hatchet determined the purpose. The principal captain of the embassy made a speech, on delivering these credentials of his authority. If the belt was accepted, nothing more was said, that act being considered a solemn promise to lend every assistance; but if neither the hatchet was lifted up nor the belt accepted, it was understood that the tribe would remain neutral. The consideration of the matter was usually circumspect and slow, and the decision regarded with no little reverence.

The lives of prisoners taken in war were rarely spared, except those of women and children, who were treated leniently and adopted by their conquerors to recruit their numbers. Male prisoners were subjected to great torture, usually by fire, and a savage cunning indeed was practiced in prolonging the sufferings of the victims. The next of kin was an avenger and might inflict death on a murderer, provided he was enabled to do so within twenty-four hours. After the lapse of that time the avenger himself was liable to death if death came by

---

[1] Heckewelder gives the following as the war song of the Lenape warriors:
"O poor me!
Who am going out to fight the enemy,
And know not whether I shall return again,
To enjoy the embraces of my children
And my wife.
O poor creature!
Whose life is not in his own hands,
Who has no power over his own body,
But tries to do his duty
For the welfare of his nation.
O thou Great Spirit above!
Take pity on my children
And on my wife!

Prevent their mourning on my account!
Grant that I may be successful in this attempt,
That I may slay my enemy,
And bring home the trophies of war
To my dear family and friends,
That we may rejoice together.
O take pity on me!
Give me strength and courage to meet my enemy.
Suffer me to return again to my children,
To my wife!
And to my relations!
Take pity on me and preserve my life,
And I will make thee a sacrifice."

his hand. A murderer was seldom killed after the first twenty-four hours were passed, but he was obliged to remain concealed ; meantime his friends endeavored to reconcile the parties, and offered a blood atonement of wampum. If peace was agreed upon it was usually accompanied by the condition that the nearest relatives of the murderer, whether men, women or children, on meeting the relatives of the murdered person, must give way to them. But an offense unatoned was unforgiven, and, though years might elapse, vengeance was certain if opportunity offered.

Great faults were charged against the Indians, and great faults they doubtless possessed when judged from the standpoint of a different civilization. Were the line strictly drawn, however, it might be shown that, as a whole, they compared favorably with nations upon whom light had fallen for sixteen hundred years. This at least appears to their credit, that among them there were none who were cross-eyed, blind, crippled, lame, hunch-backed or limping ; all were well-fashioned, strong in constitution of body, well-proportioned and without blemish. Until touched and warped by wrong treatment, wherever they were met, whether on the Potomac, the Delaware, the Hudson, or the Connecticut, they were liberal and generous in their intercourse with the whites. More sinned against than sinning, they left behind them evidences of great wrongs suffered, their enemies being the witnesses.

CHAPTER III.

National and Tribal Organizations, Totemic Classifications, Political Relations, etc.

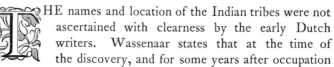HE names and location of the Indian tribes were not ascertained with clearness by the early Dutch writers. Wassenaar states that at the time of the discovery, and for some years after occupation by the Dutch, the *Maikans* or *Mahicans*, held twenty-five [1] miles on both sides of the river in the vicinity of Fort Orange; that the *Maquas*, or *Mohawks*, resided in the interior; that Fort Orange was erected on the lands of the *Mahicans*, whose castle was on the opposite (east) side of the river. De Laet writes in 1625, that the *Maquas* held the west shore, and Wassenaar concludes with a similar statement; but if it is considered that the history of the latter was written at different periods extending from 1621 to 1632, his account will be found entirely consistent with itself as well as with De Laet's. South of Fort Orange the classifications of these writers is almost wholly by chieftaincies or cantons. Van der Donck, writing twenty years later, does not appear to have obtained more definite knowledge than his predecessors.

From information subsequently obtained, however, and especially that furnished by treaties and other documentary papers, it would appear that at the time of the discovery the *Mahicans* held possession, under sub-tribal organizations, of the east bank of the river from an undefined point north of Albany to the sea, including Long Island; that their dominion extended east to the Connecticut, where they joined kindred tribes; that on the west bank of the Hudson they ran down as far as Catskill, and west to Schenectady; that they were met on the west by the territory of the *Mohawks*, and on the south by chieftaincies

[1] Seventy-five English miles.

acknowledging the supremacy of the *Minsis*, a totemic tribe of the *Lenni Lenapes*, and that the territory of the latter extended thence to the sea, and west to and beyond the Delaware river. Pending the early operations of the Dutch traders, this original classification was somewhat changed. The *Mahicans* sold a considerable portion of their lands on the west side of the river to Van Rensselaer, retaining only a castle at Cohoes falls and one at Katskill, and admitted the *Mohawks* to territorial sovereignty north of the Mohawk river. Although the latter were not in possession by castles and villages, it may be admitted that, practically, as early as 1630, three great divisions or nations were represented on the Hudson : The IROQUOIS,[1] the MAHICANS, and the LENNI LENAPES, or Delawares as they were more modernly known. The first of these nations, the IROQUOIS, was represented by a tribe called by themselves *Kayingehaga ;* by their enemies, the Mahicans, the *Maquas ;* by the Dutch, *Makwaes;* by the English, *Mohawks,* and by the French *Agniers.* The IROQUOIS CONFEDERACY[2] was, at this time, composed of five tribes under the modern names of *Mohawks, Oneidas, Onondagas, Cayugas,* and *Senecas* and bore the title of *Aquinoshioni* or *Konoshioni,* that is, Cabin-makers, or People of the Long House, as applied to their territorial possessions and national organization. That " long house " subsequently reached from the banks of the Hudson to the shores of Lake Erie, and from the Katskill range to the St. Lawrence — the Eastern door guarded by the *Mohawks* and the western by the *Senecas.*

The traditions held by the *Iroquois* respecting their origin and confederate organization,[3] are that, like the Athenian, they sprung from the earth itself. In remote ages they had been confined under a mountain near the falls of the Osh-wah-kee,

---

[1] The appellation, *Iroquois*, was first applied to them by the French, because they usually began and finished their discourses or *palaver* with the word *hiro,* which means either " I say," or " I have said," combined as an affix with the word *konë,* an exclamation expressing joy or sorrow according as it was pronounced long or short."—*Garneau's History of Canada.*

[2] *Colden's History of the Six Nations; Schoolcraft's Notes on the Iroquois; Dunlap's Hist. New York ; Yates & Moulton's History New York; O'Callaghan's New Netherland ; Brodhead's New York,* etc.

[3] The Iroquois tribes are classed by Gallatin in three divisions : eastern, western, and southern. The eastern consisted of the confederation known as the Five Nations, the western of the Wy-

or Oswego river, whence they were released by *Tharonhyjagon,* the Holder of the Heavens. Bidding them go forth to the east, he guided them to the valley of the Mohawk, and following its stream they reached the Hudson, which some of them descended to the sea. Retracing their steps towards the west, they originated, in their order and position, the *Mohawks, Oneidas, Onondagas, Cayugas, Senecas,* and *Tuscaroras,* six nations ; but the *Tuscaroras* wandered away to the south and settled on the Cautano, or Neuse river, in North Carolina, reducing the number to five nations.

Each of the tribes thus originated was independent of the others, and warred with each other, as well as with the surrounding tribes. *Tharonhyjagon* still remained with the tribes ; gave them seeds of various kinds, with the proper knowledge for planting them ; taught them how to kill and roast game ; made the forests free to all the tribes to hunt, and removed obstructions from the streams. After this he laid aside his divine character and resolved to live with the *Onondagas,* that he might exemplify the maxims he had taught. For this purpose he selected a handsome spot of ground on the southern banks of the lake called *Teonto,* being the sheet of water now known as Cross lake.[1] Here he built a cabin, and took a wife of the *Onondagas,* by whom he had an only daughter, whom he tenderly loved, and most kindly and carefully treated and instructed. The excellence of his character, and his great sagacity and good counsels, led the people to view him with veneration, and they gave him the name of *Hi-a-wat-ha,* signifying a very wise man. From all quarters people came to him for advice, and in this manner all power came naturally into his hands, and he was regarded as the first chief in all the land. Under his teachings the *Onondagas* became the first among all the original clans. They were the wisest counselors, the best orators, the most expert hunters, and the bravest warriors.

andots, or Hurons, and the Attiouanda-rons, or neutral nation, north, and the Erigas and Andastes, or Guandastogues (Guyandots), south of Lake Erie ; the southern, of the Tuscaroras, the Tùtelos, and the Nottowas, of North Carolina.

The Tuscaroras and Tutelos removed to the north, the former in 1714 and the latter in 1758, and were incorporated in the Five Nations, the former becoming the sixth member of the confederacy.

[1] *Schoolcraft's Notes on the Iroquois,* 273.

Hence the *Onondagas* were early noted among all the tribes for their preeminence.

While *Hiawatha* was thus living in quiet among the " people of the hills," the tribes were attacked by a furious and powerful enemy from the north of the great lakes. This enemy advanced into the country and laid waste the villages, and slaughtered men, women and children, until the people had no heart to oppose the invaders. In this emergency they fled to *Hiawatha* for advice, who counseled them to call together all the tribes from the east, and the west, " for," said he, " our safety is not alone in the club and dart, but in wise counsels." He appointed a place on the banks of the Onondaga lake for the meeting, and thither the chiefs, warriors, and head men forthwith assembled in large numbers, bringing with them their women and children.

The council had been waiting for three days, but as yet *Hiawatha* was absent. Messengers were dispatched to hasten his attendance, but they found him gloomy and depressed. He told them that evil lay in his path, and felt that he should be called to make some great sacrifice ; nevertheless he would attend the council. The talismanic white canoe, in which he always made his voyages, and which the people had learned to reverence, was got out and *Hiawatha* and his daughter took their seats. Gliding silently down the deep waters of the Seneca, the canoe reached the outlet and entered on the placid Onondaga. As the canoe of the venerated chief appeared, he was welcomed with loud shouts ; but while he was measuring his steps towards the council ground, a long and low sound was heard, and instantly all eyes were turned upward, where a compact mass of cloudy darkness appeared, which gathered size and velocity as it approached, and appeared to be directed inevitably to fall in the midst of the assembly. Every one fled but *Hiawatha* and his daughter, who calmly awaited the issue. The force of the descending body was like that of a sudden storm ; and hardly had *Hiawatha* paused, when an immense bird, with long distended wings, came down, with a swoop, and crushed the daughter to the earth. The very semblance of a human being was destroyed in the remains of the girl, and the head and neck of the bird were buried in the ground from the force of the fall.

Hiawatha was inconsolable for several days ; but at length took his place in the council and the deliberations opened. The subject of the invasion was discussed by several of the ablest counselors, and various plans proposed to foil the enemy. *Hiawatha* listened to the debate, and at its conclusion bade the warriors depart until the next day when he would unfold his plan, which he felt confident would ensure safety.

The council again met ; and with even more than ordinary attention the people listened to the words of their great chief. *Hiawatha* counseled them, that " to oppose these hordes of northern tribes singly and alone, would prove certain destruction ; " that to oppose them successfully, the tribes must unite in " one common band of brothers," must have one voice, one fire, one pipe, and one war club. In the confederacy which he proposed should be formed, the several tribes were assigned the position they were to thereafter occupy ; and, in conclusion, he urged them to weigh well his words ; that if they should unite in the bond he had proposed, the Great Spirit would smile upon them, and they would be free, prosperous and happy ; but if they rejected it, they would be " enslaved, ruined, perhaps annihilated forever."

The tribes received the address in solemn silence ; and the council closed to deliberate on the plan recommended. Assembling the next day, the union of the tribes into one confederacy was discussed and unanimously adopted. Pending this result, *Hiawatha*, warned by the death of his daughter that his mission was accomplished, prepared to make his final departure from earth. Before the council dispersed, he recounted the services he had rendered to his people, and urged them to preserve the union they had formed. " If you preserve this," said he, " and admit no foreign element of power, by the admission of other nations, you will always be free, numerous and happy. If other tribes and nations are admitted to your councils, they will sow the seeds of jealousy and discord, and you will become few, feeble and enslaved. Remember these words, they are the last you will hear from the lips of *Hiawatha*. The Great

Master of breath calls me to go. I have patiently waited his summons. I am ready to go. Farewell." As his voice ceased, sweet sounds, from the air, burst on the ears of the multitude ; and while all attention was engrossed in the celestial melody, *Hiawatha* was seen, seated in his white canoe, in the mid-air, rising with every choral chant that burst out, till the clouds shut out the sight and the melody ceased. Every warrior now plucked a feather from the great bird as a memorial, and took their departure.[1]

The precise date of the formation of the confederacy cannot, of course, be ascertained. Pyrlaus, a missionary among the *Mohawks*, states as the result of his investigations, that the alliance took place " one age, or the length of a man's life, before the white people came into the country." Another writer fixes the date at 1414 ; while a third confirms the statement of Pyrlaus.[2] Whatever may have been its date, it was a practical and effective alliance by which the democratic principle, which was the basis of the government of the cantons, was extended to the expression of the national will. The general head had few powers, but the determination of the tribes, in regard to matters in which they had a common interest, when announced from the general council at Onondaga, carried with it the united voice of an empire. The active government was confined to the tribes or cantons, which were independent states. Each had its own chiefs, civil and military, and its own council, and was represented in general councils by sachems exercising the power of delegates. These delegates, however, spoke the popular will of the tribes they represented, and to determine their action they were not permitted to approve any measure which the tribe had not endorsed by an unanimous vote. Indeed, the unanimous principle was the ruling one of the confederacy. Tribes might declare war and conclude peace, and exercise all powers of sovereignty on their own account,

[1] *Schoolcraft's Notes,* 278, etc.
[2] *Schoolcraft's Notes,* 118, 120, etc. " The time when the confederacy was formed is not known, but it was presumed to be of a recent date, and 'the Oneidas and Cayugas are said to have been com- pelled to join it. Those two tribes were the younger, and the three others the older members of the confederacy." — *Gallatin.* " The Oneidas and Cayugas are their children."—*Zinzendorf.*

but national or confederated action required the concurrence of all the tribes, and hence, when a decision was made, it was clothed with all the power of the most full popular will.[1] There was no female suffrage among them, and yet females had the power, by adoption, to rescue prisoners from death, and to command a cessation of war. When so determined by the matrons, the braves returned from the conflict without compromiting the character of the tribe for bravery. But this feature in their customs was common to all the Indian nations. It remains to be shown that they had any forms of government peculiar to themselves. Their power was in their confederation, and in this they apparently differed from other nations only in the number of tribes and in the perpetuity of the organization, other nations securing the same results, in case of war, by temporary alliances.

A view of their national council is furnished by Loskiel, who says that in 1745, Spangenberg, one of the Moravian bishops, spent several weeks at Onondaga, and frequently attended its sessions. " The council-house was built of bark. On each side six seats were placed, each containing six persons. No one was admitted besides the members of the council, except a few, who were particularly honored. If one arose to speak, all the rest sat in profound silence, smoking their pipes. The speaker uttered his words in a singing tone, always rising a few notes at the close of each sentence. Whatever was pleasing to the council was confirmed by all with the word *nee*, or *yes*. And at the end of each speech, the whole company joined in applauding the speaker by calling *hoho*. At noon, two men entered, bearing a large kettle filled with meat upon a pole across their shoulders, which was first presented to the guests. A large wooden ladle as broad and deep as a common bowl, hung with a hook to the side of the kettle, with which every one might at once help himself to as much as he could eat.

[1] The difference between confederated and tribal action has many illustrations in the history of the times in which they took a conspicuous part. It became very difficult indeed to secure unity of action in favor of the English at different times, and in 1755 it was entirely defeated. In 1763, Johnson did not class the Senecas among the "friendly tribes," and in 1775 the English were compelled to resort to tribal alliances, in view of the determination of the council in favor of neutrality.

The whole was conducted in a very decent and quiet manner. Indeed, now and then one or the other would lie flat upon his back and rest himself, and sometimes they would stop, joke and laugh heartily."

The second of the national divisions was the MAHICANS, called by the Dutch, *Maikans,* and, by the French missionaries, " the nine nations of *Manhingans,*[1] gathered between Manhattan and the environs of Quebec." The several nations composing the confederacy have never been designated, although certain general divisions appear under the titles of the *Mahicans,* the *Soquatucks,* the *Horicons,* the *Pennacooks,* the *Nipmucks,* the *Abenaquis,* the *Nawaas,* the *Sequins,* and the *Wappingers,* which, in confederated action, may be classed under the generic name of *Abenaqui,* or *Wapanachki,* that is, Men of the East. The representative nation of the confederacy on the Hudson, the *Mahican,* appears to have taken original position there, and to have sent out subduing colonies to the south and east, originating other national combinations. To the noble stream upon which they were found by the Dutch they gave their name, the Mahicanituck ; and kindled their ancient council-fire at Schodac, opposite the site of the present city of Albany. To trace their movements prior to the discovery, tradition and theory must be blended. It may be presumed that in the course of the ages they seized the head waters of the Connecticut, the Housatonic, and the Hudson, and from their inland position rolled a savage horde upon the sea-coast, giving birth to the Pequots and the Narragansetts,[2] and from thence overrunning the tribes on the southern part of the peninsula of New York and the adjacent islands, and reuniting with the parent stock as one independent tribe in the position in which they were found

[1] *Muhhekaneew* is the orthography of the original name as given by Dr. Edwards, for many years among them. The Dutch called them Mahikanders ; the French knew them as the Mourigans and Manhingans ; the English as the Mohiccons, Mohegans, Muhheeckanew, etc.

[2] Hubbard, referring to the Pequots, says that it was " commonly reported, about the time when New England was planted by the English," that they, " being a more fierce, cruel, and warlike people than the rest of the Indians, came down out of the inland parts of the continent, and by force seized upon the goodliest places near the sea, and became a terror to all their neighbors."—*Indian Wars,* 14. The relationship between the Mahicans and Pequots is so conclusively shown that one must have apparently originated the other.

by the Dutch under the names of *Wappingers*, *Montauks* and *Mahicans*.

The tradition which the *Mahicans* give of their origin states: " The country formerly owned by the Muhheakunnuk nation, was situated partly in Massachusetts, and partly in the states of Vermont and New York. The inhabitants dwelt chiefly in little towns and villages. Their chief seat was on Hudson's river, now it is called Albany, which was called Pempotowwut-hut-Muhhecanneuw, or the fire-place of the Muhheakunnuk nation, where their allies used to come on any business whether relative to the covenants of their friendship or other matters. The etymology of the word Muhheakunnuk, according to original signification, is great waters or sea, which are constantly in motion, either ebbing or flowing. Our forefathers asserted that they were emigrants from west-by-north of another country ; that they passed over great waters, where this and the other country are nearly connected, called Ukhkokpeck ; it signifies snake water or water where snakes are abundant ; and that they lived by side of a great water or sea, from whence they derive the name of Muhheakunnuk nation. Muhheakunneuw signifies a man of Muhheakunnuk tribe. Muhheakunneyuk is a plural number. As they were coming from the west they found many great waters, but none of them flowing and ebbing like Muh-heakunnuk until they came to Hudson's river ; then they said one to another, this is like Muhheakunnuk our nativity. And when they found grain was very plenty in that country, they agreed to kindle a fire there and hang a kettle, whereof they and their children after them might dip out their daily refresh-ment. That before they began to decay, our forefathers in-formed us that the Muhheakunnuk nation could then raise about one thousand warriors who could turn out at any emergency." [1]

The government of the *Mahicans* was a democracy. They had a chief sachem, chosen by the nation, upon whom they looked as conductor and promoter of the general welfare. This office was hereditary by the lineage of the wife of the sachem ; that is, the selection of a successor, on the death of a

---

[1] *Massachusetts Historical Society Collections*, IX, 101. In some of its parts this tradition bears the impress of the theories entertained by the early missionaries.

sachem, was confined to the female branch of the family. The sachem was assisted by counselors, and also by one hero, one owl, and one runner; the rest of the nation were called young men or warriors. The sachem, or more properly king, remained at all times with his tribe and consulted their welfare; he had charge of the *mnoti*, or bag of peace, which contained the belts and strings used to establish peace and friendship with different nations, and concluded all treaties on behalf of his people. The counselors were elected, and were called chiefs. Their business was to consult with their sachem in promoting the peace and happiness of their people. The title of hero was gotten only by courage and prudence in war. When a war-alliance was asked, or cause for war existed with another tribe, the sachem and the counselors consulted, and if they concluded to take up the hatchet; the matter was put in the hands of the heroes for execution. When peace was proposed, the heroes put the negotiations in the hands of the sachem and counselors. The office of owl was also one of merit. He must have a strong memory, and must be a good speaker. His business was to sit beside his sachem, and proclaim his orders to the people with a loud voice; and also to get up every morning as soon as day-light and arouse the people, and order them to their daily duties. The business of runner was to carry messages, and to convene councils.[1]

Precisely what relation the *Mahicans* of the Hudson sustained to the *Mohegans* under Uncas, is not known. Uncas, it will be remembered, was a Pequot chief, and as such occupied a district of country between the Thames and the Connecticut, called Mohegoneak.[2] After an unsuccessful conflict with the tribe to which he belonged, he fled, with some fifty of his

---

[1] *Stockbridge, Past and Present.*

[2] The Pequot and *Mohegan* country lay to the south and east of the *Nehanticks* (in Lyme), from Connecticut river to the eastern boundary line of the colony, and north-east or north of its northern boundary line. This tract was thirty miles square, and included the counties of New London, Windham, and the principal parts of the county of Tolland. The Pequot country proper was principally within the three towns of New London, Groton and Stonington. All the tract above this, as far north and east as has been described, was the Mohegan country; and most, if not all, the towns held their deeds from Uncas or his successors. Dr. Trumbull, in his *History of Connecticut*, expresses the opinion, that the Pequots and Mohegans were one tribe and took their names "from the place of their situation."—*Massachusetts Historical Society Collections*, IX, 79.

followers, to Hartford, where he formed an alliance with the English in 1638. In the subsequent wars between the English and the Pequots, he remained faithful to the former, and, when the Pequots were blotted out as a nation,[1] received a portion of its survivors as his reward. He subsequently became one of the most powerful chiefs of the country, and the petted favorite of the English of Connecticut. Originally of the same stock ;[2] controlled by the same traditionary hostility to the Mohawks ; influenced by the conflict for jurisdiction between the Dutch and the English to the Connecticut, it is not at all improbable that he was frequently found sustaining his brethren on the Hudson, and that they in turn recruited his numbers to some extent.[3] The organization under Uncas, however, was clearly distinct from that of the Hudson confederacy.[4] The latter were powerful in themselves, and in their recognized confederated allies, and successfully disputed the prowess of their Mohawk rivals.

The third of the great divisions or confederations represented on the Hudson was the LENNI LENAPES, a name which they applied to themselves, and which has had various interpretations, among others, that of original people, and unmixed people. [5] They were also called by the generic name of *Wapanachki*,

[1] By the terms of peace which closed the Pequot war, that nation were not to live in their ancient country, nor be called by their ancient name, but to become Narragansetts and Mohegans. The name of their ancient river was changed to Thames, and their territory was to be considered the property of the English.—*Rhode Island Historical Society Collections*, III, 177.

[2] " And the identity of name between the *Mahicans* of the Hudson and the *Mohegans* of East Connecticut, induces the belief that all those tribes belonged to the same stock."—*Gallatin*, II, 34. " The *Pequots* and *Mohegans* were apparently originally of the same race with the *Mohieans*, *Mohegans*, or *Mohicanders*, who lived on the banks of the Hudson."—*De Forest's History of the Indians of Connecticut.*

[3] " Some *Mahicanders* are at Hertford in consultation with others the rivers and Northern Indians."—*Col. Nichols*, *June* 25, 1666 ; *Colonial History*, III, 117.

[4] This fact cannot be too distinctly recognized. The *Mohegans* were an exclusively Eastern Connecticut tribe and in alliance with the government of that province ; the *Mahicans* of New York differed from them in their dialect, in the territory which they occupied, and in their alliances ; having in the latter respect a nominal representation with the authorities of New York and a positive one with Massachusetts. The *Mohegans* of Connecticut were one of the very few tribes whose organization and subsequent history is a matter of record ; the *Mahicans* of the Hudson ante-date all human knowledge.

[5] " The term *Lenape*," says Schoolcraft, " appears to carry the same meaning as *inaba*, a male, and the word was probably used nationally, and with emphasis in the sense of men." " I have called them simply *Lenape*, as they do themselves in most instances."—*Heckewelder.*

or Men of the East.[1] Their territory extended from the Katskill mountains south to the Potomac, occupying the region watered by the Hudson, the Delaware,[2] the Susquehanna and the Potomac. The site of their ancient council-fire was at what is now Philadelphia, on the bank of the *Lenapewihituk*, or Delaware river ; *Lenape*, the term given to themselves, and *ituk* a geographical equivalent for the English word domain or territory.[3]

According to tradition [4] handed down from their ancestors, the *Lenni Lenapes* resided for many centuries in a very distant country, in the western part of the American continent. Having resolved to move eastward, they set out in a body in search of a new home ; and after a long journey and many nights encampment, (i. e., halts of one year at a place), they reached the *Namaesi Sipee* (Mississippi), where they fell in with another nation, the *Mengwe*, or Iroquois, who had also emigrated from a distant country for the same purpose. The region east of the Mississippi was occupied by the *Allegewi* (Alleghany), a powerful and partially civilized people, having numerous large towns defended by regular fortifications and entrenchments.[5]

[1] " These people are known and called by all the western, northern and some of the southern nations by the name of Wappanachki, which the Europeans have corrupted into Apenaki, Öpenagi, Abenaquis, and Abenakis. All these names, however differently written, and improperly understood by authors, point to one and the same people, the Lenape, who are by this compound word called People at the rising of the Sun, or as we would say Eastlanders ; and are acknowledged by near forty tribes, whom we call nations. All these nations, derived from the same stock, recognize each other as Wappanachki, which among them is a generic name."—*Heckewelder*.

[2] Their territorial possessions on the Hudson are clearly defined. Onderis Hocque, one of their chiefs, declared to the Esopus clans, at the treaty of 1660 : " Ye must not renew this quarrel. This is not your land ; it is our land. Therefore repeat not this, but throw down the hatchet. Tread it so deeply in the earth that it shall never be taken up again."

In the controversy in reference to the Hardenbergh tract, in 1769, one Dr. Shuckburgh stated that he was present at a conference in 1734, in which the chiefs of Schoharie, Seth and Hance, " told the Esopus or Delawares that if they ever attempted to sell lands west of the Katskill hills, they would kill them." An Oneida Indian, whose father was chief sachem of Oneida, " and their oracle in all matters of antiquity," heard his " father often say that the lands on the east of the Delaware was the property of the River Indians or Delawares."—*Johnson Manuscripts*, XVII, 159.

[3] The capital of the nation was subsequently removed to Shamokin, and from thence to Wyoming.

[4] No value whatever attaches to these traditions. That which is here recited gives to them a western origin, in face of their eastern name.

[5] " It is generally believed that the *Allegewi*, or *Alleghans*, were of Welsh origin. This belief rests on the supposed voyage of Madoc to this continent in the twelfth century. The Welsh tradition is,

In this country the *Lenape*, on their arrival, asked to settle. This request was denied by the *Allegewi*, but permission was granted to pass through the territory, and seek a settlement further eastward. No sooner had they commenced to cross the Mississippi, however, than the *Allegewi*, perceiving the vast numbers of the *Lenape*, furiously attacked them. The result of this treachery was a long and bloody war between the *Lenape* and their allies the *Mengwe*, on the one side, and the *Allegewi* on the other. The latter, after protracted contest, finding themselves unable to make head against the formidable alliance, and that their very existence, as a distinct tribe, was threatened, abandoned their ancient seats and fled down the Mississippi, from whence they never again returned. Of course, their lands were divided by the conquerors.

For a long period — some say for several centuries — the *Mengwe* and *Lenape* dwelt in peace together, and both nations rapidly increased in numbers. At length some of the more enterprising of the *Lenape* huntsmen and warriors crossed the mountains, pursued their travels near to the great salt-water lake (Atlantic), and discovered the great river (Delaware). Going on still further eastward through the *Sheyickbi* country, they came to another great stream (the Hudson). On their return home they gave so flattering an account of the excellence and richness of the regions thus discovered, as to induce the general belief that this was the land which the Great Spirit designed for

that Madoc's company landed on some part of New England or Virginia, and in process of time spread over a great part of America. The investigations showing the existence of *white people* in the valley of the Mississippi, and that they were of Welsh origin, are very interesting. This people spoke the Welsh language to a considerable extent, and claimed Welsh origin. For more than a century and a half, the existence of this people in the interior of our country, has been traced."— *Yates and Moulton.* " They occupied a large portion of the western area of the State of New York, comprising the valley of the Alleghany river to its utmost source, and extending eastwardly an undefined distance. Our authorities do not leave us in doubt, that this ancient people, who occupy the foreground of our remote aboriginal history, were a valiant, noble and populous race, who were advanced in arts and the policy of government and raised fortifications for their defense, which are extended over the entire Mississippi valley, as high as latitude 43°, and the lake country, reaching from Lake St. Clair to the south shore of Lake Ontario, and the country of the Onondagas and Oneidas."— *Schoolcraft.* Priest traces the *Allegewi* from the lake country to the " vale of Mexico, where they finally and permanently rested," and where they assumed the name of *Aztecas*, or people of the lakes. The course of migration is marked by the mounds where they " rested," or dwelt temporarily on their journey.— *American Antiquities.*

their permanent abode. Though emigrating at first in small numbers, the great body of the nation at last settled on the four great rivers, Delaware, Hudson, Susquehanna and Potomac, and kindled their council-fire in the centre of their possessions. Here they became so numerous that their descendants were compelled to separate from them in branches, so that nearly forty tribes honored them with the title of *grandfather*,[1] a title which some of them continue to apply to the present day.[2]

In the government of the *Lenapes* the perfect liberty of the people was the fundamental law, and absolute unanimity the only recognized expression of the popular will. A more perfect system of checks and balances the wisdom of civilized nations has not devised. They were divided in three tribes, the *Unami*, the *Unalachto*, and the *Minsi*, or the Turtle, the Turkey, and the Wolf. Each tribe had its chief and each chief his counselors, the latter composed either of experienced warriors or aged and respectable fathers of families. In times of peace nothing could be done without the consent of the council unanimously expressed. The chiefs were required to keep good order, and to decide in all quarrels and disputes ; but they had no power to command, compel, or punish ; their only mode of government was persuasion and exhortation, and in departing from that mode they were deposed by the simple form of forsaking them. The constant restraint which they were under made them, in general, the most courteous, affable and hospitable of men. Their legislative hall was usually in a building provided for that purpose ; the counselors were called together by a servant ; in the centre of the room a large fire was kindled, and tobacco, pipes, and provisions provided, and the matter under consideration disposed of after alternate smoking, eating and deliberation, but with the utmost gravity.

In national matters the chief of the *Unami* was first in rank and constituted the head or king. For this reason, while he must be a member of that tribe, the selection of his successor, in case of his death, was made by the ruling chiefs of the other

---

[1] The tribes acknowledging this relation addressed the *Lenni Lenapes* with the title of *Mochomes*, that is to say, their *grandfather*, and were received with the appellation of *Noochwissak* or *my grandchildren.—Yates and Moulton.*

[2] Schoolcraft admits that there is some reason to acquiesce, " to a certain extent,"

tribes. He was required to maintain the peace and covenants
with other nations, and to that end to carry on a kind of corre-
spondence with them that he might always be acquainted with
their disposition towards his people.   He also sent out embassies,
with the advice and consent of the other chiefs.   He was liable
to removal in case of neglect of duty, or for suffering any of
his people to commit offenses which might involve the nation in
war.   If, after being admonished of his duty he was still neg-
lectful of it, he was forsaken and his power was at an end.
National councils were a duplication of tribal councils, except
that they were composed of representatives selected by the
chiefs and counselors of the tribes and their assemblage held at
the capital.   In times of war the powers of the civil government
were suspended.   A chief could not declare war without the
consent of his captains, nor could he accept a war-belt except
to transmit it to them, and finally, the captains could not declare
war unless by unanimous assent.   When war was formally
declared, the care of the people passed into the hands of the
captains.   When terms of peace were proposed, civil government was resumed ; the chief again took his place ; the captains
placed the proposals in his hands, and he had power to accept
or reject them.   If he accepted the proposals, he took the
hatchet from the hands of the chief captain, and desired him
to sit down.   This constituted a truce, and was followed by the
appointment of embassadors to conclude a treaty.   All the
proceedings were accompanied by the gravest demeanor, and
the most impressive dignity.   " No stranger could visit their
councils without a sensation of respect."

Law and justice, as civilized nations understand those terms,
were to them unknown, yet both they had in a degree suited to
their necessities.   Assaults, murders, and other acts regarded
as criminal offenses by all nations, were so regarded by them,
but the execution of punishment was vested in the injured
family, who were constituted judges as well as executioners,

in both the claim to antiquity and their
ancient position, in the great Algonquin
family of the *Lenapes*. He says : " It
is believed that there are no members of
this generic family of tribes, certainly

none of the existing tribes in the north
and west, who are known to us personally,
who do not acknowledge the ancient *Lenapes* under the title of grandfather."

and who could grant pardons or accept atonements. The rights of property they understood and respected ; and half their wars were retaliatory for the taking of their territory without making just and proper compensation. There was not a man among them that did not know the bounds of his own land as accurately as though defined by a surveyor's chain. Their customs were their unwritten laws, more effective than those which fill the tomes of civilized governments, because taught to the people from infancy and woven into every condition and necessity of their being. Their chiefs were poor and without revenue, yet the treasury of the nation was never exhausted. A more perfect democracy will never exist among the nations of the earth, and in this respect it was distinguished from the government of the Iroquois, the latter more nearly resembling a republic from the greater number of tribes represented in national councils, but in other respects scarcely presenting a single contrasting feature.

The names given to the *Lenape* tribes were from their totems. Each Indian nation was not only divided into tribes and chieftaincies or family clans, but had peculiar totemic classifications. Totems were rude but distinct devices or family symbols, denoting original consanguinity, and were universally respected. They were painted upon the person of the Indian, and again on the gable end of his cabin, " some in black, others in red." The wandering savage appealed to his totem, and was entitled to the hospitality of the wigwam which bore the corresponding emblem. They had other and various uses, but the most important was the representation which they made of the tribe or family to which they belonged or were made the emblems. The *Iroquois* had nine, forming two divisions, one of four tribes and the other of five. Of the first division the emblems were the Tortoise, the Wolf, the Bear, and the Beaver. The second division, and subordinate to the first, were the Deer, the Potatoe, the Great Plover, the Little Plover, and the Eagle. The *Mohawks* were represented by the totem of the Bear.[1] The *Lenni Lenapes* had three totemic tribes : the Turtle, or

[1] The Mohawk sachems who presented their condolence at Albany, in 1690, on the taking of Schenectady, said : " We are all of the race of the bear, and the bear you know never yields while one drop of blood is left. We must all be bears."—*Schoolcraft.*

Unami;[1] the Turkey, or *Unalachto*, and the Wolf, or *Minsi*. The totems of the *Mahicans* were the Bear,[2] the Wolf, and the Turtle. The Turkey and Turtle tribes occupied the sea-coast and the south-western shore of the Hudson, while the Wolf or *Minsi*, being much the most warlike of the three, served as a sort of shield to their more peaceful brethren, and watched the movements of the *Mengwe* or Iroquois. Their territory extended from the Katskill mountains to the head waters of the Delaware and Susquehanna rivers, and was bounded on the east by the Hudson; their council-fire was lighted at Minisink.[3] The Turkey tribe joined the *Minsi* on the south somewhere about Stony point. On the west bank of the river, therefore, there were but two totemic *Lenape* tribes. Above the *Minsi* came the *Mahican* totem of the Wolf, and on the east bank the Bear of that nation. Below the *Mahicans* from Roeloff Jansen's kill to the sea, the Wolf again appeared as the totem of the *Wappingers*; while the *Montauks* bore the emblem of the Turtle.[4] The prevailing totem of all the Hudson river cantons was the Wolf, borne alike by *Minsis*, *Wappingers* and *Mahicans*,[5] leading the French to call them all *Loups* or wolves, and affording Mr. Schoolcraft the basis for his

[1] "The Turtle tribe, among the *Lenapes*, claims a superiority and ascendancy over the others because of their *relation* to the great tortoise, a fabled monster, the *Atlas* of their mythology, who bears, according to their traditions, this great island, as they term the world, on his back; and also superior because he is amphibious."—*Yates and Moulton's History*. Politically the Turtle and Turkey tribes were associated in the same government, while the Minsis had a distinct organization.

[2] "The Bear tribe was considered the leading totem and entitled to the office of chief sachem."—*Mahican Tradition*. They appear to have been in occupation in the vicinity of Albany.

[3] The location was about ten miles south of Maghackemek, in the present state of New Jersey. "The third tribe, the Wolf, commonly called the *Minsi*, which we have corrupted into *Monseys*, had chosen to live back of the two other tribes, and formed a kind of bulwark for

their protection, watching the motions of the *Mengwe*, and being at hand to afford their aid in case of rupture with them. The *Minsi* were considered the most warlike and active branch of the Lenape. They extended their settlements from the Minisink, a place named after them, where they had their council seat and fire, quite up to the Hudson; and to the west, or southwest, far beyond the Susquehanna; their northern boundaries were supposed originally to be the heads of the great rivers Susquehanna and Delaware, and their southern boundaries that ridge of hills known in New Jersey by the name of Muskanecum, and in Pennsylvania, by those of Lehigh, Coghnewago, etc."—*Heckewelder*.

[4] The classification is not positive. There were other than the Turtle totem on the island.

[5] "*Mohegan* is a word, the meaning of which is not explained by the early writers; but if we may trust the deductions of philology, it needs create little uncer-

argument that the name of the Mahican confederacy was from its prevailing totemic emblem.

For dividing the territory of the *Mahicans* at Roeloff Jansen's kill, and again at Long Island, there is other than totemic authority. In regard to the former, the affidavit of King Nimham is on record, under date of October 13, 1730, in which it is stated that the deponent was "a River Indian of the tribe of the *Wappinoes*, which tribe was the ancient inhabitants of the eastern shore of Hudson's river, from the city of New York to about the middle of Beekman's patent," in the northern part of the present county of Dutchess ; "that another tribe of River Indians called the Mayhiccondas were the ancient inhabitants of the remaining eastern shore of said river ; that these two tribes constituted one nation." The testimony in regard to the *Montauks* is not so clear and positive, but is sufficiently so to indicate their status at the time of the discovery, whatever may have been their subsequent political relations. On the earliest maps the island is assigned to the *Mahicans.* DeRasieres, writing in 1626, states that its occupation was then by the " old Manhattans," and intimates that they were conquered "by the Wappenos." While all the eastern Indians were called Wappenos, [1] or Wapenacki, the reference, in this instance, is clearly specific, not general, and evidently refers to the Wappinoo or Wappinger branch of the Mahicans, who, whatever may have

---

tainly. In the *Mohegan*, as spoken at the present time by their lineal descendants, the Stockbridges of Wisconsin. *Maihtshow* is the name of the common wolf. It is called, in the cognate dialects of the Algonquin, *Myegan* by the Kenistenos, and *Myeengun* by the Chippewas, etc. In the old Algonquin, as given by La Hontan, it is *Mahingan*, and we perceive that this was the term adopted by the early French writers for the Mohegans.· The term itself, it is to be understood, by which the tribe is known to us, is not the true Indian, but has been shorn of a part of its true sound by the early French, Dutch and English writers. The modern tribe of the Mohegans, to whom allusion has been made, called themselves *Muhhekaniew.* * * *Mohegan* was a phrase to denote an enchanted

wolf, or a wolf of supernatural power. This was the badge of arms of the tribe, rather than the name of the tribe itself."—*Schoolcraft.* Compare with the statement of Capt. Hendrick, quoted *ante*, p. 42.

[1] Their various tongues may be classed into four distinct languages, namely, Manhattan, Minqua, Savanoo and Wappanoos. With the Manhattans we include those who live in the neighboring places along the North river, on Long Island, and at the Neversink ; with the Minquas, we include the Senecas, the Maquas, and other inland tribes. The Savanoos are the southern nations and the Wappanoos the eastern.—Van der Donck, *N. Y. Hist. Soc. Coll.*, 2d Series, I, 206; Wassenaar, *Doc. Hist.*, III, 46.

been their origin, seized the southern part of the peninsula and adjacent islands, and established themselves in the Highlands. Long anterior to Nimham's affidavit, however, the *Montauks* were severed from the *Mahicans*, and became tributaries to the Dutch and to the English.

The original supremacy of the IROQUOIS CONFEDERACY is assumed by almost every writer of Indian history. "From their ancient fortresses," says one of their ardent but not altogether truthful admirers, "war parties continually went forth; their war-cry sounded from the lakes to the far west, and rolled along the banks of the Mississippi and over the far-off fields of the south. They defeated the *Hurons* under the very walls of Quebec, put out the council-fires of the *Gahkwas* and the *Eries*,[1] eradicated the *Susquehannocks*[2] and placed the *Lenapes*, under tribute. The terror of their name went wherever their war canoes paddled, and nations trembled when they heard the name of Konoshioni." Another asserts that "long before European discovery, the question of savage supremacy had been settled on the waters of the Cahohatatea;" that the "invincible arms" of the *Iroquois* "humbled every native foe." In view of the undeniable fact that there is not a single well-attested case of subjugation by the *Iroquois* until nearly half a century after "European discovery," these fulsome panegyrics may very properly be subjected to analysis.

While conceding to the *Iroquois*, and to their immediate representative on the Hudson, the *Mohawks*, much of the credit which has been claimed for them, justice to other nations will compel the acknowledgment that the former were aided in their conquests and preserved in their integrity to a very great extent by their early alliances with the Europeans, and especially by their constitution, by the English of New York, as an armed police over the unarmed tribes; and further, that there is scarce a recorded conquest by them that is not tinged by the unmis-

[1] The *Eries* were seated on the southern shores of the lake which still bears their name. We only know that they were an *Iroquois* tribe, and that they were destroyed in 1655.— *Gallatin*. The *Gahkwas*, or *Kahkwahs*, were also an *Iroquois* tribe, and are supposed by some to have been the same with the *Eries*; by others that they were subsequently known as the *Hurons*.— *Schoolcraft*.

[2] The Susquehannocks were seated on the Susquehanna river and Chesapeake bay. They were defeated, in conflict with the English, at their fort near Co-

takeable fact that the subjugated tribe was contending against civilized as well as savage foes.   In their early wars the Dutch took no part, except to exchange for their furs the munitions of war which they wanted, and to cultivate with them, for the purposes of trade, peace and friendship.   To both, this friendly intercourse was desirable, and to both a necessity.   When the English came in possession of the province, the wars in which the Indians had taken part and were then engaged, the alliances which they had formed with the French, and the positions which they respectively occupied, made an alliance with the *Iroquois* but the perfection of a condition of things which had had the growth of over half a century, and which were destined to still further development.

This fact appears more clearly in connection with contemporaneous events.   The settlement of Canada was commenced in 1604, under a patent granted by Henry IV to Pierre du Gast.   In 1609, the year in which Hudson ascended the Mahicanituck, Champlain discovered the lake which now bears his name.   At this time the *Mohawks* were at war with the northern tribes, and by the mere force of the circumstances under which he was placed, he formed an alliance with the latter, even agreeing to assist them against their enemies.   The first result of this alliance was at a meeting of war parties of the *Mohawks* and *Hurons* on Lake Champlain at which the former were defeated, mainly perhaps by the power of the French arquebuses.[1]   From that period the tide of *Algonquin* success rolled

lumbia, with the loss of several hundred warriors, and in this weakened state were conquered by the Oneidas and incorporated with that tribe.   When they had forgotten their language they were sent back to the Susquehanna and became known as the Conestogas.— *Gallatin.*

[1] This battle was fought on the morning of the 30th July, 1609.   Champlain with four of his men, and accompanied by some 200 *Hurons*, were engaged in exploring Lake Champlain, when a party of hostile *Mohawks* appeared.   As the Indian practice was against fighting on the water, both parties hurried to the shore, where they pitched for battle.   The Mohawks hastily entrenched themselves with trees " at the point of a cape which runs

out into the lake from the west side." By agreement, hostilities were suspended until the next morning, when the *Hurons* led the attack.   Running to within two hundred feet in front of their enemy, they stopped and divided into bands on the right and left, leaving Champlain and his men in the centre.   The sudden appearance of the Frenchmen, and the peculiarity of their arms, produced extreme astonishment in the *Mohawk* ranks; but what was their dismay when the first report of the arquebuses fell upon their ears, and they beheld two of their chiefs fall dead and a third dangerously wounded.   The contest was of short duration.   The *Mohawks* broke and fled.   Many were killed, and some taken prisoners.   Not

along the northern frontiers of the *Iroquois*, and carried terror into the ranks of the *Onondagas*.[1] Obtaining arms and powder from the Dutch, the confederacy recovered its position, and in turn harassed the French and their Indians in wars which were yet open when the jurisdiction of the Dutch was exchanged for that of the English.

That the Dutch were neutrals is evident from their treaties with the Indians. Their first settlement was among the *Mahicans* at what is now Albany, and their intercourse was mainly, if not entirely, with that nation until 1623, when it is stated, the *Mahicans, Mohawks, Oneidas, Onondagas, Cayugas,* and *Senecas,* as well as the " far off *Ottawa* Indians," came " and made covenants of friendship " with them, bringing to commander Joris " great presents of beaver and other peltry, and desired that they might come and have constant free trade with them, which was concluded upon." [2] It is not to be presumed that the nations named were present at one time, for they were not at peace with each other ; there is no mention made by the Dutch historians of any acknowledgment of subjugation by any of the tribes, so minutely described in one of the early histories of New York,[3] and accepted apparently without examination by subsequent writers. The deducible fact is that none of the tribes were granted special privileges, and that there was not the slightest distinction made between them in the terms of the compact.

During the difficulties with the Indians in the vicinity of Fort Amsterdam in 1645, it is said that Director Kieft visited Fort Orange and made a treaty with the *Mohawks* and *Mahicans* by which their friendship was secured. Although O'Callaghan [4] magnifies the consequence of the *Mohawks* in this transaction, and assumes that their " name alone, inspired terror among all the tribes west of the Connecticut ; over whom they claimed to be sovereign, and from whom they exacted tribute,"

---

one of the *Hurons* was killed ; and they celebrated their victory on the field of battle in dancing and singing.— *Yates and Moulton.*

[1] The incursions of the French exploring parties may have been the very " northern hordes," to resist whom the confederation was formed in the manner so graphically described in the story of Hiawatha.

[2] *Wassenaar,* VII, 11 ; *Doc. Hist.,* III, 35, 51.

[3] *Yates and Moulton's Hist. New York,* 346, 347.

[4] *Hist. New Netherland,* I, 355.

his statements are defeated by the association of the *Mahicans* in the treaty, by the facts which he subsequently quotes, and by the whole tenor of contemporaneous history. In 1659, the *Mohawks* visited Fort Orange for the first time to ask special favors, and the first visit to them, in an official capacity, was made by the Dutch soon after. There is nothing in the proceedings of either conference which establishes any other fact than that the *Mohawks* desired an accommodation which the Dutch were willing to grant only to an extent that should prevent the alliance of the former with the tribes then threatening hostilities. In 1660, they were included in the peace at Esopus, but neither in its negotiation nor its terms was there distinction made between the parties to that treaty. Three years later Stuyvesant distinctly refused to employ them. The advantage to the *Iroquois* from their treaty of free trade was great, but it was made so only by the bar which their proximity to Fort Orange interposed to the supplying of other nations with whom they were at war.

The treaty between Nicolls, on the part of the English, and the *Iroquois*, was one of necessity. With the *Mahicans* the English were already in treaty ; with the *Iroquois* alone they had none. Nothing was changed by it, but the change which subsequently came was due to other causes, and those causes precisely what they were a hundred years later. It required more than half a century to develop the result of the opposing French and English Indian alliances, even admitting that the result was practically determined on this continent. The war between the French Indians and the *Iroquois* at the north was one of alternate successes and reverses, with positive advantages undetermined ; but at the south, where the French alliance was without power, the *Lenapes*, *Minsis*, *Susquehannas*, *Andastes*,[1] and other tribes became tributary to their ancient enemies. With the progress of the French in the west, and the gathering

---

[1] Note 3, *ante* p. 35. Raffeix, the French missionary, writes, in 1672 : " God preserve the *Andastes*, who have only three hundred warriors, and bless their arms to humiliate the Iroquois and preserve to us peace and our missions."— *Brodhead*, II, 193. The wars of the five nations against their own kindred, as in the case of the *Andastes*, *Eries*, *etc.*, are one of the unexplained passages in their history.

thither of tribes retreating before the civilization which was rolling upon them, the condition of even the subjugated tribes improved, while the integrity of the *Iroquois* was compromised. What the French lacked in position they made up in zeal, and pushed their priests and their fire-arms together. Their success was far greater than the English could wish. The *Mohawks* were shorn of an entire canton of converts; the flower of the *Mahicans* became the trophies of the priests; the *Senecas*, who could call out more warriors than their four associate tribes combined, were detached almost entirely, two small villages only retaining their allegiance to the English. A hundred years of war and diplomacy gave the French a very strong position, and correspondingly elevated the tribes with which they were in alliance. The English were compelled to dictate the removal of the *petticoat* from the *Lenapes*, while the *Mohawks* were reduced to numbers comparatively insignificant, notwithstanding the efforts made to recruit them. How the contest would have ended had the French remained in possession of Canada and the west, cannot be assumed; but the presumption is not unreasonable, that, while the English may not have been swept out of possession, the prowess of the *Algonquins* would have been chanted where now the notes of applause embalm the memory of the *Iroquois*.

The inquiry has its specific form in the alleged subjugation of the *Mahicans* and in the period assigned to the subjugation of the *Lenapes* as having been anterior to the advent of the Europeans. The *Mahicans* were the most formidable competitors of the *Iroquois*. Equal in courage, equal in numbers, equal in the advantages of obtaining fire-arms from the Dutch and in their subsequent alliance with the English, they marched unsubdued by the boasted conquerors of America. When the Dutch first met them they were in conflict with the *Mohawks*, and that conflict was maintained for nearly three-quarters of a century, and until the English, who were in alliance with both, were able to effect a permanent settlement. Gallatin, writing upon this subject, says: "Judge Smith, in his *History of New York*, published in 1756, says, that ʻ When the Dutch began the settlement of this country, all the Indians on Long

Island and the northern shore of the sound, on the banks of Connecticut, Hudson's, Delaware, and Susquehanna rivers, were in subjection to the Five Nations, and, within the memory of persons now living, acknowledged it by the payment of an annual tribute: " He gives no authority for the early date he assigns to that event. The subsequent protracted wars of the Dutch with the Manhattan and the Long Island Indians, and the continued warfare of the Mohawks against the Connecticut Indians, are inconsistent with that account, which is clearly incorrect with respect to the Mohikander River Indians, or Mahicans. These are mentioned by De Laet as the mortal enemies of the Maquas. It was undoubtedly the interest of the Dutch to promote any arrangement, which, by compelling the Mahicans to remain at peace, would secure their own trade. If they succeeded at any time, the peace was but temporary. We learn from the Relations of the French missionaries, that war existed in 1656, between the Manhingans and the Mohawks, and that these experienced a severe check in 1663, in an attack upon a Manhingan fortified village, and Colden admits that the contest was not at an end until 1673. 'The trade of New York,' he says, 'was hindered by the war which the Five Nations had at that time with the River Indians;' and he adds that the governor of New York 'obtained a peace between the Five Nations and the Mahikanders or River Indians.'[1] It is also certain that those Mohikander or River Indians were not reduced to the same state in which the Delawares were placed. It is proved by the concurring accounts of the French and English writers, that, subsequently to the peace of 1673, they were repeatedly, indeed uniformly, employed as auxiliaries in the wars of the Five Nations and the British against the French."[2]

This conclusion is not only abundantly sustained by the records referred to, but by an analysis of the testimony which has been relied upon as indicating an opposite result. The latter is confined, first, to traditionary reverses sustained by the *Mahicans* on Wanton island, near Katskill, and at Red Hook, in Dutchess county, the bones of the slain at the latter place

---

[1] *Colden's Six Nations*, chap. ii, 35.　　[2] *Gallatin's Indian Tribes*, ii, 43, 44.

being, it is said, in monumental record when the Dutch first settled there; and second, to the statements by Michaelius and
Wassenaar. The traditionary evidence is entirely worthless as
to the results involved, and at best can only be accepted as
proof of sanguinary conflicts; while the statements by Michaelius and Wassenaar, based as they were on information received
from others, are almost wholly at variance with positive records.
The former writer states that in the war of 1626, the *Mohawks*
were successful and that the *Mahicans* fled and left their lands
unoccupied ;[1] the latter affirms that "war broke out" again in
1628, " between the *Maikens*, near Fort Orange, and the *Makwaes*," and that the former were beaten and driven off.[2] Admitting that both writers refer to the same occurrence, and that
there is no conflict in date, the retirement spoken of could only
have included a single canton or chieftaincy. That the *Mahicans*, as a nation, did not leave their lands unoccupied nor surrender their possession, appears from the title deeds which they
gave to Van Rensselaer in 1630, the validity of which was
never questioned ; from the treaty made with them by Kieft,
and from their participation in the wars with the Dutch at Fort
Amsterdam. To these facts it may be added that deeds from
King Aepjin show that his council-fire was kept burning at
Schodac[3] as late as 1664 ; that one of the castles of the nation,
that at Cohoes, was in occupation by them as late as 1660, and
that the records of the commissioners of Indian affairs show an
organization, distinct from that which was recognized by Massachusetts but clearly subordinate to it, for over half a century
after the English succeeded the Dutch in the government.

It only remains to harmonize these facts with the statements
referred to. That, as already intimated, a canton or chieftaincy

[1] " The business of furs is dull on account of a new war of the *Maechibaeys*
(Mohawks) against the *Maikans* at the
upper end of this river. There have
occurred cruel murders on both sides.
The *Maikans* have fled and their lands
are unoccupied, and they are very fertile
and pleasant."—Michaelius, *Colonial History*, II, 769.

[2] " In the beginning of this year (1628)
war broke out between the *Maikans*,
near Fort Orange, and the *Mohawks*,
but these beat and captured the *Maikans*
and drove off the remainder, who have
retired towards the north by the Fresh
river, so called, where they begin to
cultivate the soil ; and thus the war
terminated."—Wassenaar, *Documentary
History*, III, 48.

[3] It is not certain that Schodac was the
original capital of the nation. The probabilities are that it was, and that it was
subsequently removed to Westenhuck, in
the valley of the Housatonic.

of the nation retired from the west bank of the river at or about the time spoken of by Michaelius and Wassenaar, is not only probable, but its movements can apparently be traced and the territory which it " left unoccupied " very nearly defined. The explanation is found in the title deeds which were subsequently given by the tribes who were parties to the conflict. Their examination shows that the *Mohawks* only claimed the right of conquest over lands north of the Mohawk river and in part particularly embraced in the Kayaderossera patent. South of the Mohawk river they never either claimed or sold lands on the Hudson, and even north of that point their claim, although traditionally conceded, was subsequently disputed.[1] Whatever may have been the extent of the territory which they claimed, however, it is apparent that it was limited and that it did not include or extend to the east side of the river, nor involve the subjugation of the nation. The retiring canton was an advanced post on the frontiers, pushed forward, it may be reasonably supposed, by superior prowess, and maintained until peculiarly exposed. The point to which it removed is not positively stated;[2] but the evidence is sufficient to indicate pretty certainly that it was known as the *Soquatucks* or *Socoquis*,[3] in the alliances of 1664, and in the subsequent history of the nation.

If there is no evidence of prior subjugation, there is certainly none establishing that condition after the advent of the English. The nation was almost continually in conflict with the *Mohawks*, and in its last war with them maintained itself with success. A more extended reference to this war and its results may be proper. The eastern Indians were involved in the contest as well

[1] It is asserted that the *Mahicans* admitted the conquest of the lands west of the Hudson embraced in the Saratoga (Schuylerville) tract; yet from the Johnson Manuscripts it appears that they claimed them in 1767, to " the prejudice," as Johnson says, " of *Mohawk* rights."— *Johnson Manuscripts*, IV, 170, 173.

[2] Wassenaar says, " towards the north near the Fresh river."

[3] *Brodhead's Hist.*, I, 732; *Col. Hist.*, IX, 66. Probably called *Soquatucks* from Soquans, or Suckquans, their chief sachem. Their classification as Saco Indians (*note*

Col. Hist., IX, 475), does not correspond with their assignment " towards Lake Champlain," (*Ib.*, 795), or with the very plain statement by Talon : " Two Indian tribes, one called the *Loups* (Mahicans) and the other the *Socoquis*, inhabit the country adjoining the English, and live, in some respect, under their laws, in the same manner as the *Algonquins* and *Hurons* do under those of his majesty. I perceive in these two tribes, by nature arrant and declared enemies of the *Iroquois*, a great inclination to reside among the French." After King Philip's

as the *Mahicans*.[1] In 1662, Director Stuyvesant succeeded in establishing peace between the contestants, but when the *Mohawks* carried presents to the English fort at Penobscot to confirm the same, they were attacked and slain.[2] The connection of the Hudson river chieftaincies with the war which followed cannot be distinctly traced, but there is some data upon the subject. In *Kregier's Journal of the Second Esopus War*, it is said that residents at Bethlehem, in the present county of Albany, were warned, in the fall of 1663, by a friendly Indian, to remove to a place of security ; that "five Indian nations had assembled together, namely the *Mahikanders*, the *Katskills*, the *Wappingers*, those of Esopus, besides another tribe of Indians that dwell half-way between Fort Orange and Hartford ; " that their "place of meeting was on the east side of Fort Orange river, about three (nine) miles inland from Claverack,"[3] and that they were "about five hundred strong." Again : "Hans the Norman[4] arrived at the redoubt with his yacht from Fort Orange ; reports that full seven thousand Indians had assembled at Claverack, on the east side, about three (nine) miles inland, but he knows not with what intent."[5] The intent soon became apparent. Under date of June 21, 1664, Brodhead writes : "War now broke out again. The *Mahicans* attacked the *Mohawks*, destroyed cattle at Greenbush, burned the house of Abraham Staats at Claverack, and ravaged the whole country on the east side of the North river." The operations of the Jesuit missionaries were seriously hindered ; prisoners taken on either side were burned or eaten ; the *Mohawks* were weakened and their pride humbled. Such were the results of the war at the close of 1668.[6]

In the spring of 1669, a *Mohawk* embassy visited Quebec, and asked that their nation might be " protected from the *Mahi-*

war, a portion of them appear to have returned to the Hudson, where they were incorporated with the *Mahicans* at Schaticook. The greater portion, however, ultimately found their way to Canada, where, with fragments of other tribes, they were known as the St. Francis Indians.— *Doc. Hist.*, i, 27 ; *Col. Hist.*, iii, 482, 562 ; iv, 684, 715.

[1] On the other hand, war was raging furiously between the *Mohawks* and the

Mohegans, who had been joined by the *Abenaqui* nations.—*Shea's Charlevoix*, iii, 45 ; *Drake's Book of the Indians.*

[2] *Brodhead's New York*, i, 732.

[3] The village of Claverack was five miles from the Hudson. It was known by the Indian name of *Potkoke*.

[4] Norman's kill, in Albany, takes its name from this person.

[5] *Documentary History*, iv, 83, 85.

[6] *Brodhead*, ii, 99, 146.

cans by the king of France, to whom their country now belonged by the force of arms." In this they were successful so far at least as to secure the cooperation of the Jesuit missionaries in resisting an attack by the *Mahicans* on the palisaded village of Caghnawaga. This attack was made on the eighteenth of August, 1669. The *Mahicans* retired after two hours fighting; and the *Mohawks*, descending the river in canoes, hid themselves below them in an ambuscade which commanded the road to Schenectady, at a place called Kinaquariones, where a conflict ensued in which, although at first successful, the *Mohawks* were put to flight.[1] The *Mohawks* then induced the *Oneidas*, *Onondagas* and *Cayugas* to make common cause with them; and four hundred confederate warriors went to surprise a *Mahican* fort " situated near Manhattan." But this enterprise failed, and the *Iroquois* returned home with two wounded.[2] In April, 1670, Governor Lovelace visited Albany, charged, among other things, with the duty of making peace between the *Mohawks* and *Mahicans;* but it was not until August of the succeeding year that the negotiations were consummated.[3] What the terms of peace were is not stated, and can only be inferred from the subsequent treatment of the tribes who were parties to it, who are described as being " linked together in interest," and who were uniformly treated as equals even in the selection of representative chiefs to visit England. At no stage of their history are they represented as the dependents of the Five Nations. This will more fully appear from their connection with the wars with the Dutch,

[1] Drake states that the *Mahicans* and their allies marched into the Mohawk country, led. by the principal sachem of Massachusetts (*Pennacooks ?*) named Josiah, alias *Chekatabut*, a wise man, and stout man of middle stature. After a " journey of two hundred miles," they arrived at the *Mohawk* fort, " when, upon besieging it some time, and having some of their men killed and sundry others sick, they gave up the siege and retreated. The *Mohawks* pursued them, got in their front, and from an ambush, attacked them and a great fight ensued. The *Mohawks* were finally put to flight by the extraordinary bravery and prowess of *Chekatabut* and his captains; but victory was purchased by the death of their chosen leader. This was a severe stroke, and although the war continued, it was not with that spirit in which it had been commenced."

[2] *Brodhead's New York*, II, 161.

[3] *Assize Record*, II, 732; *Brodhead's New York*, II, 181. Colden says that peace was not established until 1673. The following entry is made in *Assize Record*, IV, 116: " March 7, 1671. Mendowasse, sagamore from Hackinsack, Anmanhose from Haverstroo, Meggenmaiker, sagamore of Tappan, in behalf of themselves and Neversincks, having understood that peace had been made between the Maquas and Mahikanders, asked permission to visit, etc."

their treaties with the English and their official relations with
the governments of New York and Massachusetts.

That the *Mahicans* experienced great changes is unquestioned.
To a considerable extent their position involved this.   Though
spared on the north and east, they were exposed to the incoming civilization on the west and south.   The *Wappingers* suffered
terribly in their wars with the Dutch : from the rapacity of the
traders at Fort Orange they recoiled.   If their national council-
fire was originally at Schodac, it was subsequently removed to
the valley of the Housatonic,[1] where, under the name of
W-nahk-ta-kook, it was known to the authorities of Massachusetts and to the English missionaries ; under that of Westenhuck, to the Moravians, and under that of Stockbridge,
preserved the line of kings and linked the past with the present
history of the nation.[2]   To the English of New York, however,
this council-fire was little known.   Cut off by the boundary
line of Massachusetts it was officially recognized by that province,
while the authorities of New York maintained their official
relations with an organization which is represented as existing
"above and below Albany," and known as the *Mahicander*
or River Indians.   This organization was strengthened by the
results of King Philip's war.   In that war the *Pennacooks*[3] had
taken part, and at the close of the campaign of 1675, found
winter quarters among their kindred "near Albany."   After
the disastrous conflict of August 12th, of the succeeding year,
in which Philip was killed, they again retreated "towards
Albany," some two hundred and fifty in number, but were pursued and attacked by the English, near the Housatonic river,
and a number of them killed.   The main body of them, however, made good their retreat to the Hudson, where a portion of

[1] The Housatonic was originally known
as the Westenhook river, south of Westenhuck.— (*Sauthier's Map*).   It was
the boundary line of the neutrality which
was established by the *Iroquois* and the
Mahicans with the French Indians in
the war of 1704.   "The inhabitants of
this Province who lived on the west side
of that river followed all their occupations in husbandry as in times of peace,
while at the same time the inhabitants of
New England were in their sight exposed

to the merciless cruelty of the French
and their Indians."—*Colonial History*, vi,
371.
[2] *Stockbridge, Past and Present,* 39;
History of Missions of United Brethren,
ii, 56, 115, 130; *Memorials Moravian
Church,* i, etc.
[3] The *Pennacooks,* Schoolcraft says,
"occupied the Coos country, extending
from Haverhill to the sources of the
Connecticut."   The French classed them
among the *Mahican* tribes, and such they

them remained near the Dutch village of Claverack, and the remainder, some two hundred in number, passed over to Potick, an old *Mahican* village at Katskill.[1] The French immediately made overtures to them, through their associates who had found refuge in Canada, and Connecticut invited them to homes within her borders. Governor Andros, with equal promptness and from a similar motive,[2] invited them to settle at Schaticook, in the present county of Rensselaer, near the confluence of the Hoosic with the Hudson, in company with the *Mahicans* who were established there. This offer was accepted and a flourishing colony soon came into existence, which was patronizingly called by the *Mohawks*, our children.

The historical narrative need not be further anticipated. In passing, however, it may be remarked that it cannot be admitted that while " the *Pequots* and *Mohegans* claimed some authority over the Indians of the Connecticut, those extending westwardly to the Hudson appear to have been divided into small and independent tribes, united, since they were known to the Europeans, by no common government," as stated by Gallatin. That conclusion was based upon information less perfect than that which has since been obtained, and not only so but is in conflict with the previous findings of that author. There was nothing in their action inconsistent with the clearly understood powers of chieftaincies ; but much that implies obligation to national authority. The entire peninsula south of the Highlands was under the sovereignty of the *Wappingers*, as a tribal division of the *Mahicans*, and the offenses of the Dutch were resented by the nation and the tribe. As early as 1622, the imprisonment of the chief of the *Sequins* aroused the *Mahicans* to that extent that the offending agent of the Dutch was compelled to leave the country ; in the war of 1643, the Dutch were surprised to find their boats attacked above the Highlands, by Indians with whom they were ignorant of ever having had any

appear to have been from the statements of Gov. Moore and others pending the efforts to secure their removal to the Hudson river after their disastrous defeat in the war under King Philip. At the time of the discovery they were a powerful tribe.—*Schoolcraft's Ind. Nat.*, v, 222, *etc.*

[1] *Hubbard's Indian Wars*, 94, 98, 188 ; *Colonial History*, IV, 902, *etc.* ; *Brodhead's New York*, II, 294.

[2] The Indians began to have a value in the hands of the French as well as the English. To both parties they were the most effective soldiers that could be pro-

difficulty, and subsequently the Indian fortresses of the Highlands became the receptable of Dutch prisoners. The Dutch
knew very little of tribal organizations or tribal laws. To each
village they gave the dignity of a tribe, and undertook to hold
with them separate covenants. The *Mahicans* made a very
wide distinction between the Dutch at Fort Orange and those
at Fort Amsterdam, and it was not until Kieft made his treaty
with them in 1645, that he had peace. ·With the subsequent
crumbling up of the clans more exposed to European influences,
and the debris which remained after the retirement of their
more active members, the result was the same in all parts of the
country, whether *Mahicans*, *Lenapes*, or *Mohawks*.

In considering the political relations of the LENAPES they
should be regarded as the most formidable of the Indian con-
federacies at the time of the discovery of America, and as having maintained for many years the position which subsequently
fell to the *Iroquois*, rather than as having been subjugated by the
latter anterior to the advent of the Europeans. Their tradition
that they were "the head of the *Algonquin* [1] nations,"[2] and held
the *Mengwe* in subjection," is not without confirmation. The
precise time at which the latter condition was reversed, cannot
be stated; but the causes leading thereto are now pretty correctly ascertained. Their long house was invaded alike
by the Europeans and the *Iroquois*, with special advantages to
the latter in position, and in the facility with which they could
obtain arms.[3] The tradition which they gave of their subjuga-

cured. The great error of Massachusetts
was the war which she made upon them,
as she subsequently learned.

[1] " The primitive language which was
the most widely diffused, and the most
fertile in dialects, received from the
French the name of *Algonquin*. It was
the mother tongue of those who greeted
the colonists of Raleigh at Roanoke, of
those who welcomed the Pilgrims at Ply-
mouth. It was heard from the Bay of
Gaspe to the valley of the Des Moines,
from Cape Fear, and, it may be, from
the Savannah, to the land of the Esqui-
maux; from the Cumberland river of
Kentucky to the southern bank of the
Mississippi."— *Bancroft*, III, 237.

[2] " The Delawares were the head of all
nations. All nations except the Mingoes
and their accomplices, were united with
them and had free access to them; or in
their own words, according to their figu-
rative manner of expressing themselves,
the united nations had *one house, one fire,
and one canoe.*"—*Heckewelder*.

[3] " Clean across this extent of country
(namely from Albany to the Potomac),
our grandfather had a long house, with a
door at each end, which doors were always
open to all the nations united with them.
To this house the nations from ever so
far off used to resort, and smoke the pipe
of peace with their grandfather. The
white people coming from over the great

tion is that the *Iroquois*, finding the contest in which they were engaged, too great for them, as they had to cope on the one hand with the French, and on the other with native prowess, resorted to a master stroke of intrigue. They sent an embassy to the *Lenapes* with a message in substance as follows : That it was not well for the Indians to be fighting among themselves at a time when the whites, in even larger numbers, were pressing into their country ; that the original possessors of the soil must be preserved from total extirpation ; that the only way to effect this was a voluntary assuming, on the part of some magnanimous nation, of the position of the women or umpire ; that a weak people in such a position would have no influence, but a power like the *Lenapes*, celebrated for its bravery and above all suspicion of pusillanimity, might properly take the step ; that, therefore, the *Aquinoshioni* besought them to lay aside their arms, devote themselves to pacific employments, and act as mediators among the tribes, thus putting a stop forever to the fratricidal wars of the Indians.

To this proposition the *Lenapes* listened cheerfully, and trustfully consented ; for they believed it to be dictated by exalted patriotism, and to constitute the language of genuine sincerity. They were, moreover, themselves very anxious to preserve the Indian race. At a great feast, prepared for the representatives of the two nations, and amid many ceremonies, they were accordingly made women, and a broad belt of peace entrusted to their keeping. The Dutch, so the tradition continues, were present on this occasion, and had instigated the plot. That it was designed to break the strength of the *Lenapes* soon became evident. They woke up from their magnanimous dream, to find themselves in the power of the *Iroquois*. From that time they were the cousins of the *Iroquois*, and these were their uncle.[1]

While this tradition bears the impress of theory upon a subject in regard to which little was known, and while it is much

water, unfortunately landed at each end of this long house of our grandfathers, and it was not long before they began to pull the same down at both ends. Our grandfather still kept repairing the same, though obliged to make it from time to time shorter ; until at length the white people, who had by this time grown very powerful, assisted the common enemy, the *Maquas*, in erecting a strong house on the ruins of our grandfathers."—*Relation by an aged Mahican, given by Heckewelder*

[1] *Life and Times of David Zeisberger,* 45, 46.

less clear than that already quoted, as from a *Mahican*, it is not wholly unsupported. The *Lenapes* did, to a very considerable extent, act in the capacity of mediators, and the Dutch traders did no doubt have part in terminating the hostilities between them and the *Iroquois*. It is a singular fact, too, that of all the nations subjugated by the *Iroquois*, the *Lenapes* alone bore the name of women. While the council-fires of other nations were " put out," and their survivors merged in the confederacy, that of the *Lenapes* was kept burning, and their civil government remained undisturbed. The proposition, however, is that both of the results stated were in accordance with the terms of the peace which the English government negotiated, and not of prior *Iroquois* diplomacy.

The historic causes leading to the subjugation of the *Lenapes* is to be found in the circumstances and position of the nation, as compared with the *Iroquois* ; the one with territory invaded by Europeans at different points, the other assailed only on one border by the French, against whom they were sustained by " free trade " with the Dutch and by subsequent more positive alliance with the English. To the establishment of the lordship and manor of Rensselaerswyck, and its village of Beaverwyck, the *Iroquois* were primarily indebted for their subsequent position in the family of Indian nations. That manor was organized under an independent charter with powers not delegated to the West India Company at Fort Amsterdam, especially in the matter of the sale of fire-arms to the Indians. At its trading-houses arms could be had for furs ; there the doors were open to the *Mohawks* and the *Mahicans*, who guarded well the special advantages which they enjoyed. These advantages were great ; the former were enabled by them to push their conquests, the latter to maintain independence. This is clearly deducible from the records which were made by the Dutch, in connection with the wars at Fort Amsterdam in 1643,[1] in which it is said that the traders from Rensselaerswyck, " perceiving that the *Mohawks* were craving for guns, which some of them had already received, paying for each as many as twenty beavers, and for a pound of powder as many as ten or twelve guilders, came down to Fort

---

[1] *Journal of New Netherland, Doc. Hist.,* IV, 1, etc.

Amsterdam, in greater numbers than usual, where guns were plenty, purchasing them at a fair price, realizing in this way considerable profit. This extraordinary gain was not long kept secret. The traders coming from Holland soon got scent of it, and from time to time, brought over great quantities, so that the *Mohawks*, in a short time, were seen with fire locks and powder and lead in proportion." The record continues : " Four hundred armed men knew how to make use of their advantage, especially against their enemies, dwelling along the river of Canada, against whom they have now achieved many profitable forays where before they had but little advantage. This caused them also to be respected by the surrounding Indians even as far as the sea-coast, who must generally pay them tribute ; whereas, on the contrary, they were formerly obliged to contribute to these. On this account the Indians, in the vicinity of Fort Amsterdam, and as the record elsewhere shows, especially the *Minsis* of New Jersey and the Delaware, " endeavored no less to procure guns, and through the familiarity which existed between them and the people" at New Amsterdam, " began to solicit the latter for guns and powder, but as such was forbidden on pain of death, and could not remain long concealed in consequence of the general conversation, they could not be obtained. This greatly augmented the hatred which stimulated them to con-spire against us, beginning first with insults which they every-where indiscreetly uttered, railing at us as *materiotty*, that is to say cowards."

In regard to the time at which the subjugation of the *Lenapes* took place or was acknowledged, there is wide divergence in statement. Smith's assertion that it was prior to European occupation, is generally denied ; while Brodhead's assumption that it was in 1617, is without foundation in contemporaneous or subsequent facts. Nor could subjugation have been as early as 1643 or 1645, when Kieft made his treaty with the *Mohawks* and *Mahicans*, for the Swedes were then supplying the *Minsis* with arms. In 1660, the latter, through their chief, could declaim to their dependents at Esopus, in the presence of the *Mohawk* embassador, " this is not your land ; it is our land, therefore repeat not this," [1] and no *Mohawk* chief ever made utterance with more authority. A terrific contest was then raging between the *Senecas* and the *Minsis*, and the former came to Fort Orange and demanded, by virtue of the treaty of Esopus (1660), a higher price for their furs. "We require, said they, sixty handsful of powder for one beaver. We have a vast deal of trouble collecting beavers through the enemy's country. We ask to be furnished with powder and ball. If our enemies conquer us, where will ye then obtain beavers?" Director Stuyvesant, so the record says, replied by giving them a keg of powder, but entreated them to make peace with the *Minsis* so that the Dutch might "use the road to them in safety." Three years later the Dutch were in terrible alarm. A body of six hundred *Senecas* attacked the fort of the *Minsis* on the Delaware, and were put to flight and pursued northward for two days. Unable to cope with them single-handed, the *Senecas* solicited the aid of the *Mohawks*, and with them continued the struggle. The transition of the province from the Dutch to the English found the contest undecided, and not only so but the *Mohawks* expressly asking the English to make peace "for the Indian princes with the nations down the river," [2] as they had pleaded with the governor of Canada for protection against the *Mahicans*. In a letter from Governor Lovelace, February 24, 1665, it is said that negotiations for peace were then pending between the Esopus Indians, the South Indians, and the Novisans, on the one part, and the *Senecas* and *Mohawks* on the other, and that the magistrates of Ulster were directed to encourage the same; and under date of August 13, 1669, the same officer writes that "Perewyn lately made sachem of Hackinsack, Tappen, and Staten Island," had visited him "to renew and acknowledge the peace between them and the Christians; also, between them and the *Maquas* and *Sinnecas*, the which they say they are resolved to keep inviolable." He ordered that the matter be "put on record to be a testimony against those that shall make the first breach." [3] It was about this time that tradition gives the story of a great battle between

[1] *O'Callaghan's New Netherland*, II, 417.
[2] *Colonial History*, III, 67.
[3] *Assize Records*, II, 408.

the contestants in the Minnisink country, and the probabilities are that the peace spoken of was its result. But whatever the date, the *Minnisinks*, a north-western family of the *Minsis*, as well as the *Tappans*, were under the obligations of subjugation in 1680, for Paxinosa or Paxowan as he was sometimes called, sachem of the former, was required to furnish forty men to join the *Mohawks* in an expedition against the French.[1] In 1693-4, these tribes paid tribute to the *Senecas*.[2] The inference is that if the peace which was made with the *Minsis*[3] was not made until after the English came in possession of the province, that the subjugation of the *Lenapes* did not take place at an earlier period.

And this conclusion agrees with the almost infallible test of title to lands. The *Iroquois* never questioned the sales made by the *Lenapes* or *Minsis* east of the Delaware river, but only asserted the rights acquired by conquest in accepting, in 1743, the clearly false boundaries which the proprietaries of Pennsylvania had given to lands which had been purchased from the *Lenapes* in 1686. Whatever title the *Iroquois* had could not have been acquired when this sale was made. The findings of Gallatin in this particular are confirmed by all the title deeds in New York and New Jersey. In New Jersey the *Minsis* were paid for lands which they held *prior* to subjugation long after actual subjugation had taken place and possession ceased, for the simple reason that they were not conquered lands. In whatever aspect the question is considered, the same result is reached.

That the subjugation of the *Lenapes* was complete, there is no denial. The famous speech of Canassatiego, at Philadelphia, in 1742 : "We conquered you, we made women of you ; you know you are women ; we charge you to remove instantly ; we don't give you liberty to think about it," is not more conclusive than the admission of Tedyuscung : " I was styled by my uncles, the Six Nations, a woman, in former years, and had no

---

[1] *Council Minutes*, Aug. 7.
[2] *Colonial History*, IV, 98.
[3] The terms Minquas, Minsis, Monseys, and Munsies are convertible. The Minquas who sold lands on the Delaware were the same persons who appeared at Esopus in 1660. The treaty which was concluded by the one was concluded by the other.

natchet in my hand but a pestle or a hominy pounder." But through the thick gloom which shrouds the history of their subjugation, through all the degradation and reproach which was heaped upon them as " a nation of women," there runs a thread of light revealing their former greatness, pleading the causes of their decay, promising that their dead shall live again. Not in the eternal darkness which shuts in the *Eries* is that light lost, but from its prison house breaks in brilliancy, redeeming the past, and wringing from their ancient subjugators, shivering under adverse fortune, the greeting — BROTHERS.

CHAPTER IV.

ANALYSIS OF TRIBES AND CHIEFTAINCIES.

ASSENAAR and De Laet supply the earliest account of the subtribal divisions, or chieftaincies of Indians occupying the valley of the Hudson. The former writes : " Below the *Maikans* are situate these tribes : *Mechkentowoon* and *Tappents*, on the west side ; *Wickagjock* and *Wyeck*, on the east side. Two nations lie there lower down at Klinkersberg.[1] At the Fisher's Hook[2] are the *Pachany*, *Warenecker*, *Warrawannankoncks*. In one place, Esopus, are two or three tribes. The *Manhates* are situated at the mouth." The latter corrects the geography of his predecessor and gives the location of what he calls tribes[3] more accurately. Commencing at New York, he says : " On the east side, on the main land, dwell the *Manhattans*, a bad race of savages, who have always been very obstinate and unfriendly towards our people. On the west side are the *Sanhickans*, who are the deadly enemies of the *Manhattans*, and a much better people. They dwell along the bay, and in the interior. The course of the river is north-east and north-north-west according as the reaches extend. Within the first reach, on the west bank of the river, where the land is low, dwell the *Tappans*. The second reach of the river extends upwards to a narrow part named by our people Haverstroo ; then comes the Seylmaker's-reach, as they call it, and next a crooked reach, in the form of a crescent, called Kock's-reach. Next is Hoge-reach ; and then comes Vossen-reach, which extends to Klinkersberg. This is succeeded by Fisher's-reach, where on the east side of the river, dwell a nation of savages named *Pachami*. This reach extends to another narrow pass, where on the west, is a

---

[1] The first title given to Butter Hill.
[2] The bend in the river opposite New-burgh, forming a hook by the confluence of the Matteawan creek.
[3] A tribe was an union of families, but as here used designated families.

point of land that juts out [1] covered with sand, opposite a bend in the river, on which another nation of savages, the *Waoranecks*, have their abode at a place called Esopus. A little beyond on the west side, where there is a creek and the river becomes more shallow, the *Warranawankongs* dwell. Next comes another reach called Klaverack; then comes Backerack, John Playsier's-rack, and Vaste-rack as far as Hinnenhock. Finally the Huntenrack succeeds as far as Kinderhook; further on are Sturgeon's-hook and Fisher's-hook, over against which, on the east side dwell the *Mahicans*."

Van der Donck, who wrote thirty years later, places the *Manhattans* on the island, and above them Indian villages which he names *Saeckkill*, *Wickquaskeck*, *Alipkonck*, *Sin-Sing*, *Kestaubuinck*, *Keskistkonck*, *Pasquuasheck*, and *Noch-Peem*, south of and in the highlands. On the south side of Wappinger's kill he locates three villages under the general name of *Waoranecks*, and above them and occupying both sides of the river south of the "Groote Esopus R.," he places the *Wappingers*. On the west side he locates the *Neve-Sincks* opposite Staten Island, then the *Raritans;* opposite Manhattan Island, *Haverstroo;* below Verdrietigehoeck, the *Tappans;* between Murderer's creek and the Dans-Kammer, the *Waranwankongs;* then the *Wappingers*, and west of the Esopus, the general title of " Minnessinck of te l'Landt von Bacham." [*]

Were the question of location left to these writers and to the early maps, the inquiry might well be abandoned as hopeless. Fortunately, however, Indian treaties and title deeds supply information which, though still imperfect,[2] enables a division of territory and location of subtribes to be made with tolerable accuracy. From these sources the following classifications are mainly derived :

I. The chieftaincies of the MONTAUKS were:

1st. The *Carnarsees*, who claimed the lands now included in the county of Kings, and a part of the town of Jamaica.

---

[1] Dans-Kammer point.

[2] "There being no previous survey to the grants, their boundaries are expressed with much uncertainty, by the Indian names of brooks, rivulets, hills, ponds, falls of water, etc., which were and still are known to very few Christians. Sometimes the grant is of the land that belonged to such an Indian by name, or is bounded by such an Indian's land, but to

Their principal village was about the site of the village of Flat-lands, where there is a place which still retains the name of Canarsee, and was, perhaps, the residence of the sachem. This chieftaincy was of considerable power in 1643, when it stood at the head of the Long Island tribes who were engaged in the war with the Dutch. Penhawitz was the first sachem known to the Dutch, by whom he was styled the Great Sachem of Canarsee. The names of the chiefs in 1670, as given in a deed for the site of the present city of Brooklyn, were Peter, Elmohar, Job, Makagiquas, and Shamese.

2d. The *Rockaways*, who were scattered over the southern part of the town of Hempstead, which, with a part of Jamaica and the whole of Newtown, constituted the bounds of their claim. Their main settlement was at Near Rockaway. The first sachem known to the Dutch was Chegonoe. Eskmoppas appears to have been sachem in 1670, and Parnau in 1685.

3d. The *Merricks, Merokes*, or *Merikokes*, as they have been denominated, who claimed all the territory south of the middle of the island, from Near Rockaway to the west line of Oyster bay. Their principal village was the site of the present village of *Merick*. Their sachem in 1647, was Wantagh.

4th. The *Marsapequas* or *Marsapeagues*, who had their settle-ment at a place called Fort Neck, and thence eastward to the bounds of Islip and north to the middle of the island. At Fort Neck the remains of two Indian forts were recently still visible. One was upon the most southerly point of land ad-joining the salt meadow, nearly of quadrangular form and about thirty yards in extent on each side. The other was on the southernmost point of the salt meadow adjoining the bay, and consisted of palisades set in the meadow. The place is now covered with water. The chieftaincy was prominent in the war of 1643 and suffered severely. After this they appear to have been on friendly terms with the Dutch ; and in the Esopus war of 1663, contributed forty-six men to Kregier's forces.[1]

prove that any particular spot belonged to any particular Indian, I believe is beyond human skill, so as to make it evident to any indifferent man."— *Colden, Document-ary History*, 1, 383, 384. Nevertheless many such localities have been and can be proved with positive accuracy. In hundreds of old surveys the hills, streams, etc., by which the tracts were bounded are as clear as the marks of modern sur-veyors.

[1] *O'Callaghan*, 11, 482.

Tackapousha, sachem in 1656, was also chief sachem of the western chieftaincies on the island.

5th. The *Matinecocks*, who claimed jurisdiction of the lands east of Newtown as far as the west line of Smithtown, and probably to the west side of Nesaquake river. They were numerous and had large villages at Flushing, Glen Cove, Cold Spring, Huntington and Cow Harbor.[1] A portion of the chieftaincy took part in the war of 1643 under Gonwarrowe; but the sachem at that time remained friendly to the Dutch, and through his diplomacy succeeded in establishing peace. Whiteneymen (one-eyed) was sachem in 1643, and Assiapam in 1653.

6th. The *Nesaquakes* or *Missaquogues* possessed the country east of the river of that name to Stony brook and from the sound to the middle of the island. The principal settlement of the tribe was on the site of the present village of Nesaquake where the sachem probably resided. Coginiquant was sachem in 1656.

7th. The *Seatalcats* or *Setaukets*, whose territory extended from Stony brook to Wading river. Their village was upon Little Neck. They are said to have been a numerous family. Warrawakin sachem, 1655; Gil, in 1675.

8th. The *Corchaugs* owned the remainder of the territory from Wading river to Oyster ponds, and were spread upon the north shore of Peconic bay, and upon the necks adjoining the sound. From the many local advantages which their situation afforded, there is reason to suppose that they were, as regards numbers and military power, a respectable clan. Momometon sachem in 1648.

9th. The *Manhassets*, who occupied Shelter island, Hog island, and Ram island. Their principal settlement was on Shelter island; and the residence of their sachem on what is now known as Sachem's Neck. Tradition affirms that they could once bring into the field more than five hundred fighting men. From their exposed situation they were, like other clans on this part of the island, made tributary to the *Pequots*, *Narragansetts* and *Mahicans* alternately. Poygratasuck, a brother to

---

[1] *Thompson's Long Island.* Van Tien-   thirty families in 1650.
hoven represents them to consist of only

Wyandance, was sachem in 1648, and is spoken of as possessed of capacity and courage. Yokee, or Youghco, sachem in 1651.

10th. The *Secatogues*, who joined the *Marsapequas* on the west and claimed the country as far east as Patchogue. The farm owned by the Willett family, at Islip, is supposed to have been the site of their village. The bounds of their tract were from Connectquut river on the east to the line of Oyster bay on the west, and from the South bay to the middle of the island. They were so much reduced by wars and disease that when settlements were made among them their lands were comparatively deserted. Winnequaheagh was sachem in 1683.

11th. The *Patchogues*, or *Onchechaugs*. Their jurisdiction extended from Patchogue east to West Hampton, and their villages at Patchogue, Fire Place, Mastic, Moriches and West Hampton. Tobaccus sachem in 1666.

12th. The *Shinecocks*, who claimed the territory from West Hampton to East Hampton, including Sag harbor, and the whole south shore of Peconic bay. Nowedonah was sachem in 1648, and Quaquasho, or The Hunter, in 1691.

13th. The *Montauks*.[1] This chieftaincy was acknowledged both by the Indians and the Europeans, as the ruling family of the island. They were indeed, the head of the tribe of *Montauks*, the other divisions named being simply clans or groups, as in the case of other tribes. DeRasieres and Van der Donck class them as "old Manhattans." They were considerable in numbers ; distinguished for the hospitality which they extended to the Dutch traders and early settlers, and no less so for their subsequent hostility. Holding in their possession the treasure chest of all the Indian nations, they were especially exposed to invasion by the more powerful tribes bordering on the sound. At the time of the discovery they were a part of or under tribute to the *Mahicans*. Wyandance, their sachem, was also the grand sachem of Paumanacke, or Sewanhackey, as the island was called. Nearly all the deeds for lands were confirmed by him. His younger brothers, Nowedonah and Poygratasuck, were respectively sachems of the *Shinecocks* and the *Manhassets*. His residence was upon Montauk, and

[1] Metowacks, *Brodhead ;* Matuwacks, *Yates & Moulton ;* Montauks, *Thompson.*

10

the body of his followers lay in the immediate vicinity. During the wars of the *Mahicans*, the *Montauks* were subjugated by or compelled to pay tribute to the *Pequots*. After the destruction of the latter nation in 1637, the *Mahicans* again asserted their authority, but about that time the *Montauks* accepted the protection of the English and paid tribute to the governor of New · Haven. In 1653, they were engaged in war with the *Narragansetts*, or rather the latter attacked them " as the friends and tributaries of the English."[1] A considerable number of the *Montauks* perished in this war.

On the division of the island in 1650, between the English and the Dutch, the English taking the eastern, and the Dutch the western part, the jurisdiction of Wyandance was nominally divided, Tackapousha being elected sachem of the chieftaincies in possession of the Dutch, viz : Marsapequas, Merikokes, Carnarsees, Secatogues, Rockaways, and Matinecocks. In the winter of 1658, the small pox destroyed more than half the clan, while Wyandance lost his life by poison secretly administered. The remainder, both to escape the fatal malady, and the danger of invasion in their weakened state, fled in a body to their white neighbors, who received and entertained them for a considerable period. Wycombone succeeded his father, Wyandance, and being a minor, divided the government with his mother, who was styled the Squa-sachem. Lion Gardiner and his son David acted as guardians to the young chief, by request of his father made just before his death. At Fort Pond, called by the Indians *Konk-hong-anok*, are the remains

---

[1] Thompson ascribes the cause of this war to the refusal of the Montauk monarch to join in the plan for exterminating the Europeans. Roger Williams writes to the governor of Massachusetts in 1654 : " The cause of the war is the pride of the barbarians, Ascassascotick, the Long Island sachem, and Ninigret, of the Narragansetts. The former is proud and foolish; the latter proud and fierce."— *Thompson's Hist. Long Island ; Drake's Book of the Indians.*

Lion Gardiner, in his *Notes on East Hampton*, relates, that the Block Island Indians, acting as the allies of the *Narragansetts* attacked the *Montauks*, during King Philip's war, (1675), and punished them severely. The engagement took place on Block Island, whither the *Montauks* went in their canoes, and upon landing, fell into an ambuscade. He says : " The Montauk Indians were nearly all killed ; a few were protected by the English and brought away. The sachem was taken and carried to *Narragansett*, he was made to walk on a large flat rock that was heated by building fires on it, and walked several times over it singing his death song, but his feet being burned to the bones, he fell and they finished the tragical scene as is usual for savages."— *N. Y. Hist. Soc. Coll.*, 1849, 258.

of the burial ground of the chieftaincy, and here once stood the citadel of the monarch, Wyandance.[1]

II. The chieftaincies of the WAPPINGERS were :

1st. The *Reckgawawancs.*[2] This chieftaincy has been generally known by the generic name of *Manhattans,*[3] and is so designated by Brodhead and other historians. The site of their principal village is now occupied by that of Yonkers, and was called Nappeckamak. This village, says Bolton,[4] was situated at the mouth of the Neperah, or Saw Mill creek. On Berrien's Neck, on the north shore of the Spuyten Duyvel creek, was situated their castle or fort, called Nipinichsen. This fort was carefully protected by a strong stockade and commanded the romantic scenery of the Papirinimen, or Spuyten Duyvel, and the Mahicanituk, the junction of which two streams was called Shorackappock. It was at this castle that the fight occurred between Hudson and the Indians on his return voyage,[5] and

[1] *Thompson's History of Long Island.*

[2] Bolton gives them the name of *Nappeckamaks*, but that title does not appear in the records except as the name of their village at Yonkers.

[3] Custom would, perhaps, warrant the continuance of the name as designating a chieftaincy, but the evidence is conclusive that it was not used by the Indians in any such connection, but was a generic term designating not only the occupants of the island now called Manhattan, but of Long Island, and the mainland north of Manhattan Island. The term Manhattan indicates this, being apparently from Menohhunnet, which in *Eliot's Bible,* is given as the equivalent of islands, or as applied to the people, "the people of the islands."— (*Historical Magazine,* 1, 89). The statements of the Dutch historians confirm this interpretation. Van der Donck and Wassenaar agree that there were four languages spoken by the natives, namely, the Manhattan, Minqua, Savanoo, and Wappinoo. "With the Manhattan," says Van der Donck, "we include those who live in the neighboring places along the North river on Long Island and at the Neversink." De Rasieres, writing in 1628, as a personal witness, says : "Up the river the east side is high, full of trees, and in some places there is a little good land, where

formerly many people have dwelt, but who for the most part have died or have been driven away by the Wappenos." Again, referring to Long Island, he says : "It is inhabited by the old Manhattans (Manhatesen); they are about two hundred or three hundred strong, women and men, under different chiefs whom they call sackimes (sachems)." De Laet says : "On the east side on the main land, dwell the Manhattans." Block, whose vessel was burned in the lower bay in 1614, and who there built another, was fed and protected by the Manhattans, not on Manhattan Island, but, as appears by the statements of the Long Island Indians, this care and protection was in the territory and on the island of the latter. Under this explanation there is no contradiction in the statements of Hudson, De Laet and other writers, as compared with the *Albany Records,* that the name Manhattan, is " from or after the tribe of savages among whom the Dutch made their first settlement ; " nor with that contained in a paper describing New Netherland (*Documentary History,* IV, 115) : "So called from the people which inhabited the main land on the east side of the river."

[4] *History of Westchester County.*

[5] " Whereupon two canoes full of men, with their bowes and arrowes shot at us

it was also at this point that he first dropped anchor on his ascending voyage. They held occupation of Manhattan island and had there villages which were occupied while on hunting and fishing excursions. In Breeden Raedt their name is given as the *Reckewackes*, and in the treaty of 1643, it is said that Oritany, sachem of the Hackinsacks, " declared he was delegated by and for those of Tappaen, Reckgawawanc, Kicktawanc, and Sintsinck."

The tract occupied by the *Reckgawawancs* on the main land was called Kekesick, and is described as " lying over against the flats of the island of Manhates." It extended north including the site of the present village of Yonkers, and east to the Broncks river. Their chiefs were Rechgawac, after whom they appear to have been called, Fecquesmeck, and Peckauniens. Their first sachem known to the Dutch, was Tackarew, in 1639. In 1682, the names of Goharis, Teattanqueer and Wearaquaeghier appear as the grantors of lands to Frederick Phillipse. Tackarew's descendants are said to have been residents of Yonkers as late as 1701. The last point occupied by the chieftaincy was Wild Boar hill, to which place its members had gathered together as the Europeans encroached upon them. Traces of two burial grounds have been discovered on their lands.

2d. The *Weckquaesgeeks*.[1] As early as 1644, this chieftaincy is known to have had three entrenched castles,[2] one of which remained as late as 1663, and was then garrisoned by eighty warriors. Their principal village was on the site of Dobb's Ferry ; it is said that its outlines can still be traced by numerous shell beds. It was called Weckquaskeck, and was located at the mouth of Wicker's creek, which was called by the Indians Wysquaqua. Their second village was called Alipconck. Its

after our sterne ; in recompense whereof we discharged six muskets, and killed two or three of them. Then above an hundred of them came to a point of land to shoot at us. There I shot a falcon at them, and killed two of them ; whereupon the rest fled into the woods. Yet they manned off another canoe with nine or ten men, which came to meet us. So I shot a falcon, and shot it through, and killed one of them. Then our men with their muskets, killed three or four more of them. So they went their way."—*Hudson's Journal.*

[1] This name appears to be local, although there is some reason for regarding it as generic.

[2] " Journal of New Netherland," *Documentary History*, iv, 15.

site is now occupied by the village of Tarrytown. Their territory appears to have extended from Norwalk on the Sound, to
the Hudson, and to have embraced considerable portions of the
towns of Mount Pleasant, Greenburgh, White Plains, and Rye ;
it was very largely included in the Manor of Phillipsborough.
Their sachem, in 1649, was Ponupahowhelbshelen ; in 1660,
Ackhough ; in 1663, Souwenaro ; in 1680, Weskora, or Wes-
komen, and Goharius his brother ; in 1681, Wessickenaiuw and
Conarhanded his brother. Their chiefs are largely represented
in the list of grantors of lands.

3d. The *Sint-Sinks*. This chieftaincy does not appear to
have been very numerous. Their name is perpetuated in the
present village of Sing-Sing, which was called Ossing-Sing,
where they had a village. Another village was located between
the Sing-Sing creek and the Kitchawonck, or Croton river, and
was called Kestaubuinck. Their lands are described in a deed
to Frederick Phillipse, August 24, 1685, and were included in
his manor. The grantors were Weskenane, Crawman, Wap-
pus, Mamaunare and Weremenhore, who may or may not have
been chiefs.

4th. The *Kitchawongs*, or *Kicktawancs*. The territory of
this chieftaincy appears to have extended from Croton river
north to Anthony's Nose. Their principal village, Kitchawonck, was at the mouth of the river which bears their name.
They also had a village at Peekskill, which they called Sackhoes.
Their castle or fort, which stood at the mouth of the Croton,
is represented as one of the most formidable and ancient of the
Indian fortresses south of the Highlands. Its precise location
was at the entrance or neck of Teller's point (called Senasqua),
and west of the cemetery of the Van Cortlandt family. Their
burial ground was a short distance east of the castle ; a romantic and beautiful locality. The traditional sachem of the
chieftaincy was Croton. Metzewakes appears as sachem in
1641 ; Weskheun in 1685, and, in 1699, Sakama Wicker.
There was apparently a division of the chieftaincy at one time,
Kitchawong appearing as sachem of the village and castle on
the Croton, and Sachus of the village of Sackhoes or Peekskill.
Sirham was sachem of the latter in 1684. Their lands were

principally included in the manor of Cortlandt, from which was subsequently erected the towns of Cortlandt, Yorktown, Somers, North Salem and Lewisborough.

5th. The *Tankitekes*.[1]   The lands occupied by this chieftaincy are now embraced in the towns of Darien, Stamford, and New Canaan, in Connecticut, and Poundridge, Bedford, and Greenbush, in Westchester county. They were purchased by Nathaniel Turner, in behalf of the people of New Haven, in 1641, and are described in the deed as the tracts called Toquams and Shipham. Ponus was sachem of the former and Wasenssne of the latter. Ponus reserved a portion of Toquams for the use of himself and his associates, but with this exception their entire possessions appear to have passed under a deed without metes or bounds. The chieftaincy occupies a prominent place in Dutch history through the action of Pacham, "a crafty man," who not only performed discreditable service for Director Kieft, but was also very largely instrumental in bringing on the war of 1645.

6th. The *Nochpeems*. This chieftaincy occupied the highlands north of Anthony's Nose.[2] Van der Donck assigns to them three villages : Keskistkonck, Pasquasheck and Nochpeem on the Hudson. Their principal village, however, appears to have been called Canopus from the name of their sachem. It was situated in what is now known as Canopus hollow, one of the most fertile sections of Putnam county. The residence of Canopus is said to have been on a hill in the south-east part of

---

[1] Brodhead locates this chieftaincy at Haverstraw, but his authorities are not at all clear. For example, it is said that an offending member of the Hackinsacks, had gone "two days' journey off among the Tankitekes; "Pacham, the subtle chief of the Tankitekes near Haverstraw." Haverstraw was not two days' journey from Hackinsack, certainly. His location is also defeated in the person and history of Pacham, whose name he previously gives to a chieftaincy in the highlands. O'Callaghan locates them on the east side of Tappan bay, and Bolton in the eastern part of Westchester from the deeds which they gave to their lands. The latter is clearly correct.

[2] Wassenaar locates here the Pachany; and Brodhead, on authorities which appear to him sufficient, follows him under the name of Pachimis. In Breeden Raedt they are called Hogelanders, while in the treaty of 1644 (*O'Callaghan*, 1, 302), they are called Nochpeems, a title which corresponds with the name of one of their villages on Van der Donck's map. It is not impossible that the Tankitekes extended into the highlands on the east, and that their chief Pacham held sway there, and hence the name ; but the treaty record of 1644 appears to be a sufficient answer to this theory. It is certainly safe to designate them by a title by which they were officially known.

the town of Putnam Valley, and was included in the deeds for the manor of Cortlandt. The remainder of their lands passed into the hands of Adolph Phillipse, under a title which was the subject of controversy for years, and in reference to which a delegation of chiefs visited England accompanied by king Nimham. Those who have regarded these chieftaincies as " independent tribes, united, since they were known to the Europeans, by no common government," may examine this controversy with profit. The grantors of the deed were Angnehanage, Rauntaye, Wassawawigh, Meanakahorint, Meahem, Wrawermneuw, and Awangrawryk, and was for a tract from Anthony's Nose to the Matteawan creek, and from the Hudson three miles into the country. The latter line Phillipse stretched to twenty miles.[1]

7th. The *Siwanoys ;* also known as " one of the seven tribes of the sea-coast." This chieftaincy was one of the largest of the *Wappinger* subdivisions. They occupied the northern shore of the sound, " from Norwalk twenty-four miles to the neighborhood of Hell-gate." How far they claimed inland is uncertain, but their deeds covered the manor lands of Morrisania, Scarsdall and Pelham, from which were erected the towns of Pelham, New Rochelle, East and West Chester, North and New Castle, Mamaroneck, Scarsdall, and parts of White Plains and West Farms ; other portions are included in the towns of Rye and Harrison, as well as in Stamford. There is also some reason for supposing that the tract known as Toquams and assigned to the *Tankitekes,* was a part of their dominions. A very large village of the chieftaincy was situated on Rye Pond in the town of Rye. In the southern angle of that town, on a beautiful hill now known as Mount Misery,[2] stood one of their castles. Another village was situated on Davenport's Neck. Near the entrance to Pelham's Neck was one of their burial grounds. Two large mounds are pointed out as the sepulchres of the sachems Ann-Hoock and Nimham. In the town of West

---

[1] *Land Papers,* xviii, 127, etc.

[2] This hill is said to have acquired its present name from the fact that a large body of Indians were there surprised and cut to pieces by the Huguenots of New Rochelle, in retaliation for a descent upon their place. If such a battle took place it has no official record. The story is mythical.

Chester they had a castle upon what is still known as Castle Hill neck, and a village about Bear swamp, of which they remained in possession as late as 1689. Their ruling sachem, in 1640, was Ponus, whose jurisdiction was over tracts called Rippowams and Toquams, and the place of whose residence was called Poningoe. He left issue three sons, Omenoke, Taphance and Onox; the latter had a son called Powhag. In 1661, Shanasockerell, or Shanorocke, was sachem in the same district, and, in 1680, Katonah and his son Paping appear as such. Of another district Maramaking, commonly known as Lame Will, was sachem in 1681. His successor was Patthunck, who was succeeded by his son, Waptoe Patthunck. The names of several of their chiefs occur in Dutch history as well as in the early deeds. Among them are Ann-Hoock, alias Wampage, already noticed, who was probably the murderer of Ann Hutchinson,[1] and Mayane, spoken of in 1644 as "a fierce Indian, who, alone, dared to attack, with bow and arrows, three Christians armed with guns, one of whom he shot dead; and, whilst engaged with the other, was killed by the third," and his head conveyed to Fort Amsterdam. The occurrence served to convince the Dutch that in offending against the chiefs in their immediate vicinity, they were also offending those of whose existence they had no previous knowledge.[2] Shanasockwell is represented as " an independent chieftain of the *Siwanoys*," of the island called Manussing.

8th. The *Sequins*. This was a large chieftaincy; its principal seat was on the west bank of the Connecticut river and its jurisdiction over all the south-western Connecticut clans, including those designated by Van der Donck as the *Quirepeys*, the *Wecks*, the *Makimanes*, and the *Conittekooks*, and classified by De Forest [3] as the *Mahackenos*, *Unkowas*, *Paugussetts*, *Wepawaugs*, *Quinnipiacs*, *Monteweses*, *Sicaoggs*, *Tunxis*, etc. Their lands on the Connecticut were included in a purchase made by the West India Company, June 8, 1633, and on them was erected the Dutch trading post and fort known as " Good Hope."

---

[1] Nothing was more common among the Indians than to give to a warrior the name of his victim.

[2] *Documentary History*, IV, 14.

[3] *De Forest's History Indians of Connecticut.*

The tract is said to have been sixty miles in extent.[1] Subsequently (1643), Sequin, from whom the chieftaincy took its name, covered his deed to the Dutch by one to the English, in which he included "the whole country to the Mohawks country."[2] By the fortunes of war, the Pequots compelled the *Sequins*, the *Siwanoys*, and a portion of the *Montauks*, to pay them tribute,[3] but this condition was only temporary. In the subsequent war between the English and their allies and the Pequots, the national existence of the latter was destroyed. There are many reasons for presuming that the *Sequins* were an enlarged family of *Wappingers*, perhaps the original head of the tribe from whence its conquests were pushed over the southern part of the peninsula.[4]

9th. The *Wappingers.* North of the Highlands was the chieftaincy historically known as the *Wappingers*,[5] and acknowledged as the head of the chieftaincies of the tribal organization of that name occupying the territory from Roeloff Jansen's kill

[1] The deed recites the agreement between Van Curler, on the part of the company, "and the sachem named Wapyquart or Tatteopan, chief of Sickenames river, and owner of the Fresh river of New Netherland, called in their tongue Connetticuck," for the purchase and sale of the lands named, "on condition that all tribes might freely, and without fear or danger," resort thither for purposes of trade.—*O'Callaghan*, I, 150. The *Sickenames*, from whom the title was obtained, are described as "living between the Brownists (the Puritans) and the Hollanders," and that "all the tribes on the northern coast were tributary to them." Sequin denied the validity of their deed and sold to the English. The Dutch quarreled with the *Sickenames* (Pequots), and the latter invited the English to settle at New Haven ; subsequently quarreled with them also, and were destroyed.— *O'Callaghan*, I, 157 ; *De Forest's Indians of Connecticut.*

[2] *Farmington Town Records, De Forest.*

[3] The tradition is recited by O'Callaghan that the *Sequins* had original jurisdiction, but lost it after three pitched battles with the *Pequots*. There is a strange mixing up of tribes in the story, and especially in that of the original sale, in which the

transaction is made to appear " with the knowledge of Magaritiune," the Wappinoo chief of Sloop's bay.—*O'Callaghan*, I, 149, 150, 157. "After the overthrow of Sequin, the *Pequots* advanced along the coast and obliged several tribes to pay tribute, and sailed across the sound and extorted tribute from the eastern inhabitants of Sewan-Hackey.— *De Forest's History Indians of Connecticut*, 61.

[4] *Ante*, p. 41.

[5] *Ante*, p. 41. The chieftaincy must have borne some other name, but what is not known. Among the Moravians they were known as the *Wequehachkes*, or the people of the hill country. Governor Lovelace, in a letter to Governor Winthrop of Massachusetts, Dec. 29, 1869 (*New York Assize Record*), writes : "I believe I can resolve your doubt concerning what is meant by the Highland Indians amongst us. The *Wappingers* and *Wickeskeck*, etc., have always been reckoned so." It is entirely possible that the tribal name was *Wequehachke*, or *Wickeskeck*, or *Weckquaesgeek*, and that *Wappingers* is local. In all their official relations, however, and in the recognition of Nimham, they were known as the *Wappingers.*

11

on the north to Manhattan island on the south. What their family clans were on the north is not known, nor where their capital. On Van der Donck's map three of their villages or castles are located on the south side of the Mawenawasigh, or Great Wappinger's kill, which now bears their name. North of that stream they appear to have been known as the Indians of the Long Reach, and on the south as the Highland Indians. Among their chiefs Goethals and Tseessaghgaw are named, while of their sachems the names of Megriesken and Nimham[1] alone survive. Of their possessions on the Hudson there is but one perfect transfer title on record, that being for the lands which were included in the Rombout patent, in which " Sackeraghkigh, for himself and in the name of Megriesken, sachem of the Wappinger Indians," and other Indians therein named as grantors, conveyed the tract beginning on the south side of the Matteawan creek and running along the Hudson north to a point five hundred rods beyond " the Great Wapping's kill, called by the Indians Mawenawasigh," thence east, keeping five hundred rods north of said creek, " four hours' going into the woods," thence south to the south side of Matteawan creek, and thence west " four hours' going " to the place of beginning — a district now embraced in the towns of Fishkill, East Fishkill, etc., in Dutchess county.

Although it is so stated on Van der Donck's map of New Netherland, and assumed by Gallatin as a fact, there is no evidence that the *Wappingers* extended west of the Hudson, but, on the contrary, the conclusion is certain that they did not. The record of the Esopus wars and the sales of lands show what and who the latter were. The error of Van der Donck's informants was in confusing totemic emblems, and similarity of dialect, with tribal jurisdiction. The totem of the *Wappingers* as well as that of the Esopus clans, was the Wolf, as already stated, while below the Highlands came the Turkey of the

[1] " Daniel Nimham, a native Indian and acknowledged sachem or king of a certain tribe of Indians known and called by the name of *Wappingers*, represents that the tribe formerly were numerous, at present consists of about two hundred and twenty-seven persons ; that they have always had a sachem or king whom they have acknowledged to be the head of the tribe, and that, by a regular line of succession the government of the tribe descended to the said present sachem."— *New York Land Papers*, xviii, 127.

Lenapes, constituting a clear distinction from their neighbors on the opposite shore. Gallatin strengthens the error by introducing the fact that the *Wappingers* were a party to the treaty of Easton, but was evidently without knowledge that they were recent emigrants from New York.[1]

III. The MAHICANS.

The territory of the *Mahicans* joined the *Wappingers* and *Sequins* on the south, and stretched thence north, embracing the head waters of the Hudson, the Housatonic and the Connecticut, and the water-shed of lakes George and Champlain. The chieftaincies of the tribe have a very imperfect preservation, but its general divisions are indicated by the terms: 1. The *Mahicans*, as applied to that portion occupying the valley of the Hudson and the Housatonic; 2. The *Soquatucks*, as applied to those east of the Green Mountains; 3. The *Pennacooks*, as applied to those occupying the territory "from Haverhill to the sources of the Connecticut;" 4. The *Horikans*, who occupied the Lake George district, and 5. The *Nawaas* immediately north of the *Sequins* on the Connecticut. The first of these general divisions was again divided into at least five parts, as known to the authorities of New York, viz: 1. The *Mahicans*, occupying the country in the vicinity of Albany; 2. The *Wiekagjocks*, described by Wassenaar as "next below the *Maikens*;" 3. The *Mechkentowoons* lying above Katskill and on Beeren or Mahican Island; 4. The *Wawyachtonocks*,[2] who apparently resided in the western parts of Dutchess and Columbia counties, and 5. The *Westenhucks*, who held the capital of the confederacy. At the time of the discovery those embraced in the first subdivision had a castle on what is now known as Haver island, called by them Cohoes, on the west side of the river, just below Cohoes falls, under the name of Monemius' castle, and another on the east bank and south of the first, called Unuwat's castle.[3] At

---

[1] *Johnson Manuscript*, IV, 54.

[2] The name is local, and is applied, in a petition by William Caldwell and others in 1702, to a "tract of unappropriated lands in ye hands of ye Indians, lying in Dutchess county to ye westward of Westenholks creek, and to ye eastward of Poghkeepsie, called by ye Indians by ye name of Wayaughtanock." In the proceedings of a convention held at Albany in 1689, the name is applied to the Indians who are called the Wawyachteioks or Wawijachtenocks.

[3] Map of Rensselaerswyck, *O'Callaghan's New Netherland; Wassenaar, Documentary History*, III, 43.

or near Schodac was Aepjin's castle.[1] Nine miles east of Claverack was one of the castles of the *Wiekagjocks*, and on Van der Donck's map two of their villages, without name, are located inland north of Roeloff Jansen's kill. Potik and Beeren island [2] were for many years in the possession of the *Wechken-towoons*. The villages of the *Wawyachtonocks* are without designation, but it is probable that Shekomeko,[3] about two miles south of the village of Pine Plains, in Dutchess county, was classed as one of them, as well as that of Wechquadnach or Wukhquautenauk, described as " twenty-eight miles below Stockbridge." Kaunaumeek, where the missionary, Brainerd, labored, and which he describes as " near twenty miles from Stockbridge, and near about twenty miles distant from Albany eastward ; "[4] Potatik, located by the Moravians on the Housatonic " seventy miles inland," and Westenhuck or Wnahktakook, the capital of the confederacy, were villages of the *Westenhucks*, subsequently known as the Stockbridges.[5] That their villages and chieftaincies were even more numerous than those of the *Montauks* and *Wappingers* there is every reason to suppose, but causes the very opposite of those which led to the preservation of the location of the latter, permitted the former to go down with so many unrecorded facts relating to the tribe, as well as to their neighbors, the *Mohawks*, whose four castles only appear on record instead of seven as affirmed by the Jesuit missionaries.[6]

But these subdivisions are of no practical importance. In tribal action they were as unknown as the merest hamlet in

[1] *Brodhead*, I, 77 ; *Albany County Records ; Stockbridge Tradition.*

[2] Literally Bear's island, so called no doubt from the totem of its occupants.

[3] " Shacomico, a place in the remotest part of that county (Dutchess) inhabited chiefly by Indians, where also live three Moravian priests with their families in a blockhouse, and sixteen Indian wigwams round about it."—*Documentary History*, III, 1014.

[4] " The place as to its situation, was sufficiently unpleasant, being encompassed with mountains and woods." — *Brainerd's Diary*. The Indians removed from this village to Stockbridge, in 1744. The site of the hut which Brainerd occupied

is marked by a pine tree growing up from the centre of what was once his only room, and the bridge near by is called Brainerd's Bridge. — *Stockbridge, Past and Present*, 69.

[5] Westenhuck and Stockbridge were two distinct places. The former was among the hills south of Stockbridge. — *Sauthier's Map*. After the establishment of the reservation and mission at Stockbridge the Indian village was mainly, if not entirely, deserted. Many of the tribe removed to Pennsylvania, and others united with the mission.

[6] Local research would, it is believed, develop forty villages in the territory of the Mahicans.

the voice of a civilized state ; in other respects, as free as the most perfect democracy. Had the lands upon which they were located been sold in small tracts and opened to settlement at an early period, they would not have escaped observation and record ; but the wilderness was a sealed book for many years, and there are those who still write that it was without Indian habitations. Such, too, was the dream in regard to the lands of the *Iroquois*, until Sullivan's blazing torch lighted the hills and valleys with the crackling flames of forty burning villages.

On the 8th of April, 1680, the *Mahicans* sold their land, on the west side of the Hudson, to Van Rensselaer, or at least so much thereof as was " called Sanckhagag," a tract described as extending from Beeren island up to Smack's island, and in breadth two days' journey." The grantors were Paep-Sikene-komtas, Manconttanshal and Sickoussen. On the 27th of July, following, the same gentleman bought from Cattomack, Nawanemit, Abantzene, Sagisquwa and Kanamoack, the lands lying south and north of Fort Orange, and extending to within a short distance of Monemius' castle, and from Nawanemit, one of the last named chiefs, his grounds, " called Samesseeck," stretching on the east side of the river, from opposite Castle island to a point facing Fort Orange, and thence from Poetan-oek, the mill creek, north to Negagonse. Seven years later he purchased an intervening district " called Papsickenekas," lying on the east bank of the river, extending from opposite Castle island south to a point opposite Smack's island, includ-ing the adjacent islands, and all the lands back into the interior, belonging to the Indian grantors, and, with his previous pur-chases, became the proprietor of a tract of country twenty-four miles long, and forty-eight miles broad, containing, by estima-tion, over seven hundred thousand acres, now comprising the counties of Albany, Rensselaer, and part of Columbia.[1]

Deeds of a later period for lands in the same vicinity are re-corded in Albany county records. One is given " in the pre-sence of Aepjen and Nietamozit, being among the chiefs of the

---

[1] *O'Callaghan's New Netherland*, I, 122, 123, 124 ; *Map of Manor of Rens-selaerswyck, Documentary History*, III, 916 ; *Map of Rensselaerswyck*, *O'Cal-laghan's New Netherland*, I, 204.

Mohikanders ;" another defines the tract conveyed, as " the fast bank where the house of Machacnotas stood," and another conveys an island called " Schotack or Aepjen's island." Two immense tracts were sold to Robert Livingston, July 12th, 1683, and August 10th, 1685, and subsequently included in a patent to him for the manor of Livingston. The grantors were the following " Mahican Indian owners :" Ottonowaw, a cripple Indian ; Tataemshaet, Oothoot, Maneetpoo, and two Indian women named Tamaranchquae and Wawanitsaw, and others in the deed named.[1]   The lands between Livingston and Van Rensselaer were taken up in small parcels, some of them without purchase. Sales east of the Taghkanick mountains, in the state of Connecticut, are recorded, and among others that of a tract to Johannes Diksman and Lawrence Knickerbacker, now in the town of Salisbury, the grantors being Konaguin, Sakowanahook and others " all of the nation of Mohokandas." Almost touching the shore of the southern extremity of Lake Champlain, " Mahican Abraham" asserted his proprietorship, indicating tribal possession seventy miles north of Albany. In view of these records there is no difficulty in determining the value of the assertion that the *Mahicans* were driven back to the Housatonic " by their implacable enemies, the *Mohawks.*" The more important proposition is, how came the former west of the Hudson, if the prowess of their rivals was so supreme ?

Reference has already been made to the capital or council-fire of the nation as having been at Westenhuck. That the original capital was at Schodac is affirmed by the Dutch records and by the traditions of the tribe, and accords with the interpretation of the name itself. Like other tribes, they recoiled before the incoming civilization, and sometime between 1664 and 1734, removed their national seat to Westenhuck where it was known to the authorities of Massachusetts,[2] as well as to the Moravian missionaries. " In February, 1744," says Loskiel,[3] "some Indian deputies arrived at Shekomeko from Westenhuck, to inquire whether the believing Indians would live in friendship

[1] *Documentary History*, III, 612, 617.   [3] *History of the Moravian Missions.*
[2] *Stockbridge Past and Present.*

with the new chief." In 1751, he writes at Gnadenhutten, in Pennsylvania : " Two deputies were likewise sent to the great council of the Mahikan nation at Westenhuck, with which they appeared much pleased, and as a proof of their satisfaction made Abraham, an assistant at Gnadenhutten, a captain."[1] Again : " The unbelieving Indians at Westenhuck, made several attempts to draw the Christian Indians in Shekomeko into their party." " Brother David Bruce," it is added, " paid visits to Westenhuck, by invitation of the head chief of the Mahican nation," of whom it is said : " the above mentioned chief of Westenhuck, who had long been acquainted with the brethren, departed this life." This chief was Konapot, whose name has been preserved in the records of the Stockbridge mission, and who is described by Hopkins as " the principal man among the Muhhekaneok of Massachusetts." By the records of Massachusetts, it appears that, in 1736, the Westenhuck sachem visited Boston, accompanied by the chiefs from Hudson's river, as one people, while the former, when known as the Stockbridges, came to Albany in 1756, and were received as the actual representatives of the *Mahicans*, instead of those known as such to the authorities of New York. The fact that Westenhuck was the point selected for missionary labor, by the Society for the Propagation of the Gospel in Foreign Parts, is additional proof of its importance. Though the extremities of the nation withered under the adverse influences by which they were surrounded, the heart remained in vigor long after that of its rivals had been consumed.

IV. The chieftaincies of the UNAMIS were :

1st. The *Navisinks* or *Neversincks*. This chieftaincy inhabited the Highlands south of Sandy Hook. It was with them that Hudson had intercourse after entering the bay of New York. He describes them as civil in their deportment, and disposed to exchange such products of the country as they had for knives, beads and articles of clothing. It was at their hands, also, that John Coleman, one of Hudson's crew, lost his life

[1] Abraham, whose Indian name was Schabash, was one of the chiefs of Shekomeko. He was converted by the Moravians and removed with them to Pennsylvania, from whence he returned as stated. He subsequently became the head of the Mahicans of Pennsylvania. — *Mem. Morav. Chnrch.*

on the 6th of September, 1609. Passachquon was sachem in 1663.

2d. The *Raritans*, who occupied the valley and river which still bears their name. They were first called *Sanhikans*, or Fire-workers. They were divided, it is said, in two sachemdoms and about twenty chieftaincies. From their title deeds it would appear that the two sachems were Appamanskoch and Mattano or Mattenon.[1] Their territory on the Hudson included the valley of the Raritan, and from thence to the sea.[2] The Dutch had some difficulties with them in 1641, but soon after that year they removed to the Kittateny mountains, and were subsequently known in Dutch history only through the deeds which they gave to their lands. They were not a warlike race, but peaceable in disposition, as became the traditional totem which they bore. Their treatment under the English of New Jersey, was liberal and just. No bloodshed or violence was permitted, nor occupation of their lands without purchase. Their possessions finally dwindled down to about three thousand acres in the township of Eversham, Burlington county, on which a church was erected. This land they obtained permission to sell, in 1802, when the remnant of the clan removed to Oneida lake, N. Y., and from thence, in 1824, to a tract on Lake Michigan, where they united with the Brothertons.

3d. The *Hackinsacks*. The territory occupied by this chieftaincy was called Ack-kin-kas-hacky, and embraced the valley of the Hackinsack and Passaic rivers. Their number, in 1643, is stated at a thousand souls, of whom about three hundred were warriors. Their council-fire was kindled at Gamoenapa, the aboriginal for Communipau. They took prominent part in

---

[1] Deed for Raritan meadows, 1651; Deed to Denton and others, 1664.

[2] " The district inhabited by a nation called Raritangs, is situated on a fresh water river, that flows through the centre of the low lands which the Indians cultivate. This vacant territory lies between two high mountains, far distant the one from the other. This district was abandoned by the natives for two reasons; the first and principal is, that finding themselves unable to resist the Southern Indians, they migrated further inland; the second, because this country was flooded every spring." — *Documentary History*, IV, 29. Some of our historians, with characteristic zeal for the Mohawks, ascribe the removal of the Raritans to the incursions of the former. It is not possible to determine who the " Southern Indians" named in the text were, but it is not an improbable supposition that they were Shawanoes.

events of 1643–44, but subsequently appear only as mediators in the person of their sachem Oritany,[1] who enjoyed to a rare old age the confidence of his people and of the surrounding chieftaincies, as well as that of the Europeans. He is spoken of in 1687, as very aged, and as delegating his authority in a measure to Perro. The lands of the chieftaincy embraced Jersey City, Hoboken, a part of Staten island,[2] Wehawken, Newark, Passaic, etc.

4th. The *Aquackanonks*. Their sachem, in 1676, was Captahem or Captamin. Their territory, or at least a portion of it, was called Haquequenunck or Acquackanonk, and included the site of the present city of Paterson.[3] They are also described as occupying a considerable portion of the centre of New Jersey.

5th. The *Tappans*. The relations existing between this chieftaincy and the *Hackinsacks* were very intimate, so much so as to lead some to suppose that they were a part of Oritany's sachemdom. Their separate authority and jurisdiction, however, is clearly established. Their territory extended from the vicinity of Hackinsack river to the Highlands.[4] De Vries purchased lands from them in 1640, which he describes as "a beautiful valley under the mountains, of about five hundred acres, within an hour's walk of Gamoenapa," the principal village of the *Hackinsacks*. On some of the early maps their village is located some miles back from the river, but in the attempt, on the part of the Dutch governor, to collect tribute from them, in 1640, it appears that access could be had to them by sending up a sloop, indicating that in the summer at least they had a representative position on the Hudson. In the treaty of 1745, Sessekemick represented them and appears to have acted under the counsel of Oritany. In the sale of Staten island, Taghkospemo appeared as their sachem, and there is

[1] " I, Oratum, am sagamore, and sole proprietor of Hackingsack, lying and being on the main land over against the Isle of Manhattans."—*Deed to Edward Gove*, Oct. 5, 1664.

[2] Staten island, by the Indians called Eghquaous, appears to have been owned in partnership by the *Raritans*, the *Hackinsacks* and the *Tappans*.—*Deed to Van der Cappellen*, 1659.

[3] Deed to Hans Diderick and others, March 25, 1676. Oritany, who was then living, had no part in this deed.

[4] " Within the first reach, on the western bank of the river, where the land is low, there dwells a nation of savages, named *Tappans*."—*De Laet, New York Hist. Soc. Coll.*, 2d series, I, 298.

12

evidence that his sachemship had much earlier date. Their name survives in Tappan bay, which probably bounded their possessions on the Hudson.

6th. The *Haverstraws*. North of the *Tappans* and inhabiting a territory, the westward boundaries of which are not clearly defined, were the *Haverstraws*, so called by the Dutch,[1] but whose aboriginal name appears to have been lost.[2] They took some part in the early wars, but would seem to have been absorbed by the *Tappans* after the supremacy of the English. Stony point was the northern limit of their territory, as indicated by the deed to Governor Dongan subsequently embraced in the Evans patent. In a deed to Balthazar De Hart, July 31, 1666, confirmed to him by letters patent from Cateret, and Council of New Jersey, April 10, 1671, and subsequently by patent from the Governor of New York, the tract conveyed is described as " all the land lying on the west side of Hudson's river, called Haverstraw, on the north side of the hills called Verdrietinge hook, on the south side of the highlands, on the east of the mountains, so that the same is bounded by Hudson's river and round about by the high mountains."[3] This description embraces precisely the western boundary of Haverstraw bay. The deed was executed by Sackewaghgyn, Roansameck, Kewegham, and Kackeros. By deed to Stephen Van Cortlandt in 1683, it would appear that they had either moved further north or had more northern territory, the tract conveyed being described as lying opposite Anthony's nose, from the " south side of a creek called Senkapogh, west to the head thereof, then northerly along the high hills as the river runneth to another creek called Assinapink, thence along the same to Hudson's river." The deed was executed by " Sackagkemeck, sachem of Haverstraw, Werekepes, and Kaghtsikoos." Don-

---

[1] Named by our people Haverstroo."— *De Laet.*

[2] O'Callaghan gives the name of " Sessegehout, chief of *Reweghnome*, of Haverstroo," but it is not clear that that was the name of the chieftaincy, although the presumption is strongly in its favor.— *O'Callaghan's New Netherland*, II, 509, *note.*

[3] This purchase covered what were subsequently called " the Christian Patented lands of Haverstraw," and by that title formed the boundary in part of several patents. The original grant from Cateret was predicated on the supposition that the tract was within the limits of New Jersey.

gan's purchase in 1685 covered this tract, and had as one of its grantors Werekepes, who was also a grantor to Van Cortlandt. From Verdrietig hook to Stony point may be assumed as the territory of the *Haverstraws*.

V. The chieftaincies of the MINSIS were :

1st. The *Waoranecks*. This chieftaincy has been variously located. Van der Donck places them in the Highlands on the east side of the river and south of Matteawan creek, and De Laet on the west side as occupants of the Esopus country.[1] Wassenaar agrees with De Laet in locating them in the Fisher's hook.[2] The territory which was inhabited by them on the Hudson may be regarded as described with sufficient accuracy in what is known as Governor Dongan's two purchases (1684–'85), the first of which extended from the Paltz tract to the Danskammer, and the second from Dans-kammer to Stony point. In the first, the limits of the Esopus Indians, or *Warranawonkongs*, are defined as terminating at the Dans-kammer, and in the second the jurisdiction of what are therein called " the Murderer's kill Indians," is admitted as from the Dans-kammer to Stony point. Their western boundary cannot be so satisfactorily defined. From the fact that the same names, in part, appear as grantors of the Dongan tract, of the Cheesecock tract, and of a tract to Sir John Ashhurst,[3] the latter covering sixteen miles square, commencing at a point eight miles from the Hudson on the south side of "the Murderer's kill," it may be inferred that that boundary terminated with the natural watershed of the Hudson. Were not De Laet's location sufficiently clear, there are other reasons for assuming that the " Murderer's

---

[1] " This reach (the Fisher's) extends to another narrow pass, where, on the west side of the river, there is a point of land that juts out covered with sand, opposite a bend in the river, on which another nation of savages, the *Waoranecks*, have their abode."— *De Laet*.

[2] At Fisher's hook are *Pachany, Warenocker, Warrawannankonckx*.— *Documentary History*, III, 28.

[3] The duplication of signatures indicates what may be called overlapping boundaries. The grantors, who were principal owners, are generally so stated, and the subsequent signatures classed as "inferior owners." Thus in the Haverstraw purchase, Sackagkemeck appears as sachem or principal, and Werepekes as an "inferior owner." In the Dongan purchase, Werepekes signed as sachem, and Sackagkemeck as an inferior. In the Cheesecock and Ashhurst deeds Moringamaghan, or Moringamack, is the principal, while in the Dongan deed he appears in a subordinate position. These overlapping boundaries entered very largely into consideration in fixing the limits of the Dongan purchase.

kill Indians" of 1685, were the *Waoranecks* of 1625. The name by which they were last designated was that of the creek now called " Murderer's ; " their first name disappears from the early records almost simultaneously with the appearance of the latter,[1] and with the general classification of " Esopus Indians," while the territory assigned to them had no other known occupants, rich though it was in all the elements of favorite hunting grounds. The *Waoranecks* participated in the Esopus wars, if not in the wars at Fort Amsterdam, and at the Dans-kammer celebrated those frightful

orgies called kinte-kaying, regarded by the Dutch as devil worship. Their relations with the Esopus Indians [2] were such that there can be no hazard in classing them as one of the " five tribes," so called, of the Esopus country. Their sachem in 1685, was Werekepes, or Werepekes, and Moringamaghan [3] and Awessewa principal chiefs.

Maringoman's Castle.

2d. The *Warranawonkongs*.[4] This was the most numerous of the Esopus chieftaincies. Their territory extended from the

[1] This creek is first called Murderer's on Van der Donck's map, 1656, and was so called doubtless from events occurring during the first Esopus war.

[2] Esopus is supposed to be derived from *Seepus*, a river. Reichel says : " A Sopus Indian, or *a lowlander*."

[3] Maringoman's " castle" and Maringoman's " wigwam" are spoken of in different deeds. The first was on the north end of the Schunamunck mountain on the south side of Murderer's creek, in the present town of Bloominggrove, and is particularly described as being " opposite the

house where John McLean now (1756), dwells, near the said kill." He subsequently removed to what is called a " wigwam," which stood " on the north bank of Murderer's creek, where Col. Matthews lives." The location is in Hamptonburgh, on the point of land formed by the junction of the Otter kill and the Grey Court creek, by which Murderer's creek is formed, and which takes its name at that point, as though some dark memory was associated with the name of its owner.

[4] " A little beyond, on the west side,

Dans-kammer to the Katskill mountains, or more properly perhaps to the Saugerties, and embraced the waters of the Shawaugunk, the Wallkill and the Esopus rivers. Their principal castle was in the Shawangunk country, although a very considerable one was on the Esopus river, known as Wiltmeet. The "oldest and best of their chiefs," Preummaker, was killed in the war of 1663, as was also Papequanaehen. In their treaty with Stuyvesant, in 1664, they were represented by Sewackenamo, sachem, and Onackatin and Powsawagh, chiefs. In the subsequent treaty of 1669, the five sachemdoms of the Esopus country were represented in the persons of Onackatin, Napashequiqua, Sewackenamo, Shewotin, and Calcop. In the Dongan purchase of 1684, Pemerawaghin appears as chief sachem.

3d. The *Mamekotings.* The district inhabited by the *Mamekotings* was west of the Shawangunk mountains and is still known as the Mamakating valley. Their history is so intimately blended with that of the Esopus Indians that identification is impossible further than by title. They were evidently one of the " five tribes," and may be designated as the third.

4th. The *Wawarsinks.* The fourth of the Esopus chieftaincies, the *Wawarsinks,* inhabited the district of country which still bears their name. Separate from the Esopus Indians they have no history.

5th. The *Katskills.* The fifth and last of the Esopus chieftaincies [1] inhabited the territory north of Saugerties, forming the eastern water-shed of the Katskill mountains,[2] including the Sager's creek, the Kader's creek, and the Kats kill, from which latter they took their name.[3] They were the " loving people " described by Hudson ; a neutral and not very courageous peo-

where there is a creek, and the river becomes more shallow, the *Warranawonkongs* reside."— *De Laet.*

" These following Esopus Indians."— *Deed to Wm. Loveridge.*

[2] In giving the boundaries of the Coeyman's purchase, O'Callaghan states that the line followed Coxackie creek to its head ; then ran west until it struck the head of the waters falling into the Hudson, all the land on which belonged to the Katskill Indians ; the waters flowing west to the Schoharie creek being the property of the *Mohawks.*— *History of New Netherland,* 1, 435.

[3] Brodhead locates here some families of *Nanticokes,* and it is possible that when that nation " disappeared without glory," some of its members were induced thither either as recruits of the *Minsis* or the *Mohawks,* but their more considerable emigration was to Pennsylvania.

ple, as may be inferred from Kregier's account of them.[1] Their chief, in 1663, was known as Long Jacob. Mahak Niminaw sachem in 1682.[2] Above the *Katskills* came the *Mechkentowoons* of the *Mahicans*, but with boundary undefined.

6th. The *Minnisinks*. West of the Esopus country, and inhabiting the Delaware and its tributaries were the *Minsis* proper of whom a clan more generally known as the *Minnisinks* held the south-western parts of the present counties of Orange and Ulster, and north-western New Jersey. Van der Donck describes their district as " Minnessinck of 'tLandt van Bacham," and gives them three villages : Schepinaikonck, Meochkonck, and Macharienkonck, the latter in the bend of the Delaware opposite Port Jervis, and preserved perhaps in the name Mahackemeck.[3] On Sauthier's map, Minnisink, the capital of the clan, is located some ten miles south of Mahackemeck, in New Jersey. Very little is known of the history of the clan as distinguished from the tribe of which they were part, although the authorities of New York had communication with them, and the missionary, Brainerd, visited them. Tradition gives to them the honor of holding the capital of the tribe in years anterior to the advent of the Europeans. Defrauded and maltreated, they subsequently exacted a terrible compensation for their wrongs.

VI. The IROQUOIS.

1st. The *Mohawks*. The territory occupied by the *Mohawks* has already been sufficiently described, as well as that of their associate tribes of the Iroquois confederacy. The *Mohawks* had no villages immediately upon the Hudson, although they

---

[1] " Examined the Squaw prisoner and inquired if she were not acquainted with some Esopus Indians who abode about here ? She answered that some Katskill Indians lay on the other side near the Sager's kill, but they would not fight against the Dutch."— *Documentary History*, IV, 48.

[2] " Mahak Niminaw shall have, as being sachem of Katskill, two fathoms of duffels and an anker of rum when he comes home."— *Deed to Wm. Loveridge.*

[3] On the east bank of the Neversink river, three miles above Point Jervis, on the farm now or late of Mr. Levi Van Etten, exists an Indian burial ground, the graves covering an area of six acres. Skeletons have been unearthed, and found invariably in a sitting posture, surrounded by tomahawks, arrow-heads, etc. In one grave was found a sheet iron tobacco box containing a hankerchief covered with devices, employed doubtless to preserve the record of its owner's services. Not far from the grounds is the Willehoosa, a cavern in the rocks on the side of the Shawangunk mountain. It contains three apartments, each about the size of an ordinary room. Indian implements of various kinds have been found there.

claimed title to the lands north of the Mohawk river. Their principal villages or castles, in 1677, were on the north side of the Mohawk, in the present counties of Montgomery and Herkimer, and were : 1. Cahaniaga, or Gandaougue, by the Dutch called Kaghnewage, and more modernly known as Caghnawaga ; 2. Gandagaro, or Kanagaro ; 3. Canajorha, or Canajoharie, and 4. Tionondogue or Tionnontoguen. The first contained twenty-four houses ; the second, sixteen ; the third, sixteen, and the fourth thirty.[1] Tionondogue was the capital of the tribe. It was destroyed by the French in 1667, and rebuilt about one mile further west. It was again destroyed by the French in 1693, but does not appear to have been rebuilt, as soon after that time Canajoharie is spoken of as the " upper Mohawk castle."[2] It was at the latter that Hendrick and his brother Abraham resided, as well as Joseph Brant. The house occupied by the former, and also by the latter, was situated near what is now known as " Indian castle church," in Danube, Herkimer county. Caghnawaga was the scene of early conflict between the *Mohawks* and the *Mahicans ;* it was destroyed by the French in 1693, and subsequently by the Americans. It was long known as the " lower Mohawk castle," and occupied the site of the present village of Fonda, Montgomery county. Gandagaro passed out of existence with the second French invasion, or at least is lost to the records after 1693. In 1690, a new castle was erected at the mouth of Schoharie creek and called Tiononderoge, after the name of the ancient capital of the tribe, but was more generally known as " the castle of the praying Maquas." It was situated on the site of what was subsequently known as Fort Hunter. Its occupants were called the Schoharie Indians. It was among them that several families of Esopus Indians were settlers in 1756. After the revolution the *Mohawks* had neither castles nor villages in their ancient territory.

2d. The *Oneidas,* etc. The *Oneidas* had, in 1677, one town, " the old Oneida castle," as it was called, containing one

---

[1] *Colonial History,* III, 250; *Brodhead's New York,* II, 129. Pierron, the Jesuit missionary, it is said, visited every week seven Mohawk villages, but they are not located.

[2] *Colonial History,* VI, 850.

hundred houses; the *Onondagas*, a palisaded town of one hundred and forty houses, and a village of twenty-four houses; [1] the *Cayugas* three towns, and the *Senecas* four.[2]

The capital of the confederacy was the village of Onondaga, on the lake of that name, the principal settlement of the *Onondagas*. Bishop Cammerhof, who visited it in 1751, says, "Onondaga, the chief town of the six nations, situated in a very pleasant and fruitful country, and consisting of five small towns and villages, through which the river Zinochsaa runs." In the Relations of the Jesuit missionaries it is said: "The word *Onnota*, which signifies in the *Iroquois* tongue, a mountain, has given the name to the village called Onnontaé, or as others call it, Onnontagué, because it is on a mountain; and the people who inhabit it consequently style themselves Onnontaé-ronnons, or Onnontagué-ronnons."

[1] The great villages of the Onnontagues consists of one hundred cabins.— *Colonial History*, ix, 375.
[2] *Colonial History*, iii, 250. This was the number then known. It is subsequently stated that forty towns existed in the three western cantons.— *Journal of Sullivan's Expedition*.

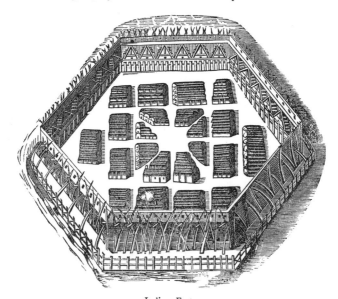

Indian Fort.
ONONDAGA, THE CAPITAL OF THE FIVE
NATIONS — 1609.

CHAPTER V.

THE INDIANS UNDER THE DUTCH — THE MANHATTAN
WARS — FROM THE DISCOVERY TO THE PEACE OF 1645.

FROM the first hour of Hudson's appearance in the waters of the Mahicanituk, to the last of the domination of Holland, there was an antagonism between the Dutch and the Indians with whom they came in contact in the vicinity of Manhattan island, and a conflict which was apparently irrepressible. While in the territory of the *Mahicans* proper Hudson met "loving men," in that of the *Wappingers* and the *Minsis*, he dyed the waters of the river which he had discovered with the blood of those who were encouraged by his overtures to a violation of laws to which they were strangers, and his exit was amid the terrifying war-cries of a people enraged by the slaughter of kindred, and clouds darkened by their quivering arrows.[1]

Subsequent events in no degree mitigated the hostility which was then awakened. When the traders followed Hudson they paused not until they had reached the jurisdiction of those with whom his intercourse had been friendly. There they maintained kindly relations with the Indians, and around their trading posts, Fort Nassau, and subsequently Fort Orange,[2] hed neutral ground between the contending *Mahicans* and *Mohawks*.[3] But this alliance of friendship did not relieve the Dutch from apprehended attacks on the part of those whom Hudson had

[1] *Hudson's Journal; ante*, p. 11.
[2] The first, or Fort Nassau, was erected on what was called Castle island, now known as Boyd's island, a short distance below the Albany ferry. It was a building twenty-six feet wide and thirty-six feet long, enclosed by a stockade fifty-eight feet square, and the whole surrounded by a moat eighteen feet wide. Its armament consisted of two large guns and eleven swivels, and the garrison of ten or twelve men. The location proved unfortunate, in consequence of the exposure to the spring freshets, and in 1618 it was removed to the banks of the Tawalsontha creek, now called the Norman's kill, from whence it was soon after removed further north and located in the vicinity of what is now South Broadway, Albany, and called Fort Orange, by which name, and that of Beaverwyck, the small settlement which gathered around it, it was known until 1664.
[3] *Ante*, p. 54.

offended, and it was deemed prudent to erect a fort on what was then known as Prince's island, and to garrison it with sixteen men for the defense of the river below."[1]

Contemporaneous circumstances contributed to keep alive this feeling. One Jacob Eelkins,[2] who had been in superintendence of the trade at Fort Nassau, in the summer of 1622 ascended the Connecticut to traffic, and while there treacherously imprisoned the chief of the *Sequins* on board his yacht, and would not release him until a ransom of one hundred and forty fathoms of wampum had been exacted. The offense was resented by all the tribes, and by none more so than by the *Mahicans*. To appease them, Eelkins was discharged, and apparently in further overture to them, Krieckbeck, the Dutch commander at Fort Orange, in 1626, joined them, with six men, on a hostile expedition against the *Mohawks*.[3]

Other causes of grievance were not wanting. The sale of fire-arms to the *Mahicans* and *Mohawks* at Fort Orange and the refusal to sell to the chieftaincies in the vicinity of Fort Amsterdam [4] was a constant irritation, to allay which the Dutch traders treated the Indians at the latter place with great familiarity, invited them to their houses, admitted them to their tables, and gave them wine, until they came to regard such civilities as their due and to resent their absence. Then the cattle of the Dutch roamed at large, " without a herdsman," and " frequently came into the corn of the Indians, which was unfenced on all sides, committing great damage there. This led to complaints on their part and finally to revenge on the

---

[1] *Wassenaar, Documentary History*, III, 35. The location of this fort has never been positively ascertained.

[2] *Wassenaar, Documentary History*, III, 45; *Brodhead*, I, 146, 168.

[3] *Brodhead*, I, 168. The expedition was not successful. Krieckbeck and three of his men were killed, and the *Mahicans* put to flight. The *Mohawks* did not resent the alliance further than to roast and eat one of the Dutch soldiers, a man named Tyman Bouwensen; but Minuit deemed it prudent, during the continuance of hostilities, to remove the Dutch families to Fort Amsterdam, and to direct the garrison at Fort Orange to observe strict neutrality in the future.

[4] Precisely to what extent the Indians in the vicinity of Fort Amsterdam were supplied with arms in 1643, does not appear. It is said by the Eight Men, in October of that year : " These Indians are, on the contrary, strong and mighty ; have, one with the other, made alliances with seven different tribes, well supplied with guns, powder and ball." (*Colonial History*, I, 190) ; yet there is not a single case of the use of fire arms by the Indians recorded. Even in their most desperate defenses bows and arrows are alone spoken of as their weapons.

cattle, without sparing even the horses." In 1626, a *Weck-quaesgeek* Indian, accompanied by his nephew, who was a "small boy," and another savage, while on their way to the fort to trade, were met and robbed by men in the employ of Minuit, the Dutch director, and in the melee the *Weckquaes-geek* was killed. The act was unknown to the Dutch at the time, but the boy treasured a revenge which he forgot not to exact in manhood.

As the Dutch settlers took up lands on Long Island and the New Jersey shore, they made frequent complaints that their cattle were stolen by the Indians. Regarding the latter as the aggressors in all cases, Director Kieft, who had in the meantime succeeded Minuit, determined, in 1639, to demand from them tribute, not only as compensation, but to aid in establishing his government over them, and for that purpose sent an armed sloop to the *Tappans* to exact contributions of corn and wampum. The Indians expressed their astonishment at this proceeding, and denounced "the sakema of the fort" for daring to attempt such exactions. Sneers and reproaches followed. "The sakema," they said, "must be a mean fellow; he had not invited them to come and live here, that he should now take away their corn." A formal conference was held with the Indians, but the latter refused to yield the contributions asked.

An open rupture soon followed. Some pigs were stolen from De Vries's plantation on Staten island, as it subsequently appeared "by the servants of the company, then (1640) going to the South river to trade, and who landed on the island to take in wood and water;" but, as Kieft professed to believe, by the Indians. He accused the *Raritans* of the offense, and, on the sixteenth of July, commissioned Secretary Van Tienhoven to proceed, with one hundred men, to their territory and demand satisfaction. The *Raritans* denied the commission of the offense, and satisfied the secretary; but the troops under him were bent on mischief, and scarcely had he left them when they made an attack, killed several of the Indians, took one of their chiefs

---

[1] *De Vries, New York Historical Society Collections,* 2d series, I, 263; *Breeden Raedt, Documentary History,* IV, 101, 102.

captive, and mangled the body of another. The *Raritans* retaliated by attacking De Vries's plantation, killed four of his planters and burned his dwelling and tobacco house. Kieft followed with a proclamation announcing the policy of extermination, and offering a bounty of ten fathoms of wampum for the head of every *Raritan* which should be brought to him. Holding their own grievances in abeyance, some of the Long Island warriors took up the hatchet against the *Raritans*, and brought in at least one head for the director's gratification, but the great body of the Indians refused the tempting offer.

Meanwhile the *Weckquaesgeek* boy had grown to manhood, and determined to exact his long meditated atonement for the death of his uncle. Taking with him some beaver skins to barter, he stopped at the house of one Claes Smit, "a harmless Dutchman," and while he was stooping over a chest in which he kept his goods, the savage seized an axe and killed him by a blow on the neck; then quickly plundering his abode, escaped to the woods. Kieft demanded satisfaction, but the *Weckquaesgeeks* refused to deliver up the murderer. He then summoned all the heads of families of Manhattan to a meeting and laid the matter before them, especially asking if it was not just that the murder should be avenged, and if in case the *Weckquaesgeeks* would not surrender the murderer, it would not be "just to destroy the whole village" to which he belonged; and if so, in what manner, when, and by whom such chastisement should be inflicted. The meeting referred the proposition to "twelve select men," who, with greater discernment of the consequences of an open rupture with the Indians than the director, reported that while the murder should be avenged they thought "God and the opportunity should be taken into consideration," and that in the meantime the director should make suitable arrangements for sustaining an attempt at inflicting punishment. In case hostilities should be inaugurated, they thought the director should "lead the van," while the community should "follow his steps and obey his commands." They advised, however, as an offset to this quiet bit of sarcasm, that before anything else was done the director should send up a shallop to the *Weckquaesgeeks* to demand of them "once, twice, yea for a third time," the surrender of the murderer in a "friendly manner."

Offended and bent on war, Kieft "would not listen." Remaining inactive until November, he consulted each of the "twelve" separately on the question of immediate hostilities ; but the latter remained firmly opposed. In the winter he repeated this consultation, and urged that the Indians were absent from their village on hunting expeditions, and that arrangements should be made at once to destroy them. The "twelve" consented, unwillingly, and on assurances that an attack should only be made after repeated solicitations had failed to secure the surrender of the murderer. Kieft did not long delay an attempt to execute his atrocious design. In March (1642), he dispatched a company of eighty men, under command of Ensign Hendrick Van Dyck, with instructions to fall upon the *Weckaquaesgeeks,* "who lay in their village suspecting nothing," and punish them with fire and sword. Fortunately the guide missed his way, and the expedition was compelled to return to Fort Amsterdam "in all the mortification of failure." The result, however, was that the Indians, on discovering the trail of Kieft's men, and detecting his intention, became alarmed and asked that peace might be maintained. Kieft consented on condition that the murderer of Smit was delivered up, and on this basis a treaty, as it was called, was concluded with them. But it was not fulfilled by either of the contracting parties ; the arrest of an Indian, whose action had been in strict accordance with the laws and customs of his tribe, was a process of very difficult accomplishment.

Soon after this occurrence the Dutch were terribly frightened. Miantonomo, the "principal sachem" of the *Narragansetts,* having a controversy pending with Uncas, visited the Manhattans with an hundred men, and passed through all the *Mahican* villages to secure their alliance for the destruction of his rival. The Dutch, however, gave to him a different mission. From a whispered suspicion it grew to public clamor, that the embassy had no less an object than to secure the union of all the Indians in a "general war against both the English and the Dutch." The story spread to New England, where its falsity was demonstrated ; [1] but in the meanwhile the inhabitants at New Amsterdam saw the hand of hostile Indians in every thing ; believed that they had attempted to destroy the settlement by setting fire to its powder-magazine, and the director by poisoning him " or enchanting him by their deviltry." [2]

The storm passed over only to be succeeded by another. The *Hackinsacks* and *Tappans* had hitherto escaped special irritating collisions with the Dutch. True, the *Tappans* had resisted the attempt to place them under tribute, but this attempt appears to have been abandoned. De Vries [3] had settled among the latter, after the disaster which befel him on Staten island, and by kindly treatment had won their confidence. Circumstances, however, forced them to take up the hatchet. Contrary to the advice of the director, and in opposition to the wishes of a majority of the *Hackinsacks*, one Myndert Van der Horst [4] purchased a tract near Communipaw and made settlement thereon. While visiting this settlement a *Hackinsack* warrior became intoxicated, and was robbed of his beaver-skin coat. When the stupor passed off and he became conscious of the imposition which had been practiced upon him, he vowed he would go home for his bow and arrows and shoot the " roguish Swannekin " (as the Dutch were called), who had taken his things, and faithfully did he keep his vow. Watching his opportunity, he shot one of the colonists, Garret Jansen Van Voorst, as he was thatching the roof of one of Van der Horst's houses. The chiefs of his tribe, anxious to keep unbroken friendly relations with the Dutch, hastened to De Vries to secure his counsel and intercession. They dared not go to Fort Amsterdam for fear Kieft would keep them prisoners, but they were willing to make the " blood atonement of money " customary among the tribes, and offered two hundred fathoms of wampum to the family of

[1] *Hubbard's Indian Wars*, 44.

[2] The superstitious fears of the Dutch and the English were alike strongly worked upon by the skill of the Indians in jugglery.

[3] De Vries purchased from the Tappans a tract of about five hundred acres in April, 1640; made settlement thereon the subsequent year, and gave to it the name of Vriesendael.

[4] Myndert Myndertsen Van der Horst purchased and located on a tract " within an hour's walk of Vriesendael." His plantation extended from Archer Cul bay north towards Tappan, and included the valley of the Hackinsack river. The head quarters of the settlement were about five or six hundred paces from the principal village of the Hackinsacks.

the murdered man as the price of peace. Persuaded by De Vries, who became answerable for their safe return, the chiefs visited the fort with him, and there repeated their offer. Kieft refused to accept the wampum, and demanded the murderer. The chiefs could not comply ; the murderer had sought refuge among the *Tankitekes*, and besides he was the son of a chief and could not be surrendered. They then renewed their expiatory offer, but it was again refused, and they returned to their homes hopeless of effecting reconciliation.

These collisions and causes of grievance culminated in the winter of 1643, when Director Kieft threw off all disguise and disgraced even savage modes of warfare by a blackening hypocrisy and a massacre more terrible than any of which their annals bear record. In February of that year a party of eighty *Mahicans*, " each with a musket on his shoulder," made a descent on some of the old Manhattan chieftaincies, for the purpose of collecting tribute which had been withheld.[1] Surprised, and wholly unable from inferiority in arms to cope with their adversaries, the assailed Indians fled to Fort Amsterdam for protection, leaving seventeen of their number dead and a considerable portion of their women and children prisoners in the hands of their enemies. The Dutch kindly cared for the fugitives and supported them for fourteen days ; but, again alarmed for their safety, they scattered themselves among the *Hackinsacks* and *Tappans*, while others fled to Vriesendael to beg assistance and protection. De Vries promised to do all in his power for them, and accordingly went, in a canoe, through the floating ice, to Fort Amsterdam, to ask Kieft to assist him with some soldiers. The director, however, claimed that he had none to spare ; and the next day the Indians left Vriesendael, some going to

[1] Brodhead and others assert that this foray was by Mohawks. The documentary proof, however, is that it was made by the Mahicans. " The *Mahican* Indians, who, surprising, slew full seventy of them "— *Colonial History*, 1, 151. " The *Mahicanders* dwelling below Fort Orange, who slew," etc.— *Ibid.*, 184. " The Indians, the *Mayekanders*, who came from Fort Orange "— *De Vries*. The conclusion that it was by the *Mohawks* is apparently based on the hypothe- sis that the *Mahicans* would not attack those regarded as their own people, and that the *Mohawks* alone were armed. The fact distinctly appears, however, that not only were the *Mahicans* armed, but that the " old Manhattans " had neglected to pay them the tribute due from conquered tribes. That no other chieftaincies than those of the Weckquaesgeek district were visited, is additional proof that it was by the *Mahicans*.

Pavonia [1] among the *Hackinsacks*, who were "full a thousand strong," and others to Rechtauck (now Corlear's hook) where they occupied some cabins which had been erected by the *Reckawancks*.

Made acquainted with these facts, the people of New Amsterdam were divided in opinion as to the proper policy to be pursued. The majority, under the lead of De Vries, counseled patience, humanity and kindness, such as had been extended to the fugitives when they first fled thither for protection. Another party, headed by Van Tienhoven, provincial secretary, masking their action under professions of indignation at the shedding of innocent Christian blood, clamored for the extermination of the Indians. A petition was circulated by the latter, and obtained some signatures, reminding the director that God had now supplied the "opportunity" which the "twelve" had suggested should be awaited, and asking permission to "attack and destroy the enemy which had been delivered into" their hands, and "that one party, composed of freemen, and another of soldiers, be dispatched to different places against them." [2] The petition was resisted by De Vries and others, who warned the director against so gross a breach of Indian and civilized laws of hospitality; but Keift, who had long before taken his position on the subject, readily complied with the request of the petitioners, and issued an order that the Indians should be attacked by two divisions, one at Pavonia and the other at Corlear's hook, the former to be by the soldiers under the command of Sergeant Rodolf, and the latter by the burghers headed by Maryn Andriaensen. [3]

---

[1] Michael Pauw purchased from the Indians the tract now included in Hoboken and Jersey City, and established there a colony to which he gave the name of Pavonia.—*Brodhead*, I, 203.

[2] *Colonial History*, III, 146; *O'Callaghan*, I, 266; *Brodhead*, I, 349. The Narrative is principally by De Vries.

"[3] We, therefore, hereby authorize Maryn Adriansen, at his request, with his associates, to attack a party of savages skulking behind Corlear's hook, or plantation, and act with them in every such manner as they shall deem proper and the time and opportunity shall permit. Sergeant Rodolf is commanded and authorized to take under his command a troop of soldiers and lead them to Pavonia, and drive away and destroy the savages being behind Jan Evertsen's, but to spare, as much as possible, their wives and children, and to take the savages prisoners.* *The exploit to be executed at night, with the greatest caution and prudence. Our God may bless the expedition. Done Feb. 24th, 1643." — *O'Callaghan*, I, 267, 268.

The plan was executed on the night of the 25th of February. The Indians had gathered behind Pauw's settlement at Pavonia, unsuspicious of attack from those to whose shelter they had fled, and were sleeping in conscious security when the work of death commenced. Loud shrieks first announced to DeVries, who was watching at Fort Amsterdam, that the slaughter had begun, but these shrieks were succeeded by the stolid indifference with which the red man always met his fate, and nothing was heard but the report of fire-arms. Neither age nor sex were spared. Warrior and squaw, sachem and chief, mother and babe, were alike massacred. DeVries describes the terrible tragedy in pointed language. Children were taken from the arms of their mothers and butchered in the presence of their parents, and their mangled limbs thrown into the fire or the water. " Other sucklings had been fastened to little boards, and in this position they were cut to pieces. Some were thrown in the river, and when the parents rushed in to save them, the soldiers prevented their landing and let parents and children drown." The next morning some of the Indians, who had escaped the midnight slaughter, came to the fort begging for shelter, but instead of receiving it, were killed in cold blood or thrown into the river.[1] Continues DeVries, " some came running to us from the coun- try, having their hands cut off ; some lost both arms and legs ; some were supporting their entrails with their hands, while others were mangled in other horrid ways, too horrid to be conceived. And these miserable wretches, as well as many of the Dutch, were all the time under the impression that the attack had pro- ceeded from their Indian enemies "— were unwilling to believe that men professing the Christian name could be guilty of so gross a violation of Christian principles.

With an aching heart, DeVries returned to his home, and had scarcely arrived when some of the fugitives gathered around him. " The Fort Orange Indians have fallen upon us," said they, " and we have come to hide ourselves in your fort." " It is no time to hide yourselves in the fort ; no Indians have done

[1] " I am told for a fact that a certain skipper, Isaac Abrahamsen, having saved a boy, and hidden him under the sails, in order to give him to one Cornelius Me- lyn, towards morning the poor child, overcome with cold and hunger, made some noise, and was heard by the soldiers, eighteen Dutch tigers dragged (him) from

14

this deed; it is the work of the Swannekens," answered De Vries, and he led the fugitives to the gate, " where stood no sentinel," and bade them seek shelter in the forest depths. Meanwhile the victorious expeditions returned to Fort Amsterdam and reported, as the result of their work, that eighty Indians had been slaughtered at Pavonia and thirty at Corlear's hook, while with them were thirty prisoners. Kieft received his freebooters and soldiers with thanks, rewards and congratulations ; while Van Tienhoven's mother, forgetful of the finer feelings which do honor to her sex, amused herself, it is stated, by kicking about the heads of the dead men which had been brought in as trophies of the midnight slaughter.[1]

The first notes of triumph had barely faded from the air, however, ere the hand of revenge was made red with the blood of the Dutch. Kieft, in the exultation of the moment, sent out foraging expeditions to collect corn. One of these expeditions seized two wagon loads from the Long Island Indians, who lost three of their number in endeavoring to save their property. In retaliation, the *Montauk* and the *Hackinsack* and *Tappan* chieftaincies made common cause with the *Weckquaesgeeks*,[2] who had suffered in the February attack, and who had learned fully that the Dutch, and not the *Mahicans*, had been the principals in the massacre of their kindred, and the tomahawk, the scalping knife and the firebrand executed the work of vengeance. " From swamps and thickets the mysterious enemy made his sudden onset. The farmer was murdered in the open field ; women and children, granted their lives, were swept off into long captivity ; houses and bouweries, hay-stacks and grain, cattle and crops, were all destroyed."[3] Even Vriesendael did

under the sails, in spite of the endeavors of the skipper, cut (him) in two and threw (him) overboard."—*Breeden Raedt*.

[1] *O'Callaghan*, I, 269. " It is a scandal for our nation," says the author of *Breeden Raedt*, " and if silence would have remedied it, I should never have mentioned it."

[2] The narrative speaks of the *Weckquaesgeeks*, the *Sint-Sings*, and the *Kicktawancs* in different places.

[3] *Brodhead*, I, 354. " Almost all the bouweries were also destroyed, so that only three remained on the Manhattes, and two on Staten island, and the greater part of the cattle were destroyed. Whatever remained of these had to be kept in a very small enclosure, except in Rensselaer's colonie, lying on the North river, in the neighborhood of Fort Orange, which experienced no trouble and enjoyed peace, because they continued to sell firearms and powder to the Indians even during the war against our people."— *Report, etc., Colonial History*, I, 151.

not escape the general calamity. The outhouses, and crops and cattle were destroyed. DeVries and his colonists, however, escaped into the manor house or fort, which had been constructed with loop-holes for musketry, and were standing on their defense, when an Indian whom DeVries had sheltered on the morning of the massacre came up to the besiegers, related the occurrence and told them DeVries was "a good chief." The Indians at once raised the siege, and expressed their regret that they had destroyed the cattle ; they would let the little brewery of their Dutch friends stand, although they longed for the copper kettle to make barbs for their arrows.[1]

The Dutch were thrown into great consternation and fled to Fort Amsterdam for protection, with bitter upbraidings on their lips against the director. He met them defiantly at first, and professed to have been controlled by the wishes of Andriaensen ; but the latter denied the assertion, and carried his determination to escape the popular condemnation into an attempt upon the life of the director.[2] But the accumulating evidences of desolation brought ruler and people to repentance. For that mercy which he had refused to extend to the helpless Indians, Kieft besought the people to ask of the Most High, and to that end appointed a day of fasting and prayer, in his proclamation confessing that the calamities which had overtaken them was doubtless owing to the sins which he and his people had committed. While the latter humbled themselves before God, they had little charity in their hearts for the direct author of their calamities, and asked one another, " Did ever the duke of Alba do more evil in the Netherlands ? "

Matters assumed a more favorable aspect in the spring. The Long Island Indians, although previously rejecting the overtures made by the director for peace, and denouncing him as a " corn thief," became more tractable when the planting season came on, and sent from the wigwams of Penhawitz, "their great chief," three delegates to Fort Amsterdam, desiring that nego-tiations might be opened. De Vries and Alferton were at once

[1] *De Vries*, 269; *New York Historical Society Collections*, 2d series, I, 269; *Brodhead*, I, 255.
[2] " What devilish lies art thou report- ing of me ? but by the promptness of the bystanders the shot was prevented, and he was arrested."— *Colonial History*, I, 184.

appointed to accompany them, and setting out on the 4th of March, came to Rechquaakie or Rockaway, where they found Penhawitz, surrounded by nearly three hundred warriors and a village of thirty wigwams. The next day they were conducted into the woods about four hundred yards off, where they found sixteen chiefs of the *Montauks*, with whom the conference was conducted in the Indian form.[1] De Vries invited the chiefs to accompany him to Fort Amsterdam, under the assurance of presents and peace. The latter embraced the offer, and, to the number of eighteen, embarked in a large canoe and reached the fort in the evening. After some days spent in negotiation a treaty was concluded on the 25th, and the chiefs dismissed with presents and solicited to bring to the fort the chiefs of the river families " who had lost so many " of their number. The Long Island sachem accordingly went to Hackinsack and Tappan, but weeks elapsed before negotiations were concluded. Oritany, sachem of the *Hackinsacks*, after consultation with his allies, finally appeared at Fort Amsterdam, clothed with authority to conclude a peace both for his own and the neighboring chieftaincies. The opportunity was embraced by the director and the following treaty agreed to :

" This day, the twenty-second of April, 1643, between William Kieft, director general and the council of New Netherland, on the one side, and Oratatum, sachem of the savages residing at Ack-kinkashacky, who declared that. he was delegated by and for those of *Tappaen, Reckawawanc, Kitchawanc*, and *Sint-Sinck*, on the other side, is a peace concluded in the following manner, to wit :

[1] " We were awakened and led by one of the Indians in the woods upwards of 400 paces from the house, where we found sixteen chiefs from Long Island, who placed themselves in a circle around us. One of them had a bundle of small sticks. He was the best speaker, and commenced his speech. He related that when we first arrived on their shores, we were sometimes in want of food; they gave us their beans and corn, and let us eat oysters and fish; and now for recompense we murdered their people. He here laid down one little stick; this was one point of accusation. The men whom in your first trips you left here to barter your goods till your return, these men have been treated by us as we would have done by our eye-balls. We gave them our daughters for wives, by whom they had children. There are now several Indians, who came from the blood of the Swannekins and that of Indians; and these their own blood were now murdered in such villainous manner. He laid down another stick."—*De Vries, New York Historical Society Collections*, 2d series, 1, 271.

" All injustices committed by the said natives against the Netherlanders, or by the Netherlanders against said natives, shall be forgiven and forgotten forever, reciprocally promising, one the other, to cause no trouble, the one to the other ; but whenever the savages understand that any nation not mentioned in this treaty, may be plotting mischief against the Christians, then they will give to them a timely warning, and not admit such a nation within their own limits."[1]

This peace was one of necessity on the part of the Indians. The *Hackinsack* sachem received his presents, but complained of their insufficiency, saying that his young men would only regard them as a trifling atonement ; and such they not only were, but they were received as the sachem had indicated. At midsummer the sachem visited Vriesendael and stated that the young men of his people were urging war ; that some had lost fathers and mothers in the February massacre, and all were mourning over the memory of friends ; that the presents which had been given to them were not worth the touch, and that they could be no longer pacified. At the request of De Vries, the sachem accompanied him to Fort Amsterdam, where, on repeating his complaint, Kieft replied that he should cause his young Indians who wanted war, to be shot. Kieft then offered him two hundred fathoms of wampum, but the sachem spurned the bribe, and, after promising to do his best to pacify his people, went his way.

With the renewal of difficulties in New England, in September (1643), war again broke out at New Amsterdam. " Pachem, a crafty man, ran through all the villages, urging the Indians to a general massacre." The first aggressive act was by the *Wappingers*;[2] who seized a boat coming from Fort Orange, killed two men and took ·four hundred beaver skins. Others followed this example, " so that they seized two boats more," but were driven off, with the loss of six of their number, in

---

[1] *O'Callaghan* i, 277. *De Vries, Collections New York Historical Society,* 2d series, i, 270. It will be observed that neither the *Weckquaesgeeks* or *Manhattans* are mentioned in the treaty, a fact which indicates the local character of both titles.

[2] *Doc. Hist.,* iv, 12. The Dutch were surprised at the attack by the *Wappingers,* and protested that they had never had any trouble with them. In this they were mistaken, as the testimony shows that nearly all their troubles were with that tribe.

attacking the fourth boat. "Nine Christians, including two women," were killed in these captured boats, one woman and two children remaining prisoners. "The other Indians," continues the narrative, "so soon as their maize was ripe, followed this example, and through semblance of selling beavers, killed an old man and woman, leaving another man with five wounds, who, however, fled in a boat with a little child on his arm, who, in the first outbreak had lost father and mother, and now grandfather and grandmother, being thus twice rescued from the hands of the Indians, first when he was two years old." Nor was this all. Under the pretense of warning from approaching danger, the Indians visited dwellings and killed the inmates, and applied the brand to factories and outbuildings. The few families who had settled in the Esopus country abandoned their farms in alarm, and universal fear pervaded the province.

Kieft now called his people together again, and a committee of "eight men" was appointed to consult with him for the defense of the colony. Before any arrangement had been made, however, the *Weckquaesgeeks* attacked the plantation of Ann Hutchinson,[1] killed that extraordinary woman and her married daughter and son-in-law, and carried off captive her youngest daughter.[2]

Throgmorton's settlement [3] was next attacked and the buildings burned, the inhabitants escaping in their boats. Eighteen victims, however, were added to the revenges of the Indians. Pavonia was attacked and four bouweries burned under the very guns of "two ships of war and a privateer." From the

---

[1] The history of Ann Hutchinson is pretty generally known. With Roger Williams, she was banished from Massachusetts, as "unfit for the society" of her fellow-citizens. She followed Williams to Rhode Island, but fearing the power of Massachusetts would reach her there, removed, in 1642, to Manhattan and settled on a point now known as Pelham's neck.

[2] "The Indians set upon them and slew her and all her children, save one that escaped (her own husband having died before), a dreadful blow! Some write that the Indians did burn her to death with fire, her home and all the rest that belonged unto her, but I am not able to affirm by what kind of death they slew her."— *Wild's Rise, Reign and Ruin of the Antinomians.* "The daughter of Ann Hutchinson remained a prisoner four years, when she was delivered to the Dutch governor at Fort Amsterdam, who restored her to her friends. She had forgotten her native tongue, and was unwilling to be taken from the Indians."— *O'Callaghan.*

[3] Throgmorton was another refugee from Massachusetts. His settlement was a few miles west from that of Ann Hutchinson, and included the point now known as Throg's neck.

highlands of the Hudson to the highlands of the sea, the war-whoop was reechoed, and at a single blow " from the *Never-sincks* to the valley of the *Tappans,* the whole of New Jersey was once more in the possession of its aboriginal lords."[1] Fort Amsterdam afforded the only place of shelter, and thither the colonists fled. " There women and children lay concealed in straw huts, while their husbands and fathers mounted guard on the ramparts above." The whole force of the Dutch was scarce two hundred and fifty men, while the Indians were repre-sented by fifteen hundred of their most expert warriors, includ-ing the *Wappingers* of the Connecticut river, under the lead of Mayane, with whom the Dutch claimed they had never had any difficulty, but who then learned " for the first time that he and his Indians had done" them " much injury."[2] The position of the Dutch was perilous in the extreme. The Indians literally hung upon their necks with " fire and sword."[3] Had they known their own strength, the last refuge of the colonists would have fallen before them, but judging from their own modes of warfare, they feared to attack the fort and contented themselves with sweeping off the exposed plantations and with the terror which their presence inspired.[4]

Director Kieft now solicited aid from New England, offering " twenty-five thousand guilders " for one hundred and fifty men, and as a further consideration that New Netherland should be mortgaged to the English for the payment of the sum offered. Relief was also solicited from Holland ; but these applications were attended with only partial success, and the Dutch were thrown on their own resources, aided by a few English volun-teers under the command of Captain John Underhill.[5] Two

[1] The prowess of the *Iroquois* is affirmed in that they once placed Quebec in siege, yet Fort Amsterdam, more formidable than Quebec, was twice laid waste by the Indians in its vicinity.

[2] *Documentary History,* IV, 14.

[3] *Colonial History,* I, 182.

[4] " They rove in parties continually around day and night on the island of Manhattans, slaying our folks not a thou-sand paces from the fort, and 'tis now arrived at such a pass, that no one dare move a foot to fetch a stick of fire wood

without a strong escort.— *Col. Hist.,* I, 206, 211.

[5] This Underhill was a terrible scourge to the Indians. Engaged in New Eng-land wars, he spared neither the aged nor the young. " He could justify putting the weak and defenceless to death, for says he, 'the Scripture declareth women and children must perish with their pa-rents '— 'we had sufficient light from the word of God for our proceedings.'"— *Trumbull.*

companies were soon organized, one of sixty-five and one of seventy-five men, and the work of retaliation commenced. The second company was composed of forty burghers under Captain Pietersen, and thirty-five Englishmen under Lieutenant Baxter ; Councillor La Montagne acting as general. This company passed over to Staten island; but found that the Indians, who had fallen back from the vicinity of the fort some time previously, had also abandoned their houses. Five or six hundred skepels of corn rewarded the invaders, but nothing was accomplished beyond its removal. Returning to the fort, the company was increased to one hundred and twenty men and sent to the Weckquaesgeek country. Landing at Greenwich in the evening, from three yachts, they marched the entire night, but found nothing. Retreating through Stamford, they were told by the English that there were Indians in that vicinity. Scouts were sent out who returned with the location of an Indian village. Twenty-five men were at once dispatched thither, and succeeded in killing a number and in capturing an old man, two women and some children. One of the captives offered to lead the expedition to the castles of the *Weckquaesgeeks.* Sixty-five men were sent with him and three castles found, but they had no tenants. Two of them were burned, and, after marching some thirty miles, the expedition returned, " having killed only one or two Indians, taken some women and children prisoners, and burnt some corn."

Meanwhile Underhill,[1] with a company of Dutch and English, had passed over to Long Island to attack the *Canarsees* under Penhawitz. After landing, the force was divided; Underhill and fourteen Englishmen were to attack a small village at Hempstead, and Captain Pieter Cock, and General La Montagne, with eighty men, were to reduce the more considerable village of Mespath. Both were successful; one hundred and twenty Indians were reported as having been killed, with a loss to the attacking forces of one man killed and three wounded.[2] Seven prisoners were turned over to Underhill by the English minister, Fordam, at Hempstead. They had been arrested for stealing pigs and had been confined in Fordam's cellar. Under-

[1] He held the rank of sergeant-major.   [2] *Documentary History,* IV, 16.

hill killed three of the seven in the cellar; two were towed in the water until they were drowned, and two were taken to Fort Amsterdam, where, after a short time, they were turned over to the soldiers "to do as they pleased with," and by whom they were dispatched in the most brutal manner.[1]

The third and last expedition was now organized. Underhill having visited Stamford and learned that a large number of Indians had assembled in one of their villages in that vicinity, a force of one hundred and thirty men was dispatched under his command to destroy them. Passing up the sound in three yachts, he landed at Greenwich, where he was compelled to remain over night, in consequence of a severe snow storm. Piloted by an Indian, he marched in the morning to the northwest "up over stony hills over which some must creep," and arrived in the evening about three miles from the village. Halting until ten o'clock, the march was resumed, and the village reached about midnight. Says the narrator : "The order was given as to the mode to be observed in attacking the Indians ; they then marched forward towards the houses, being three rows set up street fashion, each eighty paces long, in a low recess of the mountain, affording complete shelter from the north-west wind. The moon was then at the full, and threw a strong light against the mountain so that many winter days were not brighter than it then was. On arriving there the Indians were wide awake, and on their guard ; so that ours determined to charge and surround the houses sword in hand. They demeaned themselves as soldiers and deployed in small bands,

---

[1] "The first of these savages having received a frightful wound, desired them to permit him to dance what is called the kinte-kaye, a religious use observed among them before death; he received, however, so many wounds, that he dropped down dead. The soldiers then cut strips from the other's body, beginning at the calves, up the back, over the shoulders and down to the knees. While this was going forward Director Kieft and his councillor, Jan De la Montagne, a Frenchman, stood laughing heartily at the fun, and rubbing his right arm, so much delight he took in such scenes. He then ordered him to be taken out of the fort, and the soldiers bringing him to the beaver's path (he dancing the kinte-kaye all the time), threw him down, cut off his partes genitales, thrust them into his mouth while still alive, and at last, placing him on a millstone, cut off his head.   *   *   There stood at the same time some twenty-four or twenty-five female savages, who had been taken prisoners, and when they saw this bloody spectacle, they held up their arms, struck their mouths, and in their language exclaimed : 'For shame ! For shame ! such unheard of cruelty was never known among us.'" — *Documentary History*, IV, 105.

so that we got in a short time twelve dead and one wounded. They were so hard pressed that it was impossible for one to escape. In a brief space of time there were counted one hundred and eighty dead outside the houses. Presently none durst come forth, keeping within the houses, discharging arrows through the holes. The general (Montagne) remarked that nothing else was to be done, and resolved, with Sergeant Major Underhill, to set the huts on fire, whereupon the Indians tried every means to escape, not succeeding in which they returned back to the flames, preferring to perish by the fire than to die by

Massacre of the Weckquaesgeeks.

our hands. What was most wonderful is, that among this vast collection of men, women and children, not one was heard to cry or to scream. According to the report of the Indians themselves the number then destroyed exceeded five hundred; some say full seven hundred, among whom there were also twenty-five *Wappingers*, our God having collected together there the greater part of our enemies to celebrate one of their festivals,[1] from which escaped no more than eight men in all, of whom even those were severely wounded." The work of sword and

[1] The Indians had doubtless assembled for their annual festival of the first moon   following that at the end of February.— *Ante*, p. 27.

of fire having been completed in a manner so satisfactory to the humane and Christian Underhill and the equally pious Montagne, the expedition returned to Stamford bearing with them fifteen wounded. Two days after, the force reached Fort Amsterdam, where joy bells rang their welcome.[1]

The Indians now solicited peace, and a treaty was brought about through the intervention of Underhill. Mamaranack, chief of the *Sint-Sings*, Mongockonone of the *Weckquaesgeeks*, Pappenoharrow from the *Nochpeems*, and the *Wappingers* from Stamford, presented themselves at Fort Amsterdam, in the early part of April, 1644, and having pledged themselves that they would not henceforth commit any injury whatever on the inhabitants of New Netherland, their cattle and houses, nor show themselves, except in a canoe, before Fort Amsterdam, should the Dutch be at war with any other chieftaincies ; and having further promised to deliver up Pacham, the chief of the *Tankitekes*, peace was concluded, the Dutch promising, on their part, not to molest the Indians in any way.

The Long Island chieftaincies were not included in this arrangement, and the Dutch determined to employ some of the friendly Indians there against those who were hostile. Whiteneymen, sachem of the *Matinecocks*, with forty-seven of his warriors, was secured and dispatched with a commission to do all in his power " to beat and destroy the hostile tribes." The sachem's diplomacy, however, was better than his commission, and he returned to Fort Amsterdam in a few days empowered by the Long Island chiefs to negotiate a treaty of peace, which was at once concluded and pledges exchanged of eternal amity. Gonwarrowe, a chief of the *Matinecocks*, who was present, became surety for the *Hackinsacks* and *Tappans*, for whom he solicited peace,[2] which was granted, on the condition that neither canton should harm the Dutch, and that they should not afford shelter to hostile Indians.

Director Kieft then visited Fort Órange and solicited the negotiation and mediation of the *Mohawks* and *Mahicans* to secure

---

[1] " A thanksgiving was proclaimed on their arrival."— *New York Documentary History*, IV, 17.

[2] A semblance of peace was attempted to be patched up last spring, by a foreigner with one or two tribes of savages to the north.— *Col. Hist.* I, 210 ; *O'Callaghan's New Netherland*, I, 302.

peace with the remaining insurgents, and on their advice the latter agreed to conclude a treaty of which the record is in these words :

" Aug. 30, 1645. This day, being the 30th August, appeared at Fort Amsterdam before the director and council in the presence of the whole commonalty, the sachems in their own behalf, and for sachems in their own neighborhood, viz : Oratany, chief of *Ackkinkeshacky*, Sesekennick and Willem, chiefs of *Tappaans* and *Reckgawawank*, Pokam and Pennekeck, who were here yesterday, and did give their power of attorney to the former, and took upon them the responsibility for those of *Ouany* and its vicinity, viz : those of *Majauwetumemin*, those of *Marechhourick*, *Nyeck* and their neighbors, and Aepjen, who personally appeared, speaking in behalf of the *Wappinex*, *Wiquaeshex*, *Sint-Sings* and *Kitchtawanghs*.

" 1. They conclude with us a solid and durable peace, which they promise to keep sincerely, as we oblige ourselves to do in the same manner.

" 2. And if (which God in his mercy avert), there should arise any difficulty between us and them, war shall not be renewed, but they shall complain to our governor, and we to their sachems ; and if any person should be murdered or killed, justice shall be directly administered on the murderer, and henceforth we shall live together in amity and peace.

" 3. They may not come on the island Manhattan with their arms in the neighborhood of Christian dwellings ; neither will we approach their villages with our guns, except we are conducted thither by a savage to give them warning.

" 4. And whereas there is yet among them an English girl,[1] whom they promise to conduct to the English' at Stamfort, which they yet engage to do ; and if she is not conducted there, she shall be guided here in safety, while we promise to pay them the ransom which has been promised by the English.

" All which we promise to keep religiously throughout all New Netherlands. Done in Fort Amsterdam, in the open air, by the director and council in New Netherlands, and the whole commonalty, called together for this purpose ; in the presence

---

[1] Supposed to have been the daughter of Ann Hutchinson.

of the *Maquas* embassadors, who were solicited to assist in this negotiation, as arbitrators, and Cornelius Anthonisson, their interpreter and arbitrator with them in this solemn affair. Done as above."

The original was signed with the mark of Sisindogo, the mark of Claes Norman, the mark of Oratany, the mark of Auronge, the mark of Sesechemis, the mark of Willem of Tappan, the mark of Aepjen, sachem of the *Mahicans*, and William Kieft, La Montagne, and other Dutch officials and witnesses.[1]

Thus terminated a war which had been waged for over five years. Both parties had suffered severely. Sixteen hundred Indians, it is said, perished, while the Dutch pointed to " piles of ashes from the burnt houses, barns, barracks and other buildings, and the bones of the cattle," and exclaimed: " Our fields lie fallow and waste ; our dwellings and other buildings are burnt ; not a handful can be planted or sown this fall on all the abandoned places. All this through a foolish hankering after war ; for it is known to all right thinking men here, that these Indians have lived as lambs among us until a few years ago, injuring no one, and affording every assistance to our nation." [2]

[1] *Collections of the New York Historical Society,* 2d series, I, 275. *Col. Hist.* I, 210.

[2] *Colonial History,* I, 210.

The mark of Aepjen

sachem of the Mahicans.

CHAPTER VI.

THE ESOPUS WARS.— FROM THE PEACE OF 1645 TO THE
PEACE OF 1664.

SCARCELY had the peace of 1645 been concluded
before the Dutch resumed their former intercourse
with the Indians, as well as their former modes of
promoting trade. The town of New Amsterdam
was largely given up to the sale of brandy, tobacco and beer,
and Indians were daily seen " running about drunk," through
the streets. Every advantage was taken by the Dutch. The
Indians were employed as servants, and defrauded of their wages ;
they were induced to drink, and while intoxicated were robbed
of their furs or of the goods which they had purchased ; they
had standing complaint in regard to the sale of arms at Beaverwyck, and found cause of grievance in the value which the
Dutch attached to the lands which they had sold, which led
them to believe that they had not been paid a sufficient price
for them. The *Minsis* were especially aggrieved, and when
the Swedes made their appearance on the South river and offered
them arms and ammunition in exchange for their furs, their contempt for the Dutch was openly expressed.

The Dutch, on the other hand, protested their innocence of
the causes of complaint charged against them, and made up
quite a formidable bill of grievances in their own justification.
The Indians " without any cause," so far as they knew, had
" not only slain and killed many animals, such as cows, horses
and hogs," to the immigrants belonging, but had " cruelly murdered ten persons," one in the second year after the peace had
been concluded, one in the year 1651, four in the year 1652,
three in the year 1653, and one in the year 1654. The murderers had been demanded under the treaty of 1645, but the
Indians had refused to give them up, and the government, " for
the sake of peace and out of consideration for the good and ad-

vantage of the country and its people," had not attempted to enforce redress.[1] Granting that the offenses recited had been committed, they only prove that they were in retaliation for outrages inflicted on the Indians, for the testimony in all similar cases is that the latter were not wanton murderers.[2] The wrongs which they suffered found no fitting record at the hands of the Dutch, but their acts of retaliation were detailed with horror, and were exceeded, when opportunity offered, in the cold-blooded vengeance which was inflicted upon them.

Hostilities were not long delayed. A squaw, detected in stealing peaches from the garden of Hendrick Van Dyck, at New Amsterdam, had been killed by him, and her family determined to avenge her death. Availing themselves of the organization of a war party of *Wappingers*, then about to make descent upon some neighboring tribe, they prevailed upon them to stop at New Amsterdam, and aid them in enforcing the " blood atonement," which their laws demanded. On the morning of the fifteenth of September, 1655, " sixty-four canoes full of Indians," were beached on the shore, and, " before scarcely any one had yet risen," their occupants, " five hundred men, all armed," [3] scattered themselves throughout the town, and, " under the pretense of looking for northern Indians," entered dwellings by force and " searched the premises" with more than the zeal of modern officers in quest of fugitives. They offered no personal violence, however, and their sachems readily attended a conference, called by the authorities, and promised to take their departure in the evening. But they failed to do so. The object for which they came was not accomplished. In the evening they were joined " by two hun-

---

[1] Petition of October, 1655, *Dutch Manuscripts*, vol. IV, office of secretary of state, Albany, as translated by Dr. O'Callaghan in *Indian War of* 1655.

[2] The Indians promptly confessed their wrong in the first of the cases recited, and sent a deputation to the director to solicit forgiveness and renew their covenant of peace. They wished to live in friendship, but were sorely provoked by their Dutch neighbors. The director promised that he would surely punish offenders against them if the Indians

would complain directly to him. He accepted their gifts and made them presents in return, and they departed " very much satisfied."

[3] Brodhead says the Indians were supposed to number nineteen hundred men, of whom from five to eight hundred were armed. The text of the Dutch manuscript, however, is " five hundred," and even that number was a large complement for sixty-four canoes. Councillor La Montagne, upon whose " opinion," Brodhead evidently bases his statement,

dred armed Indians," and with them renewed the search. About eight o'clock, they detected Van Dyck, and an arrow was almost instantly winged to his breast. One Leendertsen, in attempting to protect him, was "threatened with an axe."[1] The cry of murder was raised by the Dutch, and the burgher guard rushed from the fort, "without any orders, some through the gate, others over the walls, so that they came into conflict with the Indians." The latter were "lying about the shore," evidently preparing to take their departure as they had promised. In the attack upon them two of the guard were killed and three wounded, while of their own number three were left dead.[2] Meanwhile they had embarked in their canoes, and, "taking their course across the river, landed on the western side ; and commenced the work of retaliation for the attack which had been made upon them and for the loss which they had suffered. A house at Hoboken was soon in flames, and those at Pavonia speedily followed. Every family, with the exception of one, was destroyed ; every man killed, "together with all his cattle," and a large number of women and children taken into captivity. Staten island was next visited, and its ninety colonists and flourishing bouweries shared the fate of those at Pavonia. For three days the carnage continued, and at its close "full fifty" of the Dutch had been "murdered and put to death ; over one hundred, mostly women and children," were in captivity ; "twenty bouweries and a number of plantations" had been burned with "full twelve to fifteen hundred skepels of grain," and five or six hundred head of cattle either killed or driven off. In addition to those killed and captured, three hundred colonists were ruined in estate, and the aggregated damages were computed at two hundred thousand guilders or eighty thousand dollars.

At the time of this occurrence, Director Stuyvesant, who had succeeded Kieft, was absent with his soldiers on an expedition to South river, and a messenger was immediately sent for his return. Meanwhile, as the tidings of the disaster spread, the

disagrees with all of his contemporaries, and was apparently determined to give good reason for the great fright which he suffered.

[1] Neither Van Dyck nor Leendertsen appear to have been killed.
[2] Opinion of Fiscal Van Tienhoven, *O'Callaghan's Indian War of* 1655, 40.

inhabitants fled in terror to the fort as to a city of refuge. The English villages on Long Island sent word that the Indians had threatened to kill the Dutch who resided there, and that the English themselves would share the same fate if they offered any assistance to the Manhattans, even to the extent of sending them food. Lady Moody's house at Gravesend was again attacked. The settlers at Esopus abandoned their farms, lest they should be cut off. Even New Amsterdam was not secure; bands of Indians wandered over the island, destroying all who came in their way. Ten Frenchmen were enrolled to guard the house and family of the absent director, while the Dutch themselves kept within the fort.

In the midst of the terror which prevailed, Stuyvesant and his soldiers returned, and the confidence of the colonists was soon restored. Soldiers were sent to the out settlements, an embargo was laid on vessels about to sail, and passengers able to bear arms were ordered not to depart " until it should please God to change the aspect of affairs." A plank curtain was thrown up, to prevent the Indians scaling the city walls, and no persons, on any account, were to go into the country without permission, nor unless in numbers sufficient to ensure their safety.

The fury of the Indians, however, had spent its force and they retreated, after dividing their prisoners, a portion of whom were taken to the highlands, and the remainder retained with the *Hackinsacks.* The latter, finding them an incumbrance, sent Captain Pos, who had been taken at Staten island, with proposals for their ransom. Not returning as soon as was expected, the Indians sent another messenger with word that all the prisoners should be brought to Paulus hook in two days. Pos returned, and in a few days brought from the chief of the *Hackinsacks* fourteen prisoners, " men, women and children," as a token of his good will, " in return for which he requested some powder and ball. Stuyvesant sent him a Wappinger and an Esopus Indian in exchange, and also some ammunition, of which he promised a further supply when other prisoners should be brought in. Pos, accompanied by two influential citizens, conveyed this message, and soon returned with twenty-eight of the captives and another message that from twenty to twenty-four

16

others would be restored on the receipt of a proper quantity of friezes, guns, wampum and ammunition, but they would not exchange the prisoners for Indians, ransom **was** the order of their laws.   Stuyvesant then asked the ransom price " for all the prisoners *en masse*, or for each individually," and received the answer, " seventy-eight pounds of powder and forty staves of lead, for twenty-eight persons."   This offer was accepted, and thirty-five pounds of powder and ten staves of lead additional sent, but no more prisoners were returned, the highland chieftaincies having determined to retain them as hostages.   No measures were taken to punish the Indians.   The Dutch were clearly at fault, in the opinion of Stuyvesant,[1] and he turned a deaf ear to those who clamored for war, and who in return charged him with winking " at this infraction of the peace."   The settlers gradually returned to their avocations, but under restraints which were more conducive to personal safety, and comparative quiet prevailed.

The Long Island tribes under Tackapousha, who had been assigned to the jurisdiction of the Dutch under the treaty with the English at Hartford in 1650, came forward and repudiated all connection with the outbreak which had occurred.   Not only were they innocent of participation in it, but since they had withheld tribute from the *Wappingers*, they had been repeatedly attacked by them.   Said their speaker : " Our chief has been twelve years at war with those who have injured you, and though you may consider him no bigger than your fist, he would yet prove himself strong enough.   He has hitherto sat, his head drooping on his breast, yet he still hoped he should be able to show what he could achieve."   Henceforth the western *Montauk* chieftaincies were the friends of the Dutch, and soon after renewed with them their treaty of alliance.[2]

[1] " We concur in the general opinion that the Indians had, on their first arrival, no other intention than to wage war against the savages on the east end of Long Island.   We have come to this conclusion from various reasons too long to be detailed here; and that a culpable want of vigilance, and a too hasty rashness on the part of a few hot-headed spirits, had diverted the Indians [from their purpose] and been the cause of the dreadful consequences   and enormous losses." — *O'Callaghan's Indian War of* 1655.

[2] The following is the treaty referred to : " Articles of agreement betwixt the governor of New Netherland, and Tackapausha, March ye 12, 1656 : " 1. That all injuries formerly passed in the time of the governor's predecessors,

But there was no general peace. The conflict was remembered, and the Indians, as well as the Dutch, stood on guard. The scene of combat, however, was changed. The settlers at Esopus,[1] who had returned after the panic of 1655, continued for some time unmolested ; but, as in other places, they soon devoted the largest portion of their time and means to the purposes of trade. The examples of the traders at New Amsterdam were readily copied. Familiarity, brandy and other liquors, were called to their aid, and with results similar to those which had already disgraced the Dutch character. The Indians suffered wrongfully, and in retaliation (1657) "one of the settlers was killed, the house and out buildings of another were burned, and the settlers were forced, by threats of arson and murder, to plow up the patches of land where the savages planted their maize."[2] The white population consisted, at that time, of between sixty and seventy persons, who were in no condition for defense. They wrote at once to Stuyvesant, imploring him to send "forty or fifty soldiers to save the Esopus." The

shall be forgiven and forgotten, since ye sd year 1645.

"2. That Tackapausha being chosen ye chief sachem by all the Indian sachems from Mersapege, Maskahnong, Secatong, Meracock, Rockaway and Canorise, with ye rest, both sachems and natives, doth take ye governor of ye New Netherland to be his and his people's protector, and in consideration of that to put under ye sd protection, on thiere lands and territoryes upon Long Island, so far as ye Dutch line doth runn, according to the agreement made att Hartforde.

"3. The governor doth promise to make noe peace with the Indians that did the spoile at ye Manhattans the 15th September last, likewise to include the sachem in it.

"4. That Tackapausha shall make no peace wh ye sd Indians, without ye consent and knowledge of the governor, and sd sachem doth promise for himself and his people to give no dwelling place, entertainment nor lodging to any of ye governor's, or thiere owne enemies.

"5. The governor doth promise, between this date and six months, to build a house or forte upon such place as they shall show upon the north side, and the house or forte to be furnished with Indian trade and commodities.

"6. The inhabitants of Hempsteede according to their patent, shall enjoy their purchase without molestation from ye sachem or his people, either of person or estate ; and the sachem will live in peace with all ye English and Dutch within this jurisdiction. And the governor doth promise for himself and all his people to live in peace with the sd sachem and all his people.

"7. That in case an Indian doe wrong to a Christian in his person or estate, and complaint be made to the sachem, hee shall make full satisfaction ; likewise if a Dutchman or Englishman shall wrong an Indian the governor shall make satisfaction according to Equity."

[1] The precise time at which settlement was made at Atkarkarton, now Kingston, is not known, although it is assumed that a fort or trading post was erected there as early as 1614. The reference in the text is to the first known European settlers who removed thither, in company with Capt. Thomas Chambers, from Panhoosic, now Troy, in 1652.

[2] *Documentary History*, iv.

governor responded by immediately visiting the scene of disturbance with a company of soldiers, where he arrived on the 30th of May. The following day, being Ascension Thursday, the settlers assembled at the house of Jacob Jansen Stol for religious service. The governor met them there and explained to them the difficulties under which they were placed, by their isolated positions, and recommended that they should unite at once in a village, which could be easily defended from the attacks of the Indians. To this they objected on the ground of want of time to give care to their crops and to remove their dwellings and erect palisades ; and asked that the soldiers be permitted to remain until after harvest. This request Stuyvesant refused ; but promised that if they would agree to palisade at once the ground to be selected for a village, he would remain with them until the work was completed.

While these proceedings were being held, some twelve or fifteen Indians, accompanied by two of their chiefs, arrived at the house of Stol, where the director was staying, with word that other sachems were deterred from coming to the conference which he had invited through fear of the soldiers. Stuyvesant gave his assurance that no harm should befall them, when about fifty additional Indians, with a few women and children, made their appearance, and seated themselves beneath an aged tree which stood without the fence, " about a stone's throw from the house.'" Accompanied only by an interpreter and two of his followers, Stuyvesant went out and seated himself in the midst of the Indians, when one of the chiefs arose, " and made a long harangue," detailing the events of the war waged in Kieft's time (1645), and how many of their tribe the Dutch had then slain, adding, however, that they had obliterated all these things from their hearts and forgotten them.[1]

Stuyvesant replied to this address, that those things had occurred before his time, and that the recollection of them had been " all thrown away" by the subsequent peace. He asked them, however, if any injury had been done them, in person or property, since he had come into the country. The Indians remained silent. Stuyvesant then proceeded to enumerate the

[1] *O'Callaghan's New Netherland*, II, 358.

various offenses which the Indians had committed on the Dutch. " Your overbearing insolence at Esopus," said he, " is known. I come to investigate this matter, and not to make war, provided the murderer be surrendered and all damage repaid. The Dutch never solicited your sachems for leave to come here. Your sachems have requested us, over and over again, to make a settlement among you. We have not had a foot of your land without paying you for it, nor do we desire to have any more without making full compensation therefor. Why then have you committed this murder? Why have you burned our houses, killed our cattle, and continue to threaten our people ?"

To this harangue the sachems made no reply, but " looked on the ground." At length one of them arose and responded : " You Swannekins have sold our children the *boisson.*" It is you who have given them brandy and made them *cachens,* intoxicated and mad, and caused them to commit all this mischief. The sachems cannot then control the young Indians nor prevent them fighting. This murder has not been committed by any of our tribe, but by a *Minnisink,* who now skulks among the *Haverstraws.* It was he who fired the two houses and then fled. For ourselves we can truly say, we did not commit the act. We know no malice, neither are we inclined to fight, but we cannot control our young men."

Stuyvesant immediately arose, and hurled defiance at the young braves. " If any of your young people desire to fight, let them now step forth. I will place man against man. Nay, I will place twenty against thirty or forty of your hot heads. Now, then, is your time. But it is not manly to threaten farmers, and women and children who are not warriors. If this be not stopped, I shall be compelled to retaliate on old and young, on women and children. This I can now do by killing you all, taking your wives and little ones captive and destroying your maize lands ; but I will not do it. I expect you will repair all damages, seize the murderer if he come among you, and do no further mischief." " The Dutch," he continued, " are now going to live together in one spot. It is desirable that you should sell us the whole of the Esopus land, as you have often proposed, and remove farther into the interior ; for it is not good for you to reside so near the Swannekins, whose cattle might eat your maize and thus cause fresh disturbances." The sachems promised to take the matter into consideration, and departed with their followers. While they were absent the settlers agreed that it would be for the best to adopt the counsel of the director, and left the selection of the site of the village to him. He " accordingly chose a spot at the bend of the kill, where a water front might be had on three sides ; and a part of the plain, about two hundred and ten yards in circumference, was staked out."[1] The erection of a stockade was immediately commenced, the Dutch, in this particular, adopting the mode of the Indians and drawing from them lessons in defensive warfare.

On the 1st of June, the sachems returned and solicited peace, expressing sorrow for what had passed. They felt deeply the shame that Stuyvesant had challenged their young men, and they had not dared to accept the wager, and hoped the fact would not be spread abroad. Presents were distributed to them in exchange for the wampum with which they had accompanied their proposals for peace ; but they were told a second time that they must surrender the murderer, and make good the damages they had committed. To these requirements they demurred ; and it was finally agreed that they should make compensation for damages, and sell the land for the projected village. They then retired, but returned again on the 4th with a final reply, which was that they would give the director the land he asked, " to grease his feet with, as he had taken so long a journey to visit them." They then renewed the assurance that they had thrown away all malice, and that hereafter none among them would injure a Dutchman. The director responded with like assurances ; and the Indians departed. The work at the village now went forward rapidly. After three weeks' labor, the lines of palisades were completed ; all the buildings removed ; a guard-house, sixteen feet by twenty-three, built in the north-east corner ; a bridge thrown over the kill, and barracks erected for

[1] *Brodhead*, 1, 649 ; *O'Callaghan*, 11, 361. The village located by Stuyvesant was about three miles north-west from the centre of the present village of Kings-ton, at a bend in the Esopus creek near the residence now, or late, of Benjamin Smith. The Indians were probably residents of the castle of Wiltmeet.

the soldiers, of whom Stuyvesant detailed twenty-four to guard the infant settlement, and then returned to Fort Amsterdam.

Stuyvesant visited Esopus again in the fall of 1658, in order to obtain from the Indians a transfer of the remainder of their lands. Calling the chiefs together, he thus addressed them : " A year and a half ago you killed two horses belonging to Madame de Hulter, and attacked Jacob Adriaénsen in his own house with an axe, knocked out his eye, mortally wounded his infant child, and not satisfied with this, burnt his house last spring. You, moreover, robbed him of his property, and killed a Dutchman in one of his sloops. You compelled our farmers to plow your land ; threatened, at the same time, to fire their houses, and repeatedly extorted money from the settlers, who have already paid you for their farms. You have added threats and insults, and finally forced the colonists, at much expense, to break up their establishments and concentrate their dwellings. Various other injuries you have committed since that time, notwithstanding your promises. For all this we demand compensation ; to enforce which, efficient measures will be taken, unless the terms we now propose be acceded to."

The demand was a bold attempt at extortion ; the terms of peace not less so. The Indians were required to make a free surrender of all the Esopus lands so far as they had been explored by the Dutch, as indemnity for the expenses which the settlers had incurred in removing their dwellings and fortifying their village ; the relinquishment of all claims held by the Indians against the settlers for labor or furs, and the payment to the latter of several hundred fathoms of wampum for damages. The Indians regarded the terms as hard, and stated that they had already been deprived of many of their maize fields without compensation. Such a demand was unexpected, and as many of their sachems were absent, they asked time for consultation. Stuyvesant generously agreed to allow them one night to consider what course they would pursue.

The next day (Oct. 16), the council again assembled, and the sachems expressed a willingness to make reasonable compensation for injuries. They would relinquish part of their claims against the settlers, and give some lands to those who had been injured ; but they were poor and had no wampum.   Then throwing down a beaver skin, the principal sachem reminded the director that he could well afford to be generous from the prospect of largely increased trade with the *Senecas*.   Offering a wampum belt, he concluded : " A horse belonging to Jacob Jansen Stol broke into our corn-fields and destroyed two of our plantations.   One of our boys shot it, for which we gave Stol seventy guilders in wampum.   But this belt we now present, so that the soldiers may let us go in peace, and not beat us when we visit this place."

Stuyvesant's proposition in relation to land was left untouched by the sachem, and the director asked : " What do you intend to propose about the land ? "   The sachem replied, that " it belonged to the chiefs who were not here to-day, and we cannot, therefore, come to any conclusion on it."   He promised, however, that they would return the next day and give their answer.   The morrow came, but the chiefs did not return. Stuyvesant dispatched messengers to their wigwams to inquire their intentions, who returned with the answer that "the chiefs had made fools of them."   Stuyvesant had overreached himself by his extravagant demand, and, chagrined and disappointed, departed for Fort Amsterdam, leaving Ensign Dirck Smith with fifty soldiers under instructions to guard the village properly, and not allow any Indians within the palisades ; to act purely on the defensive, and to detail, from day to day, a proper guard to protect the husbandmen.   A *ronduit*, or small fort, was also projected at the mouth of the Walkill, and the work of its construction commenced.   Several chiefs came in, shortly after Stuyvesant's departure, and made a present to Stol as further indemnity for the injuries he had sustained.   The offering was accompanied by a renewal of their request for the removal of the soldiers, and an exchange of presents.   The former was declined, and in response to the latter the settlers had " nothing to grease the Indian's breasts.   So the meeting was a dry one."

Notwithstanding the threatening aspect of Indian affairs, the settlement continued prosperous, and its occupants, increased in numbers and enjoying the protection of an armed force, became more and more disregardful of the rights of the red men.

During the summer of 1659, mutual distrust and suspicion prevailed. The settlers were disturbed by reports that the Indians intended a general massacre when the work of harvest should begin ; while the Indians regarded the presence of the soldiers as a menace, doubted the director's desire for peace, and feared that it was his intention to attack and destroy them, as he had not yet sent the presents he had promised them. A conference was held with the chiefs Aug. 17, but they denied that they had any hostile intentions. " We patiently submit,"' said they, " to the blows which have been inflicted on us ; yet the Dutch still plunder our corn." Laying down seventeen small sticks, the sachem added : " so many times have the Swannekins struck and assaulted us in divers places. We are willing to live in peace, but we expect your chief sachem will make us some presents. Otherwise he cannot be sincere." The conference was broken up without removing the feeling which existed between the parties ; and fresh rumors disturbed the settlers that the Indians were preparing bows and arrows and concentrating their strength for an attack. Familiar as the Dutch were with the customs of the Indians and the periods of their annual return from their hunting expeditions, and their almost constant preparation of the implements of the chase, they nevertheless now saw in them nothing but impending destruction.

Nor were the general relations existing between the Indians and the Dutch more favorable. Two soldiers, who had deserted from Fort Orange, were murdered by the *Mahicans,* and some of the *Raritans* had destroyed a family of four persons, at Mespath kil, in order to obtain possession of a small roll of wampum which, in an unguarded moment, had been exhibited to them, and excited their cupidity. The *Mohawks,* suffering under the blows of the French, had complaint against the Dutch, and sent a delegation to Fort Orange, where, on the sixth of September, 1659, the second official conference was held with them. The *Mohawk* speaker charged that the Dutch called his people brothers, and asserted that they were bound to them by a chain, but that this continued only so long as they had beavers, after which they were no longer thought of. They had favors to ask, however, and were not disposed to quarrel.

17

They were engaged in war with the French, and, finding themselves crippled by the liquor which the Dutch sold to their warriors, asked that the sale be stopped, the liquor kegs plugged
up and the dealers punished. The gunsmiths refused to repair
their arms when they had no wampum ; this was not generous,
nor was it generous to deny to them powder and lead. The
French treated their Indians more liberally, and their example
should be considered. Their principal request, however, was
for thirty men with horses, to cut and draw timber for the forts
which they were building.

The commandant at Fort Orange could give no reply, but
would submit the requests which had been made to the director,
whose arrival was daily expected. But Stuyvesant did not ar-
rive, and, after waiting several days, the authorities at Fort
Orange, now thoroughly alarmed, resolved to send embassadors
to the *Mohawks* to reply to their requests. At Caughnawaga,
on the twenty-fourth, was held the first formal council with the
Iroquois in their own country. The professions of friendship
on the part of the Dutch were warm, and no doubt sincere, in
view of their relations with other tribes. They would remain
the brothers of the *Mohawks* for all time, and would neither
fight against them nor leave them in distress when they could
help them ; but they could not force their smiths to repair
their " brothers' fire arms without pay, for they must earn food
for their wives and little ones." The sale of brandy could not
be stopped so long as the Indians would buy it. The director
was angry that such sale was made, and had forbidden it ; let
the chiefs also forbid their people. " Will ye," they asked, " that
we take from your people their brandy and their kegs ? Say so
before all those here present." Aid to build the *Mohawk* forts
could not be given ; the Dutch were all sick, and the hills were
so steep their horses could not draw the timber. But to aid
them in their work they gave them fifteen new axes ; and to
assist them in their wars, seventy pounds of powder and a hundred weight of lead were added to their stores.[1]

[1] It was at this conference that the Dutch speaker asserted that it was " now sixteen years " since an alliance had been formed with the *Mohawks*. Reference has already been made to this treaty. It will also be observed that the *Minsis* were not subjugated at that time, but were in condition to ask the alliance of the *Mohawks*.

The embassadors made no efforts to control the *Mohawks* in their wars, nor cared with whom they fought so long as the Dutch escaped ; while the *Mohawks* cared as little for their white neighbors, their sole object being to obtain the munitions of war to continue their conflict with the French and their Indians. The request of the embassadors for the release of the French prisoners, the *Mohawks* would not grant ; but they would refer the matter to their castles. They had little faith in the French, however, for they made treaties and did not observe them ; and when hunting parties of the *Mohawks* were abroad, they were attacked by the French Indians, among whom a number of Frenchmen were always skulking to knock them on the head. In their request that the *Mohawks* would not aid the Esopus clans in an attack upon the Dutch, the embassadors were more successful, the chiefs promising that they would refuse their belts and have nothing to do with them.[1]

In the meantime hostilities had broken out in the Esopus country. Chambers[2] had employed a number of Indians to husk corn, and, on the night of the termination of their labor, they had asked for and obtained some brandy. A carouse followed, in the course of which another bottle of brandy was procured. When the debauch was at its height, one of them discharged his gun, loaded only with powder, which had the effect to alarm the village. One of them, more wise than his associates, deplored the act of his companion, and proposed that they should

[1] *O'Callaghan*, II, 389, etc.

[2] Thomas Chambers was of English birth. He settled at Panhoosic, now Troy, in the jurisdiction of Rensselaerswyck, in 1651, and from thence removed to the Esopus country in 1652, where he took part in the early Indian wars, became a captain in the Dutch service, and was elected delegate to the provincial assembly in 1664. His residence was near the confluence of the Walkill with the Hudson, and was built for the double purpose of a house and a fort, being square and loop-holed for musketry. By commercial and other speculations, he acquired a considerable tract of land, which was erected, by Gov. Lovelace, in 1672, into the manor of Foxhall, with power to hold certain courts and to appoint a steward to try causes arising between the vassals. Not satisfied with these honors, he determined to perpetuate his name in another form, and accordingly passed his estate to his heirs by the most intricate entail. The manor and title was to be held only by heirs bearing the name of Chambers. To this end, his first wife having died without issue, he married a widow Van Gaasbeck and adopted her children. He died in 1698, and was buried in his vault on the site of the residence now or late of Jansen Hasbrouck, at Rondout. His remains, with those of the Van Gaasbeck family, were removed in 1854. The name of the manor and its owner only live in history.

at once leave the place, urging that " he felt a sensation in his body that they would all be killed." His companions, however, laughed at his alarm. They had never harmed the Dutch — "Why should they kill us ?" But the speaker still cherished his fears, and replied: " My heart feels heavy within me ;" and again he entreated his companions to depart, but they refused, and, in conscious security, lay down upon their blankets to sleep.

Meanwhile Ensign Smith had yielded to the request of the villagers by dispatching Sergeant Stol to reconnoitre and report the cause of the disturbance. Stol, on his return, stated the facts, when Smith gave orders that the Indians should not be molested. Notwithstanding this order, Stol went among the villagers and invited them to unite in a sortie against the Indian encampment. Enlisting some ten or eleven persons [1] in the enterprise, he left the village and stealthily approached the sleeping Indians, who were aroused from their slumbers by a volley fired among them. Jumping up to escape, one was knocked on the head with an axe, a second was taken prisoner, a third fled, and a fourth, too deeply intoxicated to awake, " was hewn on the head with a cutlass," which roused him to consciousness and he made off. Stol and his valorous associates then returned to the village and recounted their deeds of noble daring, justifying their proceedings by the assertion that the Indians' first attacked them, an assertion subsequently proved to be without foundation. [2]

Ensign Smith, finding his orders disobeyed, and hostilities actually commenced by a people whose movements he could not control, determined to leave the settlers to their fate by returning with his command to Fort Amsterdam. Learning his intention, the settlers frustrated his design by chartering, on their own account, all the sailing vessels that lay at the shore in which he and his men intended to embark. The only alternative that remained to him was to send an express to the director, detailing the state of affairs and requesting his presence. With this purpose in view he sent an armed party, eighteen or nine-

[1] His associates were Jacob Jansen Van Stoutenberg, Thomas Higgins, Gysbert Phillipsen Van Velthuysen, Evert Pels, Jan Arentsen, Barent Harmaensen, Martin Hoffman, Gilles de Wecker, Abel Dircksen, and James the mason.— O'Calla-

ghan, II, 396.

[2] A full investigation into this affair by the proper authorities attached the blame entirely upon the men engaged in the foray.

teen in number, to the shore to forward dispatches. In the meantime, the Indians had gathered in considerable numbers, determined to avenge the attack which had been made upon their kindred. Observing the party which had been sent out by Smith, an ambuscade was formed, into which, on their return, the company fell and were immediately surrounded by the Indians, to whom thirteen of the party, including the officer in command and six soldiers, surrendered without any resistance, and were borne off into captivity.

Open war was now declared. The Indians, justly incensed against their Dutch neighbors, burned all the houses, barns, and harvests within their reach, and killed all the horses and cattle that fell in their way. Four or five hundred Indians invested the village, and, after vainly attempting to set it on fire, avenged themselves by burning at the stake eight or ten of the prisoners in their hands, among whom was Stoutenberg who had taken part in the attack on the sleeping Indians. It was a horrid ceremony. The victims were fastened naked to stakes, placed at some distance from each other encircling a large fire; their heads ornamented; their bodies painted. The dance of death was then held, and the work of torture commenced. The nails of the victims were pulled out, their fingers bitten off or crushed between stones, their skin scorched with fire-brands or torches, pieces of flesh cut from their bodies, and every kind of slow torture that savage ingenuity could suggest, inflicted; and, as one by one they were released by death, their bodies were cast into the blazing fire and consumed. Terror folded her wings in the hearts of the people who beheld the spectacle which they could not prevent ; fathers gathered upon the ramparts, and mothers pressed their children to their arms, not knowing how soon the frail palisades might yield, and themselves be exposed to the pitiless mercy of the frenzied children of the forest.

For three weeks the village was held in siege, the little stockade fort on the brow of the hill resisting the skill of Indian warfare. Relief at length came. The express to Stuyvesant reached Fort Amsterdam on the 23d of September ; but everything there was in the greatest consternation. The settlements on Long island were being ravaged, and another general Indian war was feared. Considerable time was lost in enlisting a company to proceed to the assistance of the Esopus settlers, and it was not until the 10th of October, that Stuyvesant set sail. He arrived at Esopus on the 11th, with a force of nearly two hundred men. Indian runners had preceded him and apprised their friends of his approach, and, a few hours previous to his arrival, the siege was raised and the beleaguering forces melted into the forests. Thither they could not be pursued, heavy rains having swollen the streams and made the trails impassible, and, having no employment for his force, Stuyvesant directed their return to Fort Amsterdam.

The authorities at Fort Orange now interested themselves in the matter, and obtained the cooperation of some *Mohawk* and *Mahican* chiefs, who visited the settlement, and succeeded in securing an armistice and the surrender of two prisoners held by the Indians. On the 28th of November, Stuyvesant came up, with the hope of making a permanent treaty, but the sachems refused to meet him. A conference was finally held on the 18th of December, and the Indians persuaded to bring in some supplies in exchange for powder ; but they refused to make peace, denounced the truce which had been made as without binding authority, and retained their young prisoners, having killed all the others.

In the spring of 1660, peace having been concluded with the *Wappingers*, Stuyvesant determined upon active hostilities against the Esopus cantons ; but the latter, shorn to a large extent of their allies, were not disposed to continue the contest, and accordingly secured the intercession of Goethals, the chief sachem of the *Wappingers*, that they might be included in the treaty which had been made with that tribe. Stuyvesant doubted their sincerity, and Goethals replied : " The Indians say the same of the Dutch." He assured Stuyvesant that Kaelcop, Pemmyraweck, and other Esopus sachems were anxious for peace, and that it was only the *kalebackers* [1] who were not inclined to treat, but that the chiefs would make them

---

[1] Indians who possessed guns were called *kalebackers*, and were generally the most idle and vicious of the Indian people.— *De Laet.*

come in. "What security can there be for peace, if the *kale-backers* desire war?" asked the director, but Goethals could not reply. Stuyvesant then told him that the Esopus chiefs must visit him at Fort Amsterdam, if they desired peace. "They are too much frightened and dare not come," was the reply. Believing this to be true, Stuyvesant consented to visit Esopus and hold a conference with the Indians.

While these negotiations were in progress, Ensign Smith was engaged in active service against the offending Indians. On the 17th of March he advanced, with forty men, nine miles into the interior, and attacked the Indian fort Wiltmeet, which was defended by some sixty Indians who fled at the first fire, leaving four of their number dead and twelve others prisoners. A large quantity of maize, peas, and bearskins, fell into the hands of the Dutch, and the fort was destroyed.

Stuyvesant arrived at Esopus on the 18th, but soon saw that all hope of negotiating a peace was at an end. He therefore sent the prisoners and plunder to Fort Amsterdam, and directed a vigorous prosecution of the war by a formal declaration (March 25th) against the Esopus Indians "and all their adherents." Smith now followed up the advantage he had gained by posting (April 4th) forty-three men in ambuscade, "over the creek among the rocks," but the Indians discovered the snare, and a general fight ensued in which three Indians were killed, two severely wounded, and one taken prisoner. This disaster produced a material change in the deportment of the Indians, who now most earnestly entreated for peace, and again obtained the intercession of neighboring chiefs in their behalf. On the 24th of May, three *Mahican* chiefs visited Fort Amsterdam, and declared that the Esopus Indians were willing to leave that country and transfer their land to the Dutch, in indemnity for the murder of the settlers, on condition that their friends in captivity should be surrendered and peace concluded. Security was demanded that the *kalebackers* also united in the request. Laying down four belts of wampum, "these," said Aepjin, the *Mahican* chief sachem, "are a guaranty that the *kalebackers* desire peace, and that we are authorized to treat in their behalf." Stuyvesant accepted the belts, but told the chiefs that peace would be concluded only when the Esopus chiefs would present themselves at Fort Amsterdam for that purpose. The director was then requested to liberate the captive Indians ; but he declined, and in reply to the question : " What are your intentions as regards these men ? " answered, " What have been done with the Christian prisoners ? " Aepjin then requested that if the war was continued it might be confined to the Esopus country, and the director assured him that so long as his people observed peace, the Dutch would treat them as friends. The conference was concluded by the presentation of a blanket, a piece of frieze, an axe, a knife, a pair of stockings, and two small kettles, to each of the chiefs, who departed content. The next day, Stuyvesant issued an order banishing the Esopus prisoners to Curaçoa " to be employed there, or at Buenaire, with the negroes in the company's service." Two or three of the prisoners only were retained at Fort Amsterdam, to be punished " as it should be thought proper."

Meanwhile Ensign Smith pushed hostilities with vigor. On the 30th of May, guided by one of his prisoners, a force under his command discovered, " at the second fall of Kit Davit's kil," [1] about twelve miles west from the Hudson, a few Indians planting corn on the opposite bank. The stream being swollen, it was found impossible to cross, so he returned to the village, where he learned that the Indians had concentrated their force at an almost inaccessible spot about twenty-seven miles " up the river, beyond the above-mentioned fall, where it was pretty easy to ford " the kil. Thither Smith directed his force, but the Indians received notice of his approach by the barking of their dogs, and fled, leaving behind them Preummaker, " the oldest and best of their chiefs." [2] The aged sachem met his foes with the haughty demand, " What do ye here, ye dogs ? " aiming an arrow at them as he spoke. He was easily disarmed, and a consultation held as to how he should be disposed of. " As it

---

[1] Sager's kil, now called the Esopus creek. " The second fall " was the small stream entering the Esopus creek from the west, south of the old village. " Kit Davit's farm was about nine miles from Hudson's river."—*O'Callaghan*, II, 44.

[2] *O'Callaghan*, II, 411. " Preummaker's land," lying upon Esopus kil, within the limits of Hurley, was laid out for Venike Rosen, April 15, 1685.— *Land Papers*, II, 169.

was considerable distance to carry him," writes the ensign, " we struck him down with his own axe."

While Smith was thus carrying war into the heart of the Indian country, several of the sachems were seeking the mediation of the neighboring chiefs to secure a permanent peace. Sewackenamo called his warriors together to know their wishes. " We will fight no more," was the brief reply. The chief next assembled the squaws, and inquired " what seemed to them best ? " These answered, " That we plant our fields in peace and live in quiet." He then assembled the young men, who urged him to make peace with the Dutch, and declared that " they would not kill either hog or fowl any more." The sachem then proceeded to Gamoenapa to secure the assistance of the sachems of the *Hackinsacks* and *Tappans* in procuring a cessation of hostilities. While there a runner brought to him the intelligence of the death of Preummaker, which so unmanned him that " he knew not what to do." Leaving his *Hackinsack* friends to negotiate for him, he returned to his people with a heavy heart.

Oritany, of the *Hackinsacks*, bore the peace belts which were committed to him to Fort Amsterdam, and presented them to the director on the 2d of June. Stuyvesant assured him that the Dutch were disposed for friendship. " It is very strange, then," said the old sachem, whose notions of warfare differed somewhat from his hearers, " that your people were so recently engaged against the Indians, and have slain their aged chief." Stuyvesant replied, that it was customary among white men to exert all their strength until they had conquered a peace. Oritany then requested a suspension of hostilities while negotiations for peace were in progress. To this Stuyvesant consented with the proviso that the sachem should go at once to Esopus, accompanied by a Dutch interpreter, and learn for himself the wishes of the Indians. Oritany accepted the proposition, and took his leave saying, " Now I shall see for myself if the Esopus people contemplate any good." His mission was entirely successful, and he returned to Fort Amsterdam with a request to the director to visit Esopus and arrange a treaty.

18

On the 7th of July, Stuyvesant arrived at Esopus, accompanied by Captain Martin Kregier and Burgomaster Van Cortland, and sent messengers to acquaint the sachems of his arrival. Three days elapsed and no response came from the Indians. Summoning the chiefs of the *Mohawks*, *Mahicans*, *Wappingers*, *Minsis* and *Hackinsacks*, who had been invited to assist in the negotiations,[1] he addressed them as follows :

" Brothers : Ye all know well that we have not caused this war. After the Esopus savages burned three of our houses and murdered one of our men, a year ago, we forgave them and renewed the chain of friendship with them, promising the one to the other, that we should not thenceforth again wage war though a man was killed, but that the murderer should be surrendered and punished. Notwithstanding all this, the Esopus savages took some of our people prisoners, now ten moons since,[2] burnt several houses ; besieged and stormed Esopus, though they pretended, during the siege, to be inclined to peace. They then consented to receive a ransom for the prisoners, but when the ransom was brought out to the gate, they carried it away by force, retained our prisoners, and murdered eight or nine of them afterwards in an infamous manner. Brothers : this it was that compelled us to take the hatchet.

" Brothers : On the earnest entreaties of Indian friends, who solicited peace on behalf of the Esopus savages, and on the intercession of the *Maquas*, the *Mahicans*, those of the Highlands, the *Minsis*, the *Katskills*, and other tribes, we concluded a truce with our enemies, who seemed much rejoiced, and solicited us to come in person and conclude a treaty. We came with our friends, yet those of Esopus hang back. They come not to us, nor speak one word of peace. Ye see clearly that it is not our fault. Brothers : The Esopus savages play the fool with you, as well as with us.

" Brothers : Our station will not permit us to remain here in uncertainty, any longer. Even ye are tired with waiting,

[1] The chiefs present on this occasion were : *Mohawks*, Adogbegnewalquo, Requesecade, Ogknekelt ; *Mahicans*, Aepjin, Aupamut ; *Katskill*, Kefe-weig, Machacknemenu ; *Minsis*, Onderis Hocque, Kaskongeritschage ; *Wappingers*, Isseschahya, Wisachganio ; *Hackinsacks*, Oritany, Carstangh ; *Staten island*, Warehan.—*O'Callaghan*, II, 419.

[2] Stuyvesant carefully avoided allusion to the immediate cause of the war, which had already been fixed against the Dutch.

and are as willing to depart as we. We request you to remember these our words. Communicate them to all the other sachems our brothers, and to all the Indians our friends, and tell them, as we have done before, that they must not meddle with the Esopus savages, nor suffer them to live among them. And now tell the Esopus savages we will yet wait till evening.

" Brothers : When yonder sun goes down, we depart if they be not here."

The sachems received this address with alarm, and immediately sent out messengers to the Esopus chiefs, urging them to attend the council. Towards evening Kaelcop, Sewackenamo, Nasbabowan, and Pemmyraweck appeared before the gate of the village. Immediately on their arrival, a grand council of all the inhabitants of Esopus, both Christians and Indians, was held. The Esopus sachems and the sachems of the tribes in attendance, and the villagers, being seated " under the blue sky of heaven," Stuyvesant signified that he was ready to hear the Esopus chiefs. Whereupon Onderis Hocque, of the *Minsis*, arose and thus addressed the assembly :

" The Indians of Esopus complained to us that they were involved in a heavy war with the Dutch. We answered them, ' Why did ye begin it ? It is all your own fault, we cannot, therefore, help you in your necessity ; but we shall intercede in your behalf, and do all in our power to obtain for you peace.' We have now brought a present, in return for that with which they solicited our assistance for a peace, which we now request in their behalf. If they cannot obtain it now, those of Esopus must return home weeping."

Stuyvesant replied : " Out of respect for the intercession of all our friends here present, we consent to a peace, if the *Mohawks* and *Minsis*, and all the other chiefs will be security that it shall be faithfully observed."

The *Mohawk* chief, Adogbegnewalquo, then addressed the Esopus chiefs : " The whole country is now convened in behalf of you, who began this quarrel, to procure you peace.[1] If

[1] At a later period the Mohawks considered the causes of the Esopus war, and reported that "all their zaakemaakers (sachems) lay the cause of the war on us," the Dutch, and this was also the verdict of the Katskill Indians.— *O'Callaghan*, II, 396.

this be once concluded, break it not again. If ye do break it and treat us with contempt, we shall never again intercede for you."

The *Minsi* sachem, Onderis Hocque, then addressed the Esopus sachems : " Ye must not renew this quarrel ; neither kill horse nor cow, nor steal any property. Whatever ye want, ye must purchase or earn. Live with the Dutch as brothers. Ye cause us and the *Mohawks* great losses. This is not your land. It is our land. Therefore repeat not this,[1] but throw down the hatchet. Tread it so deep into the earth that it shall never be taken up again." He then presented them with a white belt, and, turning to the Dutch, he warned them not to renew this trouble, nor to beat the Esopus Indians in the face and then laugh at them. Then taking an axe from the Esopus sachem, he cast it on the ground, and trampled it in the earth saying, " Now they will never commence this quarrel anew."

Sewackenamo, the Esopus sachem, then arose and addressed the assembly : " The hatchet have we permitted to be taken from our hands ; and to be trodden in the ground. We will never take it up again."

At the conclusion of these ceremonies, Stuyvesant submitted the following as the conditions of the treaty :

" 1. All hostilities shall cease on both sides, and all injuries shall be mutually forgiven and forgotten.

" 2. The Esopus Indians, in compensation of damages, promise to transfer to the director-general all the lands of Esopus, and to directly depart thence without being permitted to return thither to plant

" 3. Further, the director-general promises to pay for the ransom of the captive Christians eight hundred schepels of maize, the half next harvest when the maize is ripe, the other half, or its value, in the harvest of the following year.

" 4. The Esopus Indians promise that they will keep this peace inviolate, and will not kill any more of our horses, cattle or hogs. Should such occurrence happen, then the chiefs oblige themselves to pay for it, or by refusal, that one of them shall remain arrested until the killed animal shall be paid for or made

[1] *Ante*, p. 67.

good ; while the director-general, on his side, promises that the Dutch shall not do them any harm.

" 5. If the Dutch kill an Indian, or an Indian kill a Dutchman, war shall not be commenced on that account. Complaint thereof shall first be made, and he who committed the murder, shall be delivered to be punished as he deserves.

" 6. The Esopus Indians shall not approach the Dutch plantations, houses, or dwellings, armed ; but may go and trade, unarmed as before.

" 7. Whereas the last war owes its origin to drinking, no Indians shall be permitted to drink brandy or any spirituous liquors, in or near any Dutch plantations, houses, or concentrations, but shall do it in their country or deep in the woods, at a great distance.

" 8. In this peace shall be included, not only the aforesaid tribes, but all others who are in friendship with the director-general, and among others, by the chiefs of Long island, Tapansaugh, with all their Indians ; and if any act of hostility be committed against them, then the director-general engages himself to assist them.[1]

" 9. The aforesaid chiefs (the *Mohawks*, *Minsis* and others already named) as mediators and advocates of the Esopus nation, remain securities, and engage themselves that it shall be kept inviolate ; and if any infraction be committed by the Esopus Indians, they engage themselves to assist the Dutch to subdue them.

" Thus done and concluded, near the concentration of Esopus, under the blue sky of heaven, in the presence of the Hon. Martin Krègier, burgomaster of the city of Amsterdam in New Netherland ; Oloff Stevensen van Cortland, old burgomaster ; Arent van Curler, commissary of the colonie of Rensselaerswyck, and all the inhabitants of Esopus, both Christians and Indians, on the 15th of July, 1660."

The day was far spent before the negotiations opened, and the shades of twilight had deepened into the night ere the ceremonies were concluded. The proposals submitted by Stuyvesant were accepted, the sachem, Sewackenamo, declaring, in

---

[1] *Ante*, p. 68.

the customary language of his people, that their friendship with the Dutch should last as long as the sun and moon gave light ; as long as the stars should shine in the firmament, and the rivers flow with water. But before this conclusion, he had asked the director for the return of his kindred. Stuyvesant, who had already disposed of the prisoners in his hands, replied that they must be considered "as dead." The answer deeply grieved the sachem, the memory of their banished brethren was graven on the hearts of his people. But though sufferers by the war, their losses were not without some compensation. Among the prisoners held by them was the son of Evert Pels, one of the men who had led the midnight foray upon them. Just as he was being bound to the stake of torture, the incident which gave to American history the name of Pocahontas had its counterpart. The daughter of a chief stepped forward, in accordance with the customs of her people, and adopted the trembling captive as her own. In the depths of the forest he became her husband, and when the delivery of prisoners came, she was " unwilling to part with him or he with her." Adopted by the tribe, he returned with them to the wilderness, content to share their fortunes and their freedom.

Meanwhile affairs at Fort Orange wore a threatening aspect. In their greedy grasping for furs, a class of what were called runners had sprung up, who penetrated the woods to meet the Indians before they reached the town and secure their peltries. Their remuneration depended on the amount of property they secured for their principals, and to increase their gains they often had recourse to violence, wresting from the Indians their property against their will, after inflicting on them, in addition, personal injuries. The evil continued, despite the efforts of the authorities to correct it, until the *Mohawks* made complaint and threatened to break their treaty and leave altogether, adding, that unless the practice was discontinued, " perhaps matters might terminate as at Esopus." Stuyvesant, finding that no enforcement of law could be secured at the hands of the Beaverwyck traders, sent La Montagne thither with an armed force to patrol the woods and prosecute offenders. On the 22d of July, he went thither himself to meet a delegation of *Seneca* chiefs.

The proceedings of the conference [1] illustrate the nature of the alliance which at that time existed between the confederacy and the Dutch, as well as the relations of the former with the Esopus clans and the *Mahicans*. The *Seneca* speaker made a long harangue, in which he stated his complaint against the runners and the difficulty experienced by the Indians in negotiating the sale of their beavers without restraint, and demanded their ancient freedom of trade. They would no longer submit to being locked up by the Dutch, or kicked by those who wished to have their beavers, until "we know not where our eyes are." Several years ago, they had visited the Manhattans, and though they had offered presents, they received no answer; "no, not even one pipe of tobacco;" and they felt now as if they were about "to run against a stone." Still, they would make a few requests. They were involved in a heavy war with the French Indians and the *Minsis*, and could not obtain either powder or ball without beavers. "A brave warrior ought to have these for nothing."

"You are," continued the orator, "the chiefs of the whole country. We all look to you. We ask a piece of cloth for a beaver, and that it may be understood and henceforward be a rule, that we shall receive thirty yards of black and sixty yards of white zeawan for one beaver. Ye have been sleeping hitherto. With these three beavers we now open your eyes. We require sixty handsful of powder for one beaver. We have a vast deal of trouble collecting beavers through the enemy's country. We ask to be furnished with powder and ball. If our enemies conquer us, where will ye then obtain beavers?

"Ye have included us and the *Mohawks*, and the *Mahicans* in the peace of Esopus. Set now at liberty the Indians ye have taken prisoners there. We are sometimes obliged to pass by that path. It is good that brothers live together in peace. The French Indians meet the *Mahicans* near the Cohoes. This we regret. Brothers: We are united by a chain; ye too ought to mourn. This our speech is designed merely to rouse you from your slumbers. We shall return next spring to receive your conclusions. Warn the Dutch not to beat the Indians; otherwise they will say, 'We know nothing of this.'"

[1] *O'Callaghan*, II, 421, etc.

Stuyvesant replied, that when the chiefs were, " for the first time at the Manhattans, some two or three years ago," the tobacco was forgotten, but a roll would now be given to them to make them remember their agreement when they returned to their own country ; that he had " made peace with the Indians at Esopus, at the solicitation of the *Mohawks*, the *Mahicans*, and other friends," so that they might use in safety the rivers and the roads ; that as they had thanked him for making that peace, he solicited that they should " make peace with the *Minsis* and cultivate it," that the Dutch " might use the road to them in safety ;" that he would now give them a whole keg full of powder, but that it " ought not to be used against the *Minsis*," but against the distant enemies from whom they captured the beaver ; that he had forbidden the Dutch to maltreat any of the Indians, and that if the latter caught them doing so, they were at liberty " to beat them on the head until it could no longer be seen where their eyes stood." The price of cloth, however, he could not regulate, as it was brought from " beyond the great lake." With these assurances the chiefs departed to renew their conflict with their savage foes.

Three years of tranquillity succeeded the peace of 1660, during which the settlement at Esopus continued to increase in population. A new village was organized on the north-eastern portion of the " great plot," and the ronduit,[1] at the mouth of the Walkill completed. The Indians, however, were far from being satisfied with their Dutch neighbors. The new village was on land which they had not given to the Dutch ; the new fort boded them no good, and the sting inflicted, by sending their brethren to exile and slavery, rankled in their breasts, and threats of vengeance were again heard. To quiet them Stuyvesant instructed the magistrates to announce that he would soon visit Esopus, give them presents and renew the peace ; but this promise he failed to fulfill with that promptness that was necessary to satisfy the Indians of his sincerity. On the 5th of June, the promise was renewed, but the Indians still doubted, and replied that " if peace was to be renewed with them, the

[1] The location of this fort is supposed to have been at the place still bearing the   aboriginal name of Ponckokie.

honorable herr director-general should, with some unarmed persons, sit with them in the open field, without the gate, as it was their custom to meet unarmed when renewing peace or conducting other negotiations.[1]

Without waiting for a reply to this condition, the Indians attacked the settlement, on the 7th of June, and, with tomahawk and fire-brand, executed the work of death. On the morning of that day, the settlers went forth to their fields as usual. About noon, bands of Indians entered the gates of both villages, and scattered themselves among the houses, ostensibly for the purposes of trade. Suddenly they attacked the inhabitants of the new village, and destroyed the buildings. " Some people on horseback" escaped and reached the old village, " crying out, ' The Indians have destroyed the new village !' " This was the signal to the Indians to attack the old village ; the war whoop rang out, and the people were murdered " in their houses with axes and tomahawks, and by firing on them with guns and pistols." Women and children were seized and carried off prisoners ; houses were plundered, and men, rushing to the defense of their families, were shot down by Indians concealed in their own dwellings. To aid in the work of destruction, the Indians set fire to the village on the windward side. The flames spread rapidly ; but when at their height, the wind suddenly changed to the west and prevented further devastation. A rally of the inhabitants was now effected by the energy of Domine Bloom. The gun at the mill-gate was cleared and discharged with effect, and the settlers coming in from the fields, soon drove the Indians out. By evening all was still again, and the bereaved inhabitants kept mournful watch, during the night, along the bastions and curtains. Twenty-one lives were lost, nine persons were wounded, and forty-five carried off captives. The new village was " entirely destroyed, except a new uncovered barn, one rick, and a little stack of seed," and in the old village of Wiltwyck twelve houses were burned.[2] Writes Bloom,[3] of the scene after the Indians had retreated : " There lay the burnt and slaughtered bodies, together with those wounded by bullets and

[1] *Documentary History,* iv, 39.   [3] *Documentary History,* iii, 962.
[2] *Documentary History,* iv, 42, 44.
19

axes. The last agonies and the moans and lamentations of many were dreadful to hear. I have been in their midst, and have gone into their houses and along the roads, to speak a word in season, and that not without danger of being shot by the Indians. The burnt bodies were most frightful to behold. A woman lay burnt, with her child at her side, as if she were just delivered, of which I was a living witness. Other women lay burnt also in their houses. The houses were converted into heaps of stones, so that I might say with Micah, ' We are made desolate ;' and with Jeremiah, ' A piteous wail may go forth in his distress.' The Indians have slain in all twenty-four souls in our place and taken forty-five prisoners."

The official record conveys in simple language a picture which leaves to the imagination but little office. Killed "in front of his house," "in his house," "on the farm," "burnt with her lost fruit," "burnt in her house," are but repeated in forms of detail until the blackened villages are again presented in the presence of the pitiless massacre, and the wails of the dying and the cries of the captives fade away in the wilderness. It was a terrible massacre ; but was it not terribly provoked ?

The fate of the redoubt was not known. On the morning of the 10th, ten soldiers were commanded to ride down and ascertain its condition. They returned with the statement that the Indians had not been seen there ; that fugitives from the new village had reached there, but the soldiers had not dared to venture to the assistance of the settlers. On the 16th, a troop of soldiers was sent to the redoubt to bring up ammunition and to convey letters to be dispatched to Fort Amsterdam for assistance. This company was attacked, on its return, at the first hill, and the skirmishing continued until after passing the second hill. One of the soldiers was killed· and six were wounded ; the remainder reached Wiltwyck with their wagons and ammunition.

Immediately on the receipt of the dispatches which had been sent to him, Stuyvesant sent a commission to Fort Orange, to raise a loan, engage volunteers, and invite from the *Mahicans*, the *Mohawks* and the *Senecas*, the assistance which they had promised, under the treaty of 1660, in case of a revolt. The commissioner, however, found that the *Mahicans* and the *Mohawks* were at war, and that the *Senecas* had taken the field against the *Minsis*. From them no concerted action could be expected, while the people of Beaverwyck were in alarm lest the assistance which they had rendered to the *Senecas* should recoil upon their own heads. " The farmers fled to the patroon's new fort, Cralo, at Greenbush; the plank fence which inclosed Beaverwyck, and the three guns mounted on the church, were put in order; and Fort Orange, with its nine pieces of artillery, was prepared against an attack." [1]

Meanwhile a reenforcement of forty-two men, under command of Ensign Niessen, was sent from Fort Amsterdam to Wiltwyck, and measures taken to enlist a more considerable force. On the 26th, Burgomaster Martin Kregier, with additional men and a force of forty-six Long island Indians, was sent forward, and on the 4th of July, assembled at Wiltwyck in a general council of war. A few days after, five *Mohawk* and *Mahican* chiefs arrived from Fort Orange, on whose mediation a portion of the Dutch captives were restored; but to proposals for peace the Indians would not listen unless they were paid " for the land, named the Great Plot," and rewarded with presents at their Shawangunk castle within ten days. Scouting parties were then sent out by the Dutch, who succeeded in bringing in a few prisoners, from whom it was ascertained that the Indians had fallen back to their castle; that this castle was " defended by three rows of palisades, and the houses in the fort encircled by thick cleft palisades with port holes in them and covered with the bark of trees; " that in form it was quadrangular, but that the angles were " constructed between the first and second rows of palisades," the third row of palisades standing " full eight feet off from the others towards the interior; " and that the whole stood " on the brow of a hill " surrounded by table-land. [2]

An expedition for the reduction of this castle was at once organized, consisting of " ninety-one men of Kregier's company ; thirty men of Lieutenant Stillwell's company ; Lieutenant Couwenhoven with forty-one Long island Indians," acting under

[1] *Ante*, p. 60; *Brodhead*, I, 711. [2] *Documentary History*, IV, 49. Appendix.

their treaty of 1656 ; six Manhattan Indians ; thirty-five volunteers from the settlers, "and seven of the Honorable Company's negroes," with "two pieces of artillery and two wagons."
The expedition started on the night of the 26th of July, under
the guidance of Rachel la Montagne, who had been taken prisoner on the 7th and escaped ; but she soon lost the trail, and the
force was compelled to bivouac "until day-break," when the
right road was found, and the march resumed. The progress was slow, however ; "much stony land and hills" inter-
vened ; long swamps and frequent kils compelled halts and the
construction of bridges, and mountain passes obliged the hauling
of "wagons and cannon up and down with ropes." When
about six miles from the castle, the expedition halted and one
hundred and sixteen men were sent forward to surprise it.
This force soon captured a squaw in a corn-field, who told them
that the Indians had deserted the fort two days before. About
six o'clock the entire expedition reached its destination, but
found no foe to contest possession.

On the morning of the 28th, the captive squaw having in-
formed them that the Indians had fallen back into the mountains with their prisoners, a company of one hundred and fifteen
men started in search of them. The place where they were
supposed to be was that from which Rachel Montagne had
escaped, but when it was reached it was found that "they had
left that place also." The Indian squaw could not tell them
where her people had gone, but pointed out a mountain some
miles distant where she thought they might be found, but the
march thither was also fruitless. The squaw then pointed out
another mountain, but as the Dutch had had quite enough of
marching, and as it had become apparent that the Indians were
fully advised of their movements, they returned to the castle.
In the afternoon the corn-fields were cut down, and the maize
and beans, which had been preserved in pits, were destroyed.
Three days were spent in ravaging the country. "Nearly one
hundred morgens (two hundred and fifteen acres) of maize"
were cut down, and "above a hundred pits of corn and beans"
burned. On the morning of the 31st, the castle and all the
houses were set on fire, "and while they were in full blaze,"

the Dutch marched out in good order, and returned to Wilt-wyck.

The settlers now engaged in harvesting their grain, and the soldiers guarded them while at work, which was prosecuted day and night. Rumors of another attack were rife. One Davids arrived from Manhattan, with a letter from Couwenhoven, who had been sent down to the Dans-kammer in a sloop to nego-tiate with the Indians, and who wrote that four hundred men were preparing to attack the fort ; that the Indians " who lay there about on the river side made a great uproar every night, firing guns and *kinte-kaying*, so that the woods rang again." Davids himself had been on shore and slept one night with the Indians, who had four captives with them, one of whom, a female, informed him that the Indians were in force watching the reapers on the Great plot, and waiting opportunity to attack them.

Couwenhoven continued his negotiations, and on the 20th of August, brought up a woman and a boy whom he had redeemed. His sloop was furnished with supplies and returned to the Dans-kammer, and instructions issued to him to continue his efforts for the release of the captives ; that failing in this, he should seize as many Indians as possible, " either on land, or by in-ducing them, with fair words," to trust themselves on his vessel. If he could do no better, if the Indians came thither with their captives, he was instructed to " endeavor to detain them on shore " " by means of intoxicating liquors," or by such other mode as he should deem expedient, until word could be con-veyed to the fort, and arrangements made to surprise and seize them." The mission was not successful. The Indians took all the powder and brandy which were offered them, and called for more ; but, beyond two children, no prisoners were released by them. To aid him, Couwenhoven employed a *Wappinger* sachem to visit them, " but when he had been two or three days with them in their new fort, two *Mohawks* and one *Minsi* came there with sewan and a long message, which rendered them so ill disposed towards him that they caused him to depart."

Kregier now determined to resume the offensive. On the 30th a council of war was called, at which it was " resolved and concluded to attack, with one hundred and twenty men, the Indians who reside in their new fort, about four hours farther than their first fort." The expedition started on the afternoon of September 3d, a young *Wappinger* prisoner acting as guide, under a promise of freedom, and Davids as interpreter. Considerable difficulty was experienced in the march, the streams being swollen and heavy rains prevailing. On the 5th, about noon, the first maize field was reached, and two squaws and a Dutch woman discovered gathering corn. Passing these without alarming them, the fort was discovered about two o'clock, "situate on a lofty plain." The force was divided for the purpose of surprise, but discovery was made by a squaw, "who sent forth a terrible scream, which was heard by the Indians," who rushed from the fort, on which they were at work, to their houses to secure their arms. From thence they sprang into their corn-fields which bordered the kil, and in almost a moment of time were on the opposite bank of the stream, where they courageously returned the Dutch fire. They soon retreated however, having lost their chief, Papequanaehen, and fourteen warriors, four women and three children killed ; and thirteen prisoners, " men and women, besides an old man," who, after accompanying his captors about half an hour, would go no further, and who was then taken aside and given " his last meal." Twenty Dutch prisoners were recovered, among whom was Mrs. DuBois and her children, around whose captivity tradition has thrown the story that at the time of the attack preparation was being made for her sacrifice at the stake, which was only delayed by the pleasure with which the Indians listened to the death-song which she chanted.[1] Unfortunately for the tradition, the Indians, at the time of the attack, were not constructing sacrificial fires or listening to death songs, but were completing their fort, which is described as " a perfect square with one row of palisades set all around, being about fifteen feet above and three feet below ground," with angles " of stout palisades, all of them almost as thick as a man's body, having two rows of port-holes, one above the other." Two of these angles were

[1] Record of the family of Louis Du Bois, 15 ; *Collections of the Ulster Histori-* *cal Society*, vol. i, part i, 44.

finished, and, when surprised, the Indians "were busy at the third angle." The Dutch found plunder in abundance, such as bear skins, deer skins, blankets, elk hides, etc., sufficient indeed to have well filled a sloop. Twenty-five guns were found, about twenty pounds of powder, thirty-one belts and strings of wampum, and indeed, all the movable wealth of the fugitives. Everything was destroyed except the ripening maize, and laden with spoil, and cheered by the gladness of the rescued captives, the expedition started for Wiltwyck. On the march one of the Indian children died, and its body was thrown into the creek ; Indians were seen hovering around, but no attack was made, and on the 7th, about noon, the fort was reached.

The Indians, meanwhile, retreated to the Minnisink country. The loss which they had suffered was severe indeed, but it had fallen upon a single chieftaincy, of whom it is said " not more than twenty-seven or twenty-eight warriors, fifteen or sixteen women and a few children survived," and that these were " without houses or huts." [1] The confederated chieftaincies, however, " showed no signs of submission," and a new expedition was sent out against them. This expedition consisted of a force of one hundred and two soldiers, forty-six *Marsapequas* and six freemen. Leaving Wiltwyck on the 1st of October, it arrived at the castle destroyed on the 2d. The Indians had, meanwhile, returned to it and thrown the bodies of their dead comrades into five pits, from which " the wolves had rooted up and devoured some of them. Lower down on the kil four other pits were found containing bodies ; and further on, three Indians with a squaw and child that lay unburied and almost wholly devoured by the ravens and the wolves." A terrible picture of desolation was spread out on either hand, where but a month before the Indian lords had exulted in their strength. The Dutch completed the work of destruction. The remains of the castle were pulled down, the wigwams burned, and all the

[1] O'Callaghan says the Indians were virtually destroyed, but the facts do not warrant the conclusion. In the attack of 1659, "the savages, estimated at four or five hundred warriors, harassed the Dutch day and night ;" in that of 1663, "their numbers were estimated at about two hundred." Their losses subsequently could not have reduced them to the sixty stated. The Dutch had no confidence in such a state of facts, for they relaxed none of their vigilance.

maize which had been left was cut up and cast into the kil. Thence marching down the kil, " several large wigwams " were found, as well as " divers maize plantations," which were also destroyed. The expedition then returned to Wiltwyck.

Negotiations for the release of the captives still remaining in the hands of the Indians were again opened. On the 5th of November, one of the chiefs agreed to return them in ten days, for which purpose a truce was granted by Couwenhoven, whose sloop remained at the Dans-kammer. On the 7th, two children were brought in by a *Wappinger* chief, who accompanied them as a friend and who promised to bring in a captive woman whom he had purchased. This woman he brought in on the 13th, and received in exchange a *Wappinger*, called Splitnose, and one of the captive squaws and her child. On the 29th, the *Wappinger* again appeared and after satisfying himself that of the Indians in the hands of the Dutch none had died, said that six of the captives held by the Indians were then at the river side ; that the seventh had been sent for, and that all would be restored in three days ; but he was unable to redeem his promise. On the 2d of December he brought up two children, and stated that of the remaining five, three were in the hunting grounds and he could not find them, while the other two were detained by a sick squaw. He would, however, return them as soon he could obtain them, for which purpose he had already purchased Albert Heyman's oldest daughter. Whether the promise was fulfilled or not does not appear.

In this condition matters remained until the spring of 1664, when the Amsterdam chamber instructed Stuyvesant to continue the war until the Indians were exterminated. But Stuyvesant had on his hands a controversy with the English towns on Long island, in which was involved the jurisdiction of the West India Company, and was under the necessity of husbanding his strength for emergencies in which he might possibly be placed. Besides, wars were pending between the *Mohawks* and the *Mahicans* on the east, and the *Senecas* and the *Minsis* on the south, destroying trade and threatening to involve the Dutch settlements in the common destruction. Under the

¹ *Documentary History*, IV, 80, 81.

circumstances he deemed it prudent to entertain the solicitations of the neighboring chiefs for the establishment of peace with the Esopus cantons, especially as it was rumored that the English were encouraging the *Wappingers* and other tribes to unite in the general revolt.

Sending an invitation to the Esopus sachems and their friends to meet him in council at Fort Amsterdam, a large delegation assembled there, and the customary preliminaries being disposed of, Sewackenamo, sachem of the *Warranawonkongs*, arose, and calling several times in a loud voice on his God, BACHTAMO, prayed unto him to conclude something good with the Dutch, and that the treaty about to be formed, in the presence of the sachems assembled,[1] should be like the stick he grasped in his hand, firmly united, the one end to the other. Sigpekenano, a Long island chief, expressed his joy that peace was about to be concluded, and that the clan he represented was to share in its provisions. He hoped it would be a peace as firm and as compact as his arms, which he folded together; and then, presenting his right hand to the director, added: " What I say is from the fullness of my heart; such is my desire and that of all my people."

The next day (May 16) Stuyvesant submitted the treaty. By its terms all that had passed was to be forever forgotten and forgiven. The land already given to the Dutch as an indemnity, and now again " conquered by the sword," including the two Shawangunk castles, became the property of the Dutch; nor were the Indians to return thither to plant, nor to visit the village of Wiltwyck, nor any remote settlement, with or without arms. They were permitted, however, to plant near their new castle, and for the then present year only by their old castle, where they had already planted some seed. To prevent collisions in the future no Indian was to approach places where the Dutch farmers were pursuing agricultural labor, nor visit the village or the residences of the settlers. They might, however, trade at

---

[1] The chiefs in attendance were: *Esopus*, Sewackenamo, Onackatin, Powsawag; *Wappinger*, Tsees-sagh-gaw; *Kitchawan*, Megetsewacks; *Haverstraw*, Sessegehout; *Weckquaesgeeks* Sawanacoque; *Hackinsacks*, Oritany; *Staten Island*, Matheno; *Marsepeqau*, and *Reckheweck*, Siegpekenano, brother of Tackapousha, with twenty others of different chieftaincies acting in the capacity of embassadors.

the redoubt, in parties of three canoes at a time, by sending a flag of truce beforehand to give notice of their approach. For their accommodation on such occasions, a house was to be built beyond the creek, where they could leave their arms. Should a Dutchman kill an Indian, or an Indian a Dutchman, war was not to be declared ; but a complaint was to be lodged against the murderer, who should be hanged in the presence of both the contracting parties. All damages by the killing of cattle, or injury of crops, were to be paid for, and the treaty annually ratified by the exchange of presents. For the faithful observance of the treaty the Hackinsack and Staten island sachems became sureties on the part of the Esopus sachems, and were bound to cooperate against either party who should violate its terms.

The signing of the treaty was announced by a salute from Fort Amsterdam, and caused universal satisfaction. In special commemoration of the event, Stuyvesant proclaimed a day of general thanksgiving, to be held throughout the province on the 31st of May. To still further strengthen the position of the Dutch, he sent a commission to the *Soquatucks* [1] to negotiate a peace between them and the *Mohawks*, for which purpose a conference was held at Narrington and a treaty concluded on the 24th. The day of thanksgiving was a day of peace throughout the settlements of New Netherland.

But the brooding clouds of war were not dispelled. While yet the Esopus conflict was pending, the *Mahicans* had been summoning their clans ; the peace of Narrington was broken by the *Abenaquis*, who murdered the *Mohawk* embassadors, "instigated thereto, it is alleged, by the English ; " the war was renewed ; the *Mahicans* overran the country, killed a number of cattle at Greenbush, and " fired a house at Claverack, belonging to Abraham Staats, in which they burnt his wife and two children " (July 11). " Proceeding, next, in a body one hundred strong, against the *Mohawks*, they gave them battle, but the latter being more numerous, routed their assailants. The *Mohawks*, elated by success, pursued their foe, with whom

[1] The record says, " between the Ma- quaas and the Mahicans and Northern   Indians."—*O'Callaghan*, II, 519, note.

they renewed the fight the next morning at break of day, but were repelled with great loss." Filled with alarm, the colonists at Fort Orange sent in hot haste to request the presence and advice of the director ; but he had other duties to perform — the guns of the English fleet were echoing over the waters of the bay — a more formidable enemy was knocking at the doors of New Amsterdam.

Indian Inscription on
Rocks at Esopus.

CHAPTER VII.

THE INDIANS UNDER THE ENGLISH.—TREATIES WITH THE
FIVE NATIONS, THE MAHICANS AND THE ESOPUS INDIANS.—
THE JESUITS AND THE WAR OF 1689.

HE English, under Richard Nicolls, took possession of Fort Amsterdam on Monday, September 6th, 1664, and immediately changed its name to Fort James. Nicolls was proclaimed deputy governor for the Duke of York, in compliment to whom he directed that the city of New Amsterdam should thenceforth be known as New York. Fort Orange surrendered on the 10th, and its name was changed to Fort Albany, after the second title of the Duke of York. Following this change came a conference with chiefs of the *Mohawks* and *Senecas*, representing the Five Nations, and the conclusion with them, and with the *Mahicans* of New York, of a treaty of peace and alliance, similar to that which had existed with the Dutch. By the terms of this treaty the independence and equality of the nations parties to it, was recognized, while the tribes not in alliance with them, but " under the protection " of, or in treaty with, the English were to be regarded as subjects of the crown, and to sustain, in that relation, the position of citizens for their protection and redress. These facts more clearly appear from its text, which is as follows :

" Articles made and agreed upon the 24th day of September, 1664, in Fort Albany, between Ohgehando, Shanarage, Soachoenighta, Sachamackas of ye *Maquaes;* Anaweed, Conkeeherat, Tewasserang, Aschanoondah, Sachamas of the *Synicks* on the one part, and Col. George Cartwright, in the behalf of Col. Nicolls, governor under his royal highnesse, the Duke of Yorke of all his territories in America, on the other part, as followeth, viz :

" 1. Imprimis. It is agreed that the Indian princes above named and their subjects, shall have all such wares and commodities from the English for the future, as heretofore they had from the Dutch.

" 2. That if any English, Dutch or Indian (under the protection of the English) do any wrong, injury or violence to any of ye said Princes or their subjects in any sort whatever, if they complain to the Governor at New Yorke, or to the officer .in chief at Albany, if the person so offending can be discovered, that person shall receive condign punishment and all due satisfaction shall be given; and the like shall be done for all other English Plantations.

" 3. That if any Indian belonging to any of the Sachims aforesaid do any wrong, injury or damage to the English, Dutch or Indians under the protection of the English, if complaint be made to ye Sachims and the persons be discovered who did the injury, then the person so offending shall be punished and all just satisfaction shall be given to any of His Majesties subjects in any colony or other English plantation in America.

" 4. The Indians at Wamping and Espachomy and all below the Manhattans, as also all those that have submitted themselves under the protection of His Majesty, are included in these articles of agreement and Peace.

" In confirmation whereof the parties above mentioned have hereunto sett their hands the day and year above written. Signed, etc."

To the Five Nations proper some special concessions were made, which were included in the following supplemental articles, viz. :

" These articles following were likewise proposed by the same Indian Princes and consented to by Col. Cartwright in behalfe of Col. Nicolls, the 25th September, 1664.

" 1. That the English do not assist the three nations of the Ondiakes (Abenaquis), Pinnekooks, and Pacamtekookes, who murdered one of the Princes of the *Maquaes*, when he brought ransomes and presents to them upon a treaty of peace.[1]

" 2. That the English do make peace for the Indian Princes with the Nations down the River.[2]

" 3. That they may have free trade, as formerly.

---

[1] The Abenequis, or Eastern Indians.   [2] The Minquas, Esopus and Navison clans of Lenapes.

" 4. That they may be lodged in houses, as formerly.

" 5. That if they be beaten by the three nations above mentioned they may receive accommodation from ye English." [1]

This treaty, to be correctly interpreted, must be considered in connection with the former relations of the Indians to the governments of New Amsterdam and New England. The *Mahicans* proper were under treaty with both the English and the Dutch, but representative cantons immediately on the Hudson held a recognized intercourse with the latter. These were included in the treaty under the terms, "the Indians of Wamping and Espachomy, precisely as were those of Long island, who had recognized treaties, and who were specified "as below the Manhattans;" but the Massachusetts *Mahicans* required no such recognition, the change in the government not having affected the treaty which existed between them and the English. The fact that the treaty was made with representatives of the Five Nations has no significance other than that with them the English had no previous treaty. Whatever special terms there were in its provisions with them were included in the supplemental articles, and these related only to the questions of war and peace pending with tribes with whom the English were under treaty, and in reference to which negotiations were at once opened.[2] The new treaty made no other change in relation to the position of the representative tribes than was necessarily involved in the change of government. This clearly appears from the subsequent records of the commissioners of Indian affairs, in which the *Mahicans* uniformly appear as having not only formed a treaty with the Dutch in 1609, and to have renewed that treaty with the English, but as being " linked together in interest with the Five Nations," and consulted with and treated as allies of the government in the capacity of an independent nation.[3]

---

[1] *Colonial History*, III, 67.

[2] The war which was pending at the time this treaty was made was instigated by the English.— *O'Callaghan*, II, 519. The governor of New York and the governor of Massachusetts were the parties to the treaty between the *Mohawks* and the *Mahicans*. Governor Lovelace writes to Governor Winthrop, in 1669: " If all my letters arrived in your hands you will find them all of one tenor, viz : the earnest desire of the Maquas to conclude firm peace with the Mohicands."— *New York Assize Record*.

[3] *Colonial History*, IV, 744, 902, etc. In an address to the Massachusetts commis-

But English possession brought with it additional changes in the connection of the Indians with provincial authorities. To the boundary lines of territorial governments, which had already passed through and subdivided the *Mahicans* and the *Lenapes*, court districts and county lines were added. Indians of the same tribal families, who had hitherto been held responsible to and had their treaty relations with different governments and provinces, while consolidated in some respects, were further separated by special assignment to the charge of different court districts. Thus the *Wappingers* and those residing south of the highlands and Long island, had their treaty intercourse with the governor and authorities at New York ; those north of the highlands on the east, and north of the highlands and south of the Katskills on the west, including principally the Esopus clans, were placed under the justices at Kingston, and the *Mahicans* on the east and those on Beeren island and north of the Katskills on the west, came directly under the authorities at Albany, at which place the general council-fire was lighted and intercourse held with the Five Nations and the *Mahicans*. While these divisions were the result in part of the established centres of population and treaty intercourse under the Dutch, they subsequently added materially to the disintegration of the river tribes, and gave to them much of that character of independent cantons which has been assumed as representing their political status. From this disintegration the Five Nations escaped, with results to their consolidated recognition ,which cannot be too highly estimated. That they would have been similar sufferers had they been similarly situated, the records of the negotiations with them after the war of the revolution, are a sufficient indication. Considered only as a whole and treated as a whole, they were a power; but treated with as independent tribes they were shorn of their strength. With them the history of the *Mahicans* and the *Lenapes* repeated itself with fearful emphasis.

The policy adopted by the English was liberal and reasonable, and contributed at least to the temporary improvement of the

sioners in 1744, the chiefs used the following language : " We are united with the Six Nations in one common covenant, and this is the belt- which is the token of that covenant."

condition of the Indians. The frictions which had prevailed during the Dutch administration were very largely removed by a law declaring that " no purchase of lands from the Indians, after the first day of March, 1665," should be " esteemed a good title without leave first had and obtained from the governor and after leave so obtained ; " that purchasers should bring before the governor " the sachem or right owner " of lands which were purchased " to acknowledge satisfaction and payment " for the same, when all the proceedings were to be entered on record and constitute a valid title. " All injuries done to the Indians of what nature soever," were made punishable on complaint and proof in any court, without cost to the complainant, " in as full and ample a manner as if the case had been between Christian and Christian." The contraband trade in fire-arms was broken up, and only those who were licensed were permitted " to sell guns, powder, bullets, lead, shot, or any vessel of burthen or row boat (canoes excepted)." The sale or gift to the Indians of " rum, strong waters, wine and brandy," without license, was forbidden under penalty of " forty shillings for each pint so sold or disposed of." To prevent difficulties arising from cattle straying upon the unfenced lands of the Indians, and to encourage the latter to fence their fields, the colonists were directed to assist them in " felling trees, riving and sharpening rails " and setting posts, allowing " one Englishman to three or more Indians." These reforms were eminently satisfactory to the Indians, although many abuses were subsequently perpetrated by those who were licensed under them. Not less so was the treaty stipulation that the privileges of trade were to be uniform, in all English plantations, to Indians in alliance with the government, and the fact that such alliance secured the friendship of the " great sachem." Tranquillity was soon established, and although the *Mohawks* and the *Mahicans* and *Abenaquis*, at the east, and the *Senecas* and *Minsis*, at the south, continued their struggle, the conflict was not around the centres of civilization. Gradually the *Minsis*, more immediately represented on the Hudson, yielded to the superior advantages possessed by their enemies, or to the inducements which the English offered ; while those more remote made common cause with the French.

The annual renewal of the treaty with the Esopus Indians, required by its terms, was delayed until October, 1665, when, as their intercourse in the future was to be with the English, the treaty was rewritten in the English language, with such changes in its terms as the change in government required,[1] as appears from its text :

" An agreement made between Richard Nichols, Esq., Governor, under his Royall Highness the duke of York, and the Sachems and People called the Sopes Indians :

" That no act of hostility shall at any time bee committed on either part, or if any damage shall happen to be done by either party to the Corn, Cattle, Horses, Hoggs, Houses, or any other goods whatever of the other party, from the goods of the other party shall return be given upon demand for the same.

" 2. That if any Christian shall wilfully kill an Indyan, or any Indyan a Christian, hee shall bee put to death. And the said Sachems do promise on their part, to bring any such Indyan to the officer in chiefe at the Sopes to receive his punishment there.

" 3. That a convenient House shall bee built where the said Indyans may at any time lodge, without the Forts of the said Town, in which House the Indians are to leave their armes, and may come without molestation to sell or buy what they please from the Christians.

" 4. That in case any Christian should kill an Indyan, or any Indyan a Christian, the peace shall not be broaken, or any Revenge taken before satisfaction is demanded by the one party and refused by the other, allowing a competent time for the apprehending of the offender, in which case the Indyans are to give Hostage, till the offender is brought to punishment, the said Hostage to be kindly treated and shall receive no other punishment but imprisonment.

[1] Compare with synopsis of treaty of 1664. The statement that Nicolls made the treaty the occasion for the purchase of additional lands, apparently indicated by the fifth section, appears to have been the expression in definite terms of the general language of the treaty of 1664, " the lands now conquered by the sword." The original manuscript of the treaty, and the wampum belt which the Indians gave in accepting it, are preserved in the office of the clerk of Ulster county. It was renewed at different periods until the Indians ceased to exist or had entirely removed to the west.

" 5. That the said Sachems and their subjects now present do, and in the names of themselves, and their heirs forever, give, grant, alienate and confirm all their right and interest, claim oŕ demand to a certain Parcell of Land, lying and being to the west and south west of a certain creek or River, called by the name of Kahanksen, and so up to the head thereof, where the old Fort was ; And so with a direct line from thence through the woods and crosse the Meadows to the Great Hill, lying and being to the west or south west thereof, which Great Hill is to be the true west or south west Bounds of the said Lands. And the said creek called Kahanksen, the north or north east Bounds of the said Lands, herein mentioned, to be given, granted, and confirmed unto the said Richard Nicolls, governor under his Royal Highness, the Duke of York, or his assigns, by the said Sachems, and their subjects, forever, and to hold and enjoy the same as his free land, and Possession against any claim here-after to bee madee by the said Sachems or their subjects, or any their heirs and successors.

" In token of the aforesaid Agreement, the aforesaid Sachems do deliver two small sticks, and in confirmation thereof, do deliver two more small sticks, to the said Richard Nicholls.   And in the name of the Indyans their subjects, one of the subjects do deliver two other round small sticks, in token of their assent to the said agreement.   And the said Richard Nicholls does deliver as a present to their Sachems three laced redd coates.

" 6. The said Sachems doth engage to come once every year, and bring some of their young People, to Acknowledge every part of this agreement in the Sopes, to the end that it may be kept in perpetual memory.

" 7. That all past Injuryes are buried and forgotten on both sides.

" 8. That the young Sachem called Ningeerinoe hath Liberty for three years to plant upon a small neck of land, over against a small creek called Choughkanakanoe, unless the said young Sachem be warned off by order to remove, and give place to such Christians as shall have Order from the said Richard Nicolls, or his assignees, to plant there, at which time the said young Sachem is to receive a Blankett, by way of Curtesie, and to remove to the other side of the Creek, without delay, or claiming any future interest thereupon.

"9. In consideration of the premises, the said Richard Nicolls doth farther give and pay to the said Sachems and their subjects, forty blanketts, twenty Pounds of Powder, twenty knives, six Kettles, Twelve Barrs of Lead, which payment we acknowledge to have received, in full satisfaction, for the premises, and do bind ourselves, our heirs and successors forever, to perform every part of this agreement, without any fraud or reservation of mind; and further, that we will maintain and justify the said Richard Nicolls, or his assigns, in the full and peaceable Possession of the said Tract of Land, Royaltyes and Privileges for ever, against any Nation of Indyans whatsoever, pretending right to the same.

" In testimony whereof we have sett our markes to two several writings, the one to remaine in the hands of the Sopes Sachems, the other upon record, this 7th day of October, 1665."

The parties to the treaty on behalf of the Indians were sachems Onackatin,[1] Naposhequiqua, Senakonama (Sewakanamo), and Shewotin. The signature of Nicolls and of the sachems was witnessed by " Jeremias Van Rensleiar, Philip Pieterson Schuyler, Robert Nedham, S. Salisbury and Edw. Sackville," and by the following " Esopus young men " : Pepankhais, Robin Cinnaman "a Pekoct sachem," Ermawamen, and Rywackus. One of the chieftaincies was apparently without a sachem ; the full number was completed in 1670, when, on the 11th of April, "a new made sachem of the Esopus Indians, named Calcop," appeared before the justices of Ulster and confirmed the agreement.

The *Minsis* proper maintained hostilities until 1675, when they yielded to what Dr Colden denominates " the full play of the warlike genius" of their enemies, but more properly, as already intimated, to the fearful disadvantages under which they were placed by the refusal of the English to supply them with firearms and powder, in accordance with the treaty with the *Senecas* and *Mohawks*, and were made tributary to the *Senecas*. In the east the contest still raged. Peace was made in 1675, but it

[1] Oghgotacton; his lands were near the present village of Walden. See appendix.

was one of accommodation on the part of the *Abenaquis* and their allies, many of whom sympathized with King Philip and eagerly shared his fate. Nor were they disheartened when, on the 12th of August, 1676, that great leader gave up his life. In that remarkable struggle for the restoration of the Indians to independence, one of the branches of the formidable alliance, the *Pennacooks*, was crushed and its fugitives, bleeding and torn, sought refuge in the friendly villages of their kindred on the Hudson. Reference has already been made to the immediate subsequent history and organization of these fugitives as the *Schaticooks*.[1] After their settlement, the authorities made no little effort to increase their number by inducing those who had found refuge elsewhere to remove to the lands assigned, and in this were partially successful. At the close of the French war of 1698, and subsequently, these efforts were renewed;[2] meanwhile a very considerable number of them had reached Canada, and were encouraged by the French to invite their brethren of New York, as well as their old *Mahican* allies, to unite with them. The result of these efforts was the organization of what was known as the St. Francis Indians.

Meanwhile an element other than that of war had been introduced to divide the Indian tribes. With the French, religious zeal and commercial ambition walked hand in hand, and the banner of the cross became the pioneer of that of France. No sooner had Champlain discovered the territory of the St.

[1] *Ante*, p. 62. The date of this organization, as well as the original classification of the elements of which the *Schaticooks* were composed, is distinctly stated by Earl Bellomont, the governor, in 1698 : " Our Skackoor or river Indians and which river Indians having been formerly driven out of those eastern parts by the people of New England."— *Colonial History*, IV, 380, 715. Colden fixes the date of their settlement as 1672, while one of their chiefs, speaking in 1700, states the occurrence as happening " six and twenty years ago," or in 1674.— *Colonial History*, IV, 744. As there was no war against the New England Indians by which an exodus of this kind would be made necessary prior to the downfall of Philip in 1676, and as the fugitives from that conflict are described by Hubbard as having fled towards Albany, the conclusion is that the *Schaticooks* were no other than the Indians described by him. There was another organization of Schaticooks, composed of New England and Hudson river Indians. They were located on Ten Mile river, so called, in the present county of Dutchess. This organization is particularly described by De Forest (*History Indians of Connecticut*, 407), as having been commenced by one Gideon Manwehu, a Pequot, sometime about 1735, and who succeeded in calling about him a hundred warriors.

[2] *Colonial History*, IV, 380, 715, 744, 902.

Lawrence than he was found declaring, that while the aggrand-
izement of France was earnestly to be desired, yet " the salvation
of a soul was worth more than the conquest of an empire."
At his instance, La Carnon, an ambitious Franciscan priest,
entered the field as a missionary, and in 1616, penetrated the
Mohawk country, passed to the north into the territory of the
Wyandots and reached the river of Lake Huron. In 1633,
the Society of Jesus succeeded the Franciscans with fifteen
missionaries, the history of whose labors is connected with the
origin of every established town in the annals of French America ; " not a cape was turned, nor a river entered, but a Jesuit
led the way." [1]   The converts of these missionaries were at first
from among the enemies of the Five Nations ; the latter regarded
them as foes, and in their incursions upon the *Hurons*, spared
them not. The fate of the missionary village of St. Joseph and
of Fathers Daniel, Lallemand and Brebeuf, and the captivity of
Father Jogues, are but types of the toil and sacrifice which
attended their labors, and of the heroism with which they met
death. The fruit of their efforts was the possession by France
not only of New France and Acadia, Hudson's bay and New-
foundland, but a claim to a moiety of Maine, of Vermont, and
to more than a moiety of New York, to the whole valley of
the Mississippi, and to Texas even, as far as the Rio Bravo del
Norte, whither the flag of France followed their footsteps and
reared colonies.

The Dutch gave very little attention to the movements of
the missionaries, or to the extension of the dominion of France.
Intent upon trade and having no ambition to extend their possessions beyond the three rivers which they claimed, the
conversion of the Indians scarcely received from them a thought.[2]
The missionaries improved their advantage, and in 1654, appeared
in the territory of the *Onondagas*, where they found many *Huron*
captives who had formerly received their instruction. Missions

---

[1] *Bancroft*, III, 122.

[2] Domine Megapolensis, who came
over in 1643, under an agreement with
Van Rensselaer, made some effort to
learn the *Mohawk* language, with a
view to preach to them in their castles, but
without much success. A few Indians

attended his preaching at Albany, but
without understanding a word that he
said. The claim that he was the predecessor of Eliot, has very little foundation, and none whatever in the aid which
the government extended to him. *Brodhead*, I, 375, 376.

to the *Oneidas* and *Senecas* speedily followed ; chapels sprang into existence, and long before the English obtained possession of New Amsterdam, the solemn services of the Roman church were chanted in the heart of their future province. The possession of these privileges, however, was not destined to be permanent. The *Oneidas* murdered three Frenchmen (1657), and the French retaliated by seizing *Iroquois*. Two years later the missionaries had abandoned the country, and the French and the Five Nations were again at war. Finding success hopeless without stronger military support, the aid of the king of France was invited, and scarcely had the English succeeded in planting the flag of St. George on the walls of Fort Orange, ere the colony of New France was protected by a royal regiment, and Courcelles, a veteran French soldier, established as its governor. The missionaries now renewed their work, and reestablished themselves in the territory of the *Senecas* and *Onondagas*, and converted one of the villages of the *Mohawks*.[1]

The progress of the French soon became more formidable. Serious inroads were made on the territory claimed by the English, and the *Iroquois* were gradually yielding to the efforts of the Jesuits. Except in the valor and good faith of the Indians more immediately under English influence, the province had no protection. The Jesuit fathers became spies, and, in 1682, were enabled to advise the governor of Canada, that circumstances had materially changed ; that they were now accustomed to the woods, were acquainted with all the roads through them, and that the French could, from Fort Frontenac, fall on the *Senecas* in forty hours and crush them by an unexpected blow.[2] When Colonel Dongan came over, in 1683, as governor of New York, matters wore a threatening aspect indeed. He was under instructions to preserve friendly relations with the French, and besides this, was himself an earnest Catholic ; but he was not blind to the danger which menaced the province, or slow to use his power to avert it. Wherever the French priests traveled they set up the arms of France in token of French

---

[1] Although the priests had no little difficulty with the *Mohawks*, they ultimately succeeded in converting the village or castle of Caghnawaga.

[2] *Documentary History New York*, I, 97.

possession ; Dongan gave to his *Iroquois* allies medals showing that they were British subjects, and caused the arms of the Duke of York to be erected in all their castles. The French invited their converts to Canada ; Dongan solicited them to remain, and obtained a promise from those who had already gone to return. He would give them lands and priests and built them a church. In the fall of 1686, he sent fifty citizens of Albany and New York to winter with the *Senecas*, and used his influence with the *Mahicans* to join the *Iroquois* in an alliance for mutual defense.

Meanwhile the Duke of York (1685), under the title of James II, had succeeded the sensual Charles II, as king of England. The duke was an intense Catholic, and his elevation gave courage to the Jesuit fathers, who could now ask, with additional force, his aid in extending their work. Dongan appealed to him and endeavored to arouse him to the necessity of protecting the province and of maintaining the alliance with the *Iroquois*. "The Five Nations," said he, "are a bulwark between us and the French and all other Indians. This government has always been, and still is, at a great expense to keep them peaceable and annexed to this government, which is of that moment that upon any occasion I can have three or four thousand of their men upon call." The interests of trade also required this alliance, in his opinion, not less than the security of the English. To this end he asked for Catholic priests in the interests of the English, in order to oblige the French priests to retire to Canada and the " country be divested of the pretense for their presence." But James had already bound himself to Louis XIV in a treaty of neutrality ; to that treaty his attention had been called by Louis, on complaint from La Barre, the governor of Canada, and if he had the disposition to aid Dongan, he was under obligations to avoid a rupture with France.

La Barre's administration was not a success. The *Senecas* attacked some French trading canoes, and after organizing a considerable force to proceed against them, he had fallen back without conflict, terrified at the rumor that Dongan had promised them the aid of " four hundred horse and four hundred foot " if they were attacked. The only fruit of his expedition was a treaty which he concluded with the *Onondagas, Oneidas* and *Cayugas,* the force of which may be inferred from the fact that only six hours were spent in its negotiation. His subordinates were disgusted at his proceedings, and refused to restrain their " sovereign contempt for the general's person." " His design," says Demeneles, " was to attack the *Senecas,* but instead of showing him any civility, they did not even condescend to come and meet him, and gave an insolent answer to those who proposed it to them. If people had anything to say to them, let them take the trouble to come and meet them." De Lamberville, the Jesuit missionary at Onondaga, alone sustained him. The difficulties of prosecuting war against the *Senecas* were not, in his opinion, properly estimated. The Indians would not be found in their villages or forts, but would prowl everywhere, " killing without if possible being killed." For the conflict they were ready ; nay, had received " with joy " the intelligence that they were to be attacked, confident that in such an event they would be able to strip, roast and eat the French. The result of the affair was the removal of La Barre, the appointment of De Denonville as his successor, and the receipt by Dongan of instructions to observe strict neutrality.

The French were fully determined to attempt the destruction of the power of the *Iroquois.* Louis himself was convinced that such a step was necessary. De Denonville had examined the situation thoroughly, and had informed his royal master that the reputation of the French had been " absolutely destroyed " among the Indians, whether friends or enemies, by La Barre's conduct, and that unless this was arrested, nothing could avert a general rebellion, the ruin of trade and the extirpation of the French. War was necessary, too, " for the establishment of religion," which could not otherwise be successfully prosecuted. " Merit in the eyes of God," and the " possession of an empire of more than a thousand leagues in extent," from which " great commercial advantages" would eventually be derived, demanded the effort and the expense which it involved. The king responded with an addition to the French force ; gave his entire approval to the war, and, in addition to the means to be employed, advised that prisoners be taken and sent to him for service as galley-slaves.

The work entrusted to Denonville was not long delayed. Treachery was resorted to, to secure prisoners. De Lamberville succeeded in decoying a considerable number of *Iroquois* chiefs into Fort Frontenac, on Lake Ontario, from whence they were removed in irons to Quebec and hurried to France ;[1] Indian allies were called in, and arrangements for an aggressive movement consummated. He had no contemptible foe to encounter. " The *Iroquois* force," by his own authority, consisted of "two thousand brave, active men, more skillful in the use of the gun than the Europeans, and all well armed ; besides twelve hundred *Mahicans* (Loups), another tribe in alliance with them as brave as they,"[2] to say nothing of the English whom he expected to assist them.

In July, 1687, he marched into the territory of the *Senecas*, and took formal possession " in the name of the king." On his way he was attacked by the *Senecas* with such vigor that he was obliged to bivouac on the field, and witness, without being able to prevent, the tortures which the *Senecas* inflicted on the prisoners who had fallen into their hands. In the morning the *Senecas* retreated, and on reaching their village it was found that they had destroyed it and abandoned their fort. The French cut up the growing corn without molestation, and successfully completed the construction of Fort Niagara. The campaign cost the lives of one hundred Frenchmen, ten French or Catholic Indians, and eighty *Senecas*. The latter appealed to Dongan, who supplied them with powder, lead and arms, and

---

[1] The number taken was twenty-seven, of whom " Taweeratt, the chief warrior of Cayouge," was one.— *Colonial History,* III, 560, 579. Father Millett was charged with being a party to their capture.—*Ib.* 621. The French account is that forty chiefs were taken prisoners, one of whom is called Orehaoué, " one of the most considerable chiefs of their nation." — *Colonial History,* IX, 464. " The general in chief of the entire Iroquois nation."— *Ibid.,* 465.

[2] The cooperation of the *Mahicans* with the *Iroquois* is frequently referred to in the French records, and in language indicative of their importance. The alliance referred to in the text, is spoken of as having existed for some time. In 1674, the *Mahicans* were at war with the *Ottawas,* and the *Senecas* became arbitrators to establish peace. In 1684, it is said "six or seven hundred *Mohegans* were preparing to go to the assistance of the *Iroquois,* as the *Ottawas* were aiding the French." The number of their warriors stated in the text is no doubt exaggerated, but there is no question that they could at any time bring more warriors to the field than the *Mohawks.*— *Colonial History,* IX, 259, 460, 466, etc.

called upon their allies to unite together to defend the territory which France had invaded. In addition to this a special meeting of the council was held at Fort James, and a bill passed for levying a tax of a " penny in the pound out of the estates of the freeholders," to aid in defraying expenses. Palisades were ordered for fortifying Albany and Schenectady, and the Five Nations were requested to send down " their wives, children and old men, lest the French fall upon them in winter; that they who come be settled, some at Katskill, and along the river," where they would be in security and in readiness to assist in the common defense should it be necessary. Every tenth man of the militia was ordered to Albany, and other measures taken for defensive war. " I will do what is possible for me to save the government from the French," said Dongan to De Denonville, " until I hear from the king, my master ;" and " advise Monsieur Denonville to send home all the Christians and Indian prisoners, the king of England's subjects, you unjustly do detain."

Meanwhile the *Senecas* remained on the war path. Dongan had offered his mediation for peace on condition that the captive chiefs should be restored, the fort in the *Seneca* country razed, and the spoils taken from that nation restored. To these propositions De Denonville would not listen. In July, 1688, the *Iroquois* advanced to dictate the terms. Haaskouaun, their chief, with five hundred warriors sat down before Quebec. Twelve hundred warriors remained within call. If in four days the French would concede to Dongan's terms, the place would be spared; if not, it would be overwhelmed. The French governor yielded, and on the sixth of September following abandoned Fort Niagara and the possession of the country south of the great lakes. The imprisoned chiefs, however, he did not restore.

In this situation matters remained until January, 1689, when James was driven from the throne of England by William, the Prince of Orange. France espoused the cause of the deposed king, and declared war against England, and on both continents the conflict was opened. Before the formal declaration came, however, the *Iroquois* had resumed hostilities. Visiting Albany in July, they acquainted the magistrates that the French had not returned their chiefs, and that they were resolved to be revenged.[1] From thence they proceeded to Canada, and on the twenty-fifth of August, fifteen hundred in number, they landed on the south side of the island of Montreal, burned the houses, sacked the plantations, and put to the sword all the men, women and children without the fortifications. "In less than an hour, two hundred people met death under forms too horrible for description. Approaching the town of Montreal, they made an equal number of prisoners, and after a severe skirmish became masters of the fort, and of the whole island, of which they remained in possession until the middle of October. In the moment of consternation, De Denonville ordered Fort Frontenac, on Lake Ontario, to be evacuated and razed. From Three Rivers to Mackinaw, there remained not one French town, and hardly even a post."[2]

Anticipating an aggressive movement on the part of the English and their allies, representation had already been made to Louis. Governor Andros, who had succeeded Dongan,[3] promptly declared his determination to regard his Indian allies as "subjects of the crown of England," and the French gave up all hope of detaching them even through the influence of their priests. To retain possession of the territory was their only expectation, coupled with a determination to inflict such injury as they could. Under these instructions Count de Frontenac was appointed governor-general, and with a considerable force landed at Quebec within forty days after the attack of the *Iroquois* on Montreal, and the first news he met, on entering the St. Lawrence, was an account of it. He determined to retaliate, not by marching against the *Iroquois*, but against their English allies who had furnished them with arms and were their supporters.[4] To carry out this determination an expedition was organized to be conducted in three divisions, the first to rendezvous at Montreal and proceed towards Fort Orange; the second, at the Three Rivers and make a descent on

[1] *Colonial History*, III, 599.
[2] *Bancroft*, III, 179. *Colonial History*, III, 621.
[3] New York was annexed to New England, under the government of Sir Edmund Andros, in 1688.
[4] Frontenac brought with him, as a peace offering to the *Iroquois*, the chiefs who had been treacherously betrayed and taken to France. They were subsequently restored to their people.

New England, and the third, to proceed by water for the reduction of Fort James. Count de Frontenac was to conduct
the land expedition against Fort James, where he was to be
met by the fleet under the command of Caffiniere, while the
governor, De Callieres, was to conduct the expedition against
Albany. The latter expedition left Montreal at the commencement of February, 1690. The point of attack was concealed
from the Indian allies, by whom it was accompanied, until the
place of destination was nearly reached, when a council was
held and the destination announced. The Indians objected,
and the conclusion was finally taken to attack Schenectady instead of Albany. Thither the invaders directed their steps,
and on the morning of Sunday, February 10th, repeated the
massacre by the *Senecas* and their allies at Montreal. The attacking force separated in two divisions, and entered the gates
in two directions. At the point of junction, the shrill whoop
of the savage burst upon the air, and the implements of death
and the blazing torch completed the work of destruction. No
house were spared in the town, except one belonging to Major
Condre (Sanders), the commandant, who, with his men, surrendered to the French division on the promise of quarter, and
that of a widow and her six children, in whose care the French
commander, who had been wounded, was placed. The lives
of between fifty and sixty persons, old men, women and children, who escaped the fury of the first attack, were spared.
Upwards of eighty well built and well furnished houses were
destroyed. Sixty men, women and children were killed, and
twenty-seven carried away prisoners. A few succeeded in escaping and fled through the snow to Albany, a distance of
twenty miles, and gave the alarm. Before the local forces
could be rallied and the *Mohawks* and their allies called in,
however, the French were far on the retreat. They were pursued by the *Mohawks*, who fell upon their rear and harassed
them until they reached Montreal. The second expedition
reached Salmon Falls, in New Hampshire, which place was
burned; but the attack on New York was abandoned.

The people of New York were divided in sentiment in regard
to the claims of William and James. Immediately following

the announcement of the accession of William, Jacob Leisler, a captain of the militia, at the instigation of the friends of the Protestant king, took forcible possession of Fort James, in the name of William and Mary, while Nicholson, who had been appointed governor, fled to Europe. It was in the midst of these civil commotions that the atrocities at Schenectady terrified the people and calmed the domestic factions. New York, Massachusetts, and Connecticut united for the reduction of Montreal and Quebec. An expedition by land and water was agreed upon. Sir William Phipps was placed in command of the fleet, and the land forces assigned to the command of General Winthrop of Connecticut. The fleet arrived before Quebec about the middle of October, 1690, but the land forces only penetrated as far as Wood creek, in the present county of Washington, when sickness, want of provisions and dissensions among the officers, compelled a return. In the meantime, Quebec had been strengthened by the French, and bade defiance to the English fleet, which soon returned to Boston.

In 1691, Colonel Sloughter was appointed governor of the province, and, immediately on his arrival, Governor Leisler and his son-in-law Milborne, were arrested and executed for treason. This, with the renewing of the covenant chain with the *Iroquois*, was the only act of his administration, death having suddenly ended his career. His successor was Benjamin Fletcher, under whom, in the succeeding year, the English, with their Indian allies, carried on the war against the French, Capt. John Schuyler making a successful attack on the French settlements beyond Lake Champlain. In February, 1693, Frontenac invaded the *Mohawk* territory, surprised and burned their castles, killed many and took three hundred prisoners. The invasion cost the invaders thirty men, but the *Mohawks* were completely dispersed. The forces at Albany, accompanied by such *Mahicans* as could be rallied, hastened to their relief, pursued the retreating enemy and recovered most of the prisoners. Governor Fletcher reached Albany soon after, and so pleased were the stricken chiefs at the celerity of his movements that they gave to him the flattering title of Lord of the Great Swift

Arrow.[1] The tide of war then rolled along the frontiers of New England, and the settlements at Oyster river in New Hampshire, and Haverhill in Massachusetts, were destroyed, Hatfield and Deerfield, on the Connecticut, shared the same fate. In 1696, Frontenac invaded the territory of the *Onondagas*, but without much success,[2] while Indians in detached bands warred for the respective powers with which they were in alliance. In the year following the war terminated in September, by the peace of Ryswick, and the principal combatants withdrew. Collisions and acts of hostility continued between the *Iroquois* and the allies of the French, however, until two years later. Governor Bellomont was exceedingly anxious to so order the termination of these hostilities that the *Iroquois* should be placed in acknowledged supremacy over their foes, and the French governor was not less mindful of his own and the interests of his allies. The latter triumphed, and both parties laid down the hatchet at his feet on terms of equality. Through a feeling springing in part from this result, and in part from the antagonisms which had been engendered by the part which they had taken in the war, the assembly of New York, in 1700, made a law for hanging every Catholic priest that should come voluntarily into the province.

The part which the *Mahicans* and *Minsis* of the Hudson took in this war, is only incidentally stated. The alliance between the *Iroquois* and the former, was of no little magnitude in the opinion of the French, as has already been stated. That alliance appears to have been suggested by the *Mohawks*.[3] In reference to the more detached bands, the *Mohawk* speaker in the conference of 1683, advised : " The *Schahook* Indians, in our opinion, are well placed where they are — they are a good guard ;

[1] These castles were three in number, and were destroyed on the 7th and 8th of February. — *Colonial History*, IV, 16, 20, 22. The *Mohawks* never forgot their punishment, but in after years repeated that they knew what it was "to be whipped and scourged by the French."

[2] *Bancroft*, III, 170.

[3] At a subsequent period the aid of the *Mahicans* was asked by the council at Onondaga. " Arnout Vielle, from On-ondaga, Feb. 18, 1694-5, brought this message : The whole Five Nations send seven hands of wampum to inform the *Mahikanders*, or River Indians, that the Count Frontenac would fall upon the *Onondagas* in the spring. They desired the assistance of three hundred Christians, with as many River Indians and *Mahikanders* as can be got together."—*Colonial History*, IV, 123.

they are our children, and we shall take care that they do their duty. But you must take care of the Indians below the town so that they may be of more service to you. We advise you to bring all the river Indians to be under your subjection at Albany to be ready on all occasions." A portion of the *Minsis*, who had settled among the *Ottawas*,[1] had joined the French alliance. Governor Dongan asked the aid of the *Iroquois* to bring them home. "One of them," said he, "is worse than six of the others, therefore all means must be used to bring them home." The confederates accepted the mission, and induced a considerable number to return.[2] Governor Andros was not less positive in his personal overtures to them. When he visited the province in May, 1688, he invited their aid, and promised to give lands to those who might desire to locate their families.[3] At a meeting of the council, September 17th, 1689, it was ordered that Robert Sanders use his endeavors to procure the "Indians of the Long Reach, Wawyachtenok and Esopus to come up here (Albany) to lie out as scouts upon the borders of this county," and that the "Justices of the Peace of Ulster county assist him in persuading the Indians." On the 22d of February, 1690, it was ordered by the same body, "that the Indians living at Beere island and Katskill be persuaded to go and live at Katskill,[4] and be ready on all occasions to be employed as scouts or otherwise." In April following, the *Tappans*

---

[1] The *Ottawas* occupied the southwestern part of Canada at this time. They were almost constantly at war with the Five Nations, and also with the *Mahicans*. Their relations with the Esopus *Minsis* were intimate and friendly, and many of them came thither to trade with the English at Kingston. In 1691, a company of them, while visiting the Esopus country, fell victims to the small-pox.— *Colonial History,* III, 776, 778. In the *Land Papers,* official record is made that Punganis, whose land was near Walden, in Orange county, pledged the same to Robert Sanders as security for the payment of £70, that he had then (1689) been absent with the *Ottawas* for ten years, and that his brother "intending to go to the wars," wished Sanders to keep the land "till his brother pays him for it."—*Land Papers,* III, 22.

[2] *Colonial History,* III, 808.

[3] "Several Indians living on both sides Hudson's river came to His Excellency, some at Albany, and others at a town nigh the river called Kingstone; he commanded them to demean themselves quietly towards the Christians their neighbors, invited such as were gone elsewhere to return with their families, and that if they wanted land it should be laid out for them in convenient places."—*Colonial History,* III, 568.

[4] On a map accompanying *Proud's History of Pennsylvania, Katsban* is applied to a village immediately north of Saugerties creek, and *Katskill* to a village at the junction of the *Kader's* and the *Katskill* creek, west of the present village of Katskill. These two villages perhaps explain the text.

reported that they had sent twelve men to the *Senecas*, and should send more," and the *Kicktawancs* and other Westchester families stated that they had sent six of their number.[1] The *Schaticook* Indians were actively employed. In addition to their services as scouts, a large number of them joined in the pursuit of the French after the destruction of Schenectady, and also in the several expeditions against Canada. When the expedition under Winthrop returned, Captain John Schuyler voluntarily embarked, at Wood creek, with a company consisting of " twenty-nine English soldiers, one hundred and twenty Mohawk and Scahook Indians,[2] to go to Canada and fight the enemy." This force made the successful attack on the French beyond Lake Champlain, already noticed, and returned to Albany with nineteen prisoners and six scalps. The *Wappingers*, or " Indians of the Long Reach," as they were called, accepted the invitation to unite in the war, and with their head sachem and " all the males of the tribe able to bear arms," went to Albany,[3] and from thence to the field. A portion of them, however, appear as the allies of the French, and as such to have destroyed Hatfield and Deerfield, under the lead of Ashpelon, one of their chiefs.[4] While those who were allies of the English were absent, a large portion of their lands, embracing the present county of Putnam, were fraudulently entered by Adolph Phillipse, and after their return a fifty years' controversy was opened in regard thereto. The *Minnisinks* hesitated at first to embark in the war, and sent Paxinos, their chief, to New York to consult with Governor Dongan in regard to the

[1] April 5, 1690. The Indian Sachems of *Kightowan, Wossecamer, Wescawanus*, did promise to send six men to go against the French."— *Documentary History*, II, 237.

" April 19, 1690. The sachems of *Tappan*, called Mendoassyn, and a captain called Wigworakum, said that they had sent, fifteen days ago, twelve men to ye Maquase and Sinnekas, and when returne shall send more, being strong, in all sixty young men."— *Ibid.*

[2] " Mohawks, 92 ; River Indians, 66 ; the latter under Estewapo, Estowacamo, Wannesackes and Magataw."—*Colonial History*, III, 800, 802. The ranks of the Mohawks were frequently swelled in this manner.

[3] *Colonial History*, VII, 868.

[4] *Hubbard's History of New England*. An Indian called Quaetseitts, " who formerly lived on Hudson's river," is also mentioned as one of those who had " lately done mischief in Connecticut."— *Colonial History*, III, 562, 563. The governor of Canada, in 1698-'99, demanded of the Five Nations, among other conditions, the return of " a Mahikander Indian who is at Onondaga, a prisoner."— *Ib.*, IV, 498. These Indians had joined the French prior to or during the war.

matter.¹ They subsequently contributed their quota, however, and rendered important service.²

The losses sustained by the *Iroquois* and their allies aggregated nearly one-half of the number engaged. The *Mohawks*, *Oneidas* and *Senecas* lost over one-half of their warriors, the latter being reduced from thirteen hundred to six hundred. The river Indians, however, were the greatest sufferers, having lost nearly two-thirds of the force which they contributed to the war.³ Fifteen hundred Indians fell victims to the interests of the English, while the loss sustained by the allies of the French probably equalled that number. In addition to those lost in conflict, the *Iroquois* suffered the permanent detachment of the Praying Indians, who took up permanent residence " about four leagues above Montreal," and laid the foundation of that " formidable and fatal reduction " subsequently known as the *Caghnawaga* nation,⁴ and more modernly as the *St. Regis* Indians. Assimilating with the French in faith, they soon did so in politics. They went off in small bodies, secretly, and after they had become located, drew to them considerable numbers of *Schati-*

¹ Paxinos has been classed as a Shawanoe chief, but such was not the case at this time, whatever •he may have been subsequently.

² " Ordered, that a message be sent to Minnisinks to order them to send up their young men to Albany to join with the Five Nations against the French."— *Council Minutes*, May 6, 1688.

³ This includes only those residing in the then county of Albany. The following return made to Gov. Fletcher in 1698, gives the strength and losses of the several tribes :

	Strength, In 1689.	In 1698.	Loss.
Mohawks,	270	110	160
Oneidas,	180	70	110
Onondagas,	500	250	250
Cayugas,	320	200	120
Senecas,	1300	600	700
River Indians,	250	90	160
Total,	2820	1320	1500

Colonial History, IV, 337.

⁴ " The French debauched many of our Five Nations to their Religion and Interest, actually drew several off to go and live in Canada, and laid the foundation of that formidable and fatal reduction which now forms the Cagnawaga na-

tion."— " Four hundred of our best Indians." — *Colonial History*, *of the State of New York*, III, 836. " In the time of the last war the clandestine trade to Montreal began to be carried on by Indians from Albany to Montreal. This gave rise to the Konuaga or Praying Indians, who are entirely made up of deserters from the *Mohawks* and river Indians, and were either enticed by the French Priests or by our merchants in order to carry goods from Albany to Montreal, or run away from some mischief done here. These Indians now consist of about eighty fighting men and live about four leagues above Montreal. They neither plant nor hunt, but depend chiefly upon this private trade for their subsistence. These Indians in time of war gave the French intelligence of all designs here against them."—*Colden*, *Colonial History*, V, 732. " They became a thorn to the frontier towns and settlements of New England during the whole of the French war, and of the American Revolution."— *Schoolcraft*. They numbered, in 1745, two hundred and thirty fighting men.

23

cooks as well as of *Mohawks* and *Oneidas*.[1] The *Mohawks* felt the loss deeply, and exhausted every effort to reclaim the wanderers, but without avail.

Not only was foundation laid for the subsequent weakness of the *Iroquois* by the defection of the Praying Indians, but by the settlement among the *Lenapes* of the *Shawanoes* of Maryland and Virginia. At the outbreak of the war the *Shawanoes* were contesting the advance of the *Iroquois* in the south, and were also engaged in war with the *Cherokees*. In the latter they suffered severely, and but for the timely aid of the *Mahicans*, would have been destroyed. The *Lenapes* invited them to remove to their country ; the invitation being accepted, the *Minsis* brought the matter to the attention of the government of New York, in September, 1692, on an application to permit their settlement in the Minnisink country. The council gave its assent on condition that they should first make peace with the Five Nations.[2] This was soon effected, and the messengers departed, accompanied by Arnout Vielle, an interpreter, and three Christians, to visit the country of the *Shawanoes* and consummate the transfer.[3] On the 6th of February (1694), Major Peter Schuyler announced to the Five Nations, in conference at Albany, that " one of the Christians " had returned with the intelligence that seven nations or chieftaincies, " in all a thousand souls," were on their way.[4] Confirmation came also from

---

[1] The leader of the *Caghnawagas* was known to the French by the name of Kryn. A party led by him was prominent in the attack on Schenectady, and also on Salmon Falls. On their return from the latter expedition they were attacked by a party of *Algonquins* and *Abenaquis*, who, mistaking them for English *Mohawks*, killed two and wounded ten. " Among the slain was Kryn, the 'great *Mohawk* ;' whose death was the more deplored, because Frontenac and the Jesuits hoped that through his influence all the New York *Mohawks* would eventually be drawn to Canada."—*Brodhead*, II, 618 ; *Colonial History*, IX, 467.

[2] River Indians returned from a residence with the Shawanoes, brought with them some Shawanoes who intended to settle with the Minnisinks, asking permission to that end. Council directed that the Shawanoes, must first make peace with the Five Nations.— *Council Minutes*, Sept. 14, 1692.

[3] " We are glad that the Shawanoes, who were our enemies, did make their application to you last fall for protection, and that you sent them hither to endeavor a peace with us ; also, that you have been pleased to send Christians along with them to their country to conduct them back again. We wish they were come to assist us against the common enemy."— *Answer of Five Nations*, July 4, 1693, *Colonial History*, IV, 43.

[4] " It seems the heavens are propitious unto us, for this day we have the forerunners of the Shawanoes Farr Indians come to town with one of our Christians that was sent thither, who gives us an

another quarter.   Captain Arent Schuyler visited the *Minnisinks*
in February, and there learned that the *Shawanoes* were expected
early in the ensuing summer.¹   This expectation was realized,
and the *Minsis* of the Hudson as well as those of the Delaware
received to their embrace "the second son of their grandfather," after having given their pledge "to be faithful subjects
of the king." ²

   At the time of the incorporation of the *Shawanoes* with the
Minsis, the latter were at the lowest point in their history.
Broken by their long wars with the *Senecas* and *Mohawks*, and
scourged by the small pox,³ they were but a remnant indeed of
that proud people who had once successfully disputed the sovereignty of the continent.   Their warriors hunted in fear; their
chiefs trembled at the anger of the *Senecas*.⁴   The *Shawanoes*
were proud, warlike and cruel to an extent sufficient to draw

account that they are coming with seven
nations of Indians, with women and
children, in all a thousand souls, and are
upon their way hither with Arnout, the
interpreter."— *Colonial History*, IV, 90.
"In the intrim that they were treating
with them (the Five Nations), Gerret
Luykasse, with two of the Far Indians
called Shawanoes arrives who brings news
that Arnout, the interpreter, with a considerable number of those heathen, will
be here next summer."— *Schuyler, Colonial History*, IV, 97.
   ¹ "Enquiring after news, they told me
that six days ago three Christians and two
Shawans Indians, who went about fifteen
months ago, with Arnout Vielle, into
the Shawans country, were passed by the
Mennissincks going for Albany to fetch
powder for Arnout and his company:
and further told them that said Arnout
intended to be there with seven hundred
of the said Shawans Indians, loaden with
beaver and pelteries, at the time the Indian
corn is about one foot high, which may
be in the month of June."— *Colonial
History*, IV, 98.
   ² *Council Minutes*, 1694.
   ³ This malady was not confined to
any district of country. Charlevoix says
that in 1690 not less than fifteen hundred
Indians perished in the Canada wilderness; and Ledwick writes in 1692, that
of those residing in the vicinity of New

Amsterdam: "The small pox took many
of them away lately." Loskiel says that
the Indians discovered a remedy in what
he calls "fossil oil" (petroleum). He
adds, "an old Indian in the small pox
lay down in a morass to cool himself,
and soon recovered. This led to the discovery of an oil spring in the morass, and
since that time many others have been
found, both in the country of the Delawares and the Iroquois." About the
time spoken of by Loskiel, the epidemic
was severe in the Esopus country. An
entire company of *Ottawas* visiting there
were among its victims. *Garneau's History of Canada*, I, 228; *New York Historical Collections*, 2d series, II, 249;
Loskiel's Moravian Miss. 117.
   ⁴ The Mennissinck sachems further said
that one of their sachems and other Indians were gone to fetch beavor and
pelteries which they had hunted, and
having heard no news of them are afraid
that the Sinneques have killed them for
the lucar of the beavor, or because the
Mennissincks have not been with the
Sinneques as usual to pay their duty; and
therefore desire that your excellency will
be pleased to order that the Sinneques
may be told not to molest or hurt the
Mennissincks, they being willing to continue in amity with them — *Schuyler*,
Feb. 1693, *Colonial History*, IV, 98.

from their enemies the name of Satans. On terms of peace with, but unsubdued by the *Iroquois*, their presence inspired the *Minsis*, and opened up to them a future in which their united war cry challenged the best efforts of their English and Indian foes. Half a century later they could say to their former rulers, the *Senecas :* " We have once been women and ashamed to look down at our petticoats, but as you have taken them off and encouraged us to begin a quarrel with the English, we are determined never to submit again to that ignominious state while there is one óf us alive," [1] while a thousand warriors,

> " Quivered and plumed, and lithe and tall,
> And seamed with glorious scars,"

responded with rude but earnest approval.

[1] *Johnson Manuscripts*, IV, 131.

INDEX

ERRATA

page 9, 9th line, for *then,* read than
" 9, 19th line, for *hospitality,so,* read hospitality. So he
" 18, 11th line, for *Agassis,* read Agassiz
" 24, 9th line, for *make,* read also.
" 27, 21st line, for *sacrifice and fires,* read sacrificial fires
" 27, 22nd line, for *Kitzinacka* read Kitzinacka
" 27, 29th line, for *were,* read where
" 29, 26th line, for *presents be,* read presents were
" 29, 27th line, for *it,* read was
" 32, 5th line, for *called,* read asked
" 63, 3rd line, for *at,* read above
" 66, 14th line, for *causes,* read cause
" 87, 10th line, for *1680,* read 1630
" 154, 24th line, for *soon he,* read soon as he
" 172, 27th line, for *concede,* read accede
" 176, 13th line, for *permanent,* read their

SUGGESTED READING

A HISTORY OF ULSTER UNDER THE DUTCH by A.H. Van Buren
Starts with a good over-view of the Indians before Dutch settlement,
then shows how they were affected by the first whites. P 146pp $13.95

ALGONQUIN LEGENDS   A collection of Algonquin Indian
mythology and folklore. P $ 8.95

HOW INDIANS USE WILD PLANTS by Francis Densmore. Tells of
the traditional Native American uses of plants for food, medicine and
crafts. P   110 pp $4.95

THE INDIANS by A. G. Bevier.   Memoirs of massacres and Indian
raids in Wawasink (Ulster Co.) before the Rev.War. P 79pp $ 4.50

IROQUOIS BOOK OF RITES by H.E. Hale. The magnum opus of
this esteemed pioneer ethnographer and linguist. A landmark of
Iroquios anthropology. P 367pp $14.95

IROQUOIS, THEIR ART AND CRAFTS by Carrie Lyford. Deals
primarily with their technology and skill both before and after their
contact with the whites. P 128pp $9.95

LEGENDS OF THE LONGHOUSE by J.J. Cornplanter. The first
paperback reprint of the classic 1938 book on Iroquois folktales.
Written and illustrated by an Iroquois. P 200pp $10.95

MYTHS OF THE IROQUOIS by E.A. Smith. A collection of 56
stories, many found nowhere else. P 84pp $5.95

SCALPING AND TORTURE: Native American Warfare Practices
The first and only collection of three scholarly studies examining the
misunderstanding and distortion surrounding the controversy of Indian
perpetrated atrocities and their origins. P 109pp $7.95

NEW

INDIAN TRIBES OF HUDSON'S RIVER from 1700 to 1850
by E.M. Ruttenber. A continuation of his monumental history of the
origin, manners and customs of eastern New York Indians. This half
includes extensive biographical sketches as well as a complete account
of the French and Indian War and the Revolutionary War. Publication
date TO BE ANNOUNCED ... Inquire...

Please include NY sales tax and $1.50 shipping for each book ordered.
Prices and titles subject to change. For the best selection of New York
State regional history books write for a catalogue HOPE FARM PRESS
7321 Rt 212 Saugerties NY 12477 or call 914-679-6809 for message .